PLAYING
GOD

Seven Fateful Moments
When Great Men Met
to Change the World

Charles L. Mee, Jr.

SIMON & SCHUSTER
New York · London · Toronto · Sydney · Tokyo · Singapore

SIMON & SCHUSTER
Simon & Schuster Building
Rockefeller Center
1230 Avenue of the Americas
New York, New York 10020

Designed by Edith Fowler
Manufactured in the United States of America

10   9   8   7   6   5   4   3   2   1

Library of Congress Cataloging-in-Publication Data

Mee, Charles L.
   Playing God: seven fateful moments when great
men met to change the world / Charles L. Mee, Jr.
      p.   cm.
   Includes bibliographical references and index.
   1. Summit meetings—History.   2. World
politics.   3. International relations.   I. Title.
D32.M44   1993
327'.09—dc20   93-1599   CIP
ISBN 0-671-67888-4

ACKNOWLEDGMENTS

I am greatly indebted for their readings of my manuscript and their good advice to Professors Jay P. Anglin, Lionel Casson, Arther Ferrill, Ronald Steel, George Scheber, Suzanne Alchon; to my colleagues Lewis Lapham, Timothy Foote, Elizabeth Schleikert, Robert Cowley, Shirley Abbott; and, above all, to my editor, Alice Mayhew.

For Alice Mayhew, my mentor

CONTENTS

PROLOGUE
The Art of Making History

What stands in the way of a person who wants to change the course of history, not by the force of arms, but by the peaceful means of charm, wit, persuasion, flirting, backstabbing, patience, skillful negotiation, foresight, deceitfulness, and all the other arts of peaceful human exchange?

The question comes up every day in thousands of contexts of daily life and high diplomacy, at PTA meetings, and in corporate boardrooms.

But the question shows itself with perhaps greater clarity in one context than in all the others: at summit meetings, where two leaders meet, with the presumed power, by uttering a word, altering a position, relinquishing a claim, offering trust, telling a lie, taking a gamble, remaining firm, to transform the course of events.

In such circumstances, they naturally consider the substantial obstacles that stand in the way of their desires: the sizes of each other's armies, the resources of their economies, their geographical positions, and other material facts of the world. Both contemporary people and historians make much of such things, constructing entire theories around the importance of the means of production, the raw materials, and the skills of work forces available in various nations. But, in truth, these are the simple elements to weigh, and, by themselves, they are rarely the factors that cause people to make great miscalculations.

The sources of the big, repeated mistakes in history are the conceptual pitfalls that undo the best made plans of the most able practitioners. There are many such pitfalls, large and small. This book deals with seven of the most common and upsetting of them all.

The first involves the difficulty of knowing the facts, the foundation of the historical field in which any of us ever operates, and not only when powerful leaders come together to bargain or confront one another. Most sources of information—in our daily lives as in the archives we leave behind for historians to sort through—are dreadfully inadequate, incomplete, filled with error, biases, giving weight to certain facts because they happen to be the only ones that have survived, and ignoring others because they have been lost or discarded or shredded, or never deemed worth gathering in the first place. Is there a missing piece of evidence that would transform our understanding of John Kennedy's assassination in Dallas, or the Iran–Contra scandal, or of what Manuel Noriega of Panama did in the name of assisting American policy in Latin America? Do we have such a certain grasp of the effects of American policy that we know what will maintain good relationships with Arab countries and what will ruin them? "History," as the historiographer Michael Stanford has written, like an understanding of the present, and "unlike mathematics, is not a science of certainties, and only rarely are a historian's reasonings empirically confirmed. . . . " Meanwhile, we act, presumably, on the basis of what we know; and what we know is invariably incomplete, or wrong.

Second, as if ignorance of facts were not disabling enough, we are further incapacitated by the appearances we mistake for reality, and by those appearances that we create in order to bewilder others. We add to that the belief that by changing the appearance of things, we have changed the nature of things, or that, in time, thinking will make it so. Thus, when the Chinese massacred their citizens in a public square, President George Bush carried on with business as usual, on the premise that if the massacre went unnoticed it would not disturb the progress of China toward an open society. Of course we know that appearances do matter: that the Soviet Union seemed to be a powerful colossus fueled an immense American military budget right up to the very last moment of the Cold War. But there is a limit to the efficacy of appearances. Not all the parades of Russian tanks and missiles and soldiers could keep the Soviet Union, at the end of its economic resources, from collapse.

Third, we must face up to the fact that the ancients were right about the role of chance in human affairs. Aristotle and Plato spoke of the operations of Nature, Chance, and Art, or the exercise of practical skills in human history. St. Thomas, in his *Summa contra gentiles,* spoke similarly of nature, luck, and will. In our modern hubris, believing that with sufficient research and rational analysis we can comprehend all pertinent factors, we forget that, inevitably, absolutely unpredictable events occur to rout even the finest, most sophisticated, computer-modeled calculations about the ever-changing historical situation. If that were not the case, the stock markets of the world would not be so liable to crash, intelligence evaluations of the possibility of deposing foreign rulers would not so often be wrong, and a sandstorm would not have made such a humiliating mess of President Jimmy Carter's attempt to rescue American hostages in Iran.

Fourth, there is the disagreeable fact that events depend on the principle of contingency, which states that everything depends on everything else. As the historian Paul Veyne has written, there are no laws of history, or if there are they are couched along the lines of "a rise in the price of bread will cause a revolution except when it doesn't." And so, not only are there no rules to follow in the making of history, but there is, as a consequence, no telling, before the fact, even which factors in a given situation will turn out to be the crucial ones.

Fifth, there is the puzzle that the only thing worse than not learning from the mistakes of the past is to learn from them—and apply the wrong lessons to the wrong events at the wrong time.

From World War II, we learned the lesson of Munich: that aggressors must be firmly opposed, or they will proceed to greater and greater conquests. We applied the lesson of Munich to Vietnam—certain that the United States could not afford to show behavior that would be interpreted as weakness or timidity—and created a tragedy. Generals are famous for applying the lessons of the previous wars to future ones: thus the Maginot Line was built across France after World War I to keep tanks from rolling across French fields; and in World War II, armor outflanked the Maginot Line. The hardest lesson of all for us to learn is the lesson that every moment in history is a separate constellation of events, never to be repeated; no lesson of the past can ever be applied exactly to the present or future.

Sixth, there is the near certainty, no matter what decision is taken, that it will produce unintended as well as intended consequences. The peace treaty that wrote an end to World War I led to the rise of Hitler and so to World War II. Britain's victories in World War I and World War II helped to drain the British Empire of its wealth and to reduce it to a second-rate power. The long-desired end of the Cold War let loose the long-repressed nationalist passions of eastern Europe and removed the economic support the Soviet Union and the United States gave to the Philippines, South Vietnam, Zaire, Somalia, Cuba, Ethiopia, and other nations that now teeter on the brink of economic and political anarchy.

And finally, once all these factors are combined, they create the seventh and most confounding obstacle of all: because we cannot have a certain knowledge of what the world is or is becoming, and because the precondition of realism is an ability to suit one's actions to the world as it is and as it is becoming, it is not possible to be a confident realist. We need to embrace, in the place of mere realism, a more robust and complex view of the world, what we might call meta-realism, which recognizes a context more intricate and subtle than we had hoped would be necessary, that also takes into account some values, beliefs, wishes, and hopes that are completely unrealistic. This meta-realism might finally be indistinguishable from the elusive and contradictory tenets of ethics, which are, finally, no more nor less than the accumulated practical folk wisdom of millennia of human experience.

Each of these puzzles is considered in one of the seven chapters of this book.

The problem of the knowability of the historical field is seen in the first chapter as a particular puzzle faced by Pope Leo I and Attila the Hun when they met in the north of Italy in A.D. 452. Leo's task was to say something to Attila to persuade the barbarians not to attack Rome. Leo had no certain knowledge that what he might say would be effective; Attila had no way of knowing whether he could count on what Leo told him. Yet, on the basis of their conversation, the future of the center of western civilization —for that moment—depended.

The illusion of power—the spectacle of politics—as it is used to dazzle one's own followers, to fool an opponent, and to bemuse oneself, has never been displayed more grandly than in the meeting in 1520 of England's King Henry VIII and the French King Francis I on the Field of the Cloth of Gold, where the two kings made peace, but only for a relative moment.

And the operations of chance have not been more strikingly and catastrophically revealed than in the encounter of Hernando Cortés and his followers with the Emperor Moctezuma and the Aztecs in 1519, when the fate of an entire civilization depended on a surprise that neither of the men considered, or could have imagined.

The principle of contingency, embodied in the extraordinarily complex interrelationships of the people and the nations they represented at the Congress of Vienna in 1815, was understood by all the participants at the Congress—and, to their efforts' ultimate undoing, ignored.

The fifth chapter, addressed to the false lessons of history, recounts the story of the Paris conference of President Woodrow Wilson, Prime Minister Lloyd George, and Premier Georges Clemenceau, and the writing of the peace treaty at the end of World War I. Each of the participants had learned well and thoroughly from history lessons that were tragically wrong.

The sixth chapter, about the rule of unintended consequences, speaks of the Yalta Conference in 1945—which marked the end of World War II, and the beginning of the Cold War and all its consequences.

The seventh and final chapter—dealing with the difficulty of basing one's actions on an accurate reading of the "real world"— tells of a recent meeting of the so-called G7, the heads of the seven great industrial powers of the world, and Premier Mikhail Gorbachev, who asked for financial help to prevent the final disintegration of the Soviet Union.

The examples chosen for each of these puzzles are of course not the only ones—and perhaps not the most involved and intricate —that could have been chosen. History contains a vast store of such examples. Indeed, the Vietnam War by itself is an illustration of every single one of the seven pitfalls. But the events shown in the following chapters, from a broad span of time, are among the most exemplary, and, taken together, are bracing, and humbling, reminders of the complexity and mystery of human affairs.

One

THE
PROBLEM
OF KNOWING

Historians are painfully aware of how difficult it is to come by reliable facts in any period of study. And it is not only a historian's problem. Those who are in the midst of the events themselves are often as much at a loss for reliable information as those who attempt to reconstruct and interpret events after the fact.

Would the American State Department have instructed April Glaspie, the ambassador to Iraq in 1990, to appear as friendly to Saddam Hussein, to have refrained in their last meeting from warning him against attacking Kuwait, if the State Department had known of his plans? Or if the Americans did know Hussein's plans and wished to lure him to attack so that his nuclear weapons development could be halted, what did President Bush's advisors know about their ability to destroy Hussein's nuclear capability in the war or its aftermath?

Two professors who teach would-be Washington insiders at the Kennedy School at Harvard, Richard Neustadt and Ernest May, like to recall that President John Kennedy used to tell of hearing in college about a former German chancellor who, when asked the reasons for World War I, replied, "Ah, if we only knew."

When the "facts" are known the trouble does not so much end as begin, for we bring our own interpretive point of view to whatever incomplete facts we may possess, and that point of view may include conscious or unconscious biases. Centuries ago, some believed that earthly events were caused by God, and data was interpreted accordingly. This was regarded as the only correct understanding of the world. In the nineteenth and twentieth centuries, there were those who understood that events and even ideas and feelings arose from the material relationships described by Karl Marx, and histories were written to correspond to that view. Others assumed the truth of Thomas Carlyle's view that historical events were shaped by the acts of "great men." In the twentieth century, most of us have been more comfortable with multifactorial, pluralist explanations that recognize the complexities of a multitude of interacting factors that initiate and give distinctive shape to events. We are especially content if we are able to integrate those factors into a statistically based computer model. We accept that the older views are simply wrong, and our current view is the best possible.

Moreover, we bring to the "facts" we accumulate certain assumptions buried in language or logic or even our neurological makeup, in the sorts of percepts our minds are able, by their nature, to form. In fact, we make fundamental choices just by placing our facts into a narrative, whether it is a simple narrative of individual actions or a more abstract analysis of historical forces. Historiographer David Lowenthal wrote that "No account can recover the past as it was, because the past was not an account," no more of course than the present. Both past and present are sets of events and situations about which we compose stories that cannot be understood as definitive any more than a novel can.

There are any number of examples of this vexing difficulty of seeing the facts of the matter clearly, by the participants at the time or by those of us who try to reconstruct the event after the fact. During the Kennedy administration, as Neustadt and May have written, some thought that the Cuban Missile Crisis of 1962 had been resolved, in part, because of a strategy of "graduated escalation" in diplomatic maneuvering. Some of these same people, when they served Lyndon Johnson as president, in 1965, thought that "graduated escalation" would be effective in the war in Vietnam. As that strategy was applied, with ever-increasing force, certainty about its effectiveness became elusive and then dissipated.

When the Cold War ended with the collapse of the Soviet Union, many rushed forward to take credit for an American victory. It was confidently said that the Soviet Union was bankrupted because it could not sustain the arms race that the United States economy could afford. George Kennan, who defined the containment policy after World War II, relying on the same facts, wrote that "Nobody—no country, no party, no person—'won' the Cold War. It was a long and costly political rivalry. . . . It greatly overstrained the economic resources of both countries, leaving both, by the end of the 1980s, confronted with heavy financial, social and, in the case of the Russians, political problems." Franklyn Holzman, a professor of economics at Tufts University and a fellow at Harvard's Russian Research Center, looking at the same evidence as Kennan, wrote, "While there is an element of truth in this [explanation of the bankrupting of the Soviet Union by military expenditures], it is not the real explanation. . . . The real causes of the continuously declining growth rate of the Soviet Union, of the poor quality of its products and of its many other deficiencies are to be found in central planning by direct controls." In short, the Soviet Union would have collapsed without the Cold War, without an arms race. Everyone had the same access to the same broad set of facts—during the Cold War, and in retrospect—and intelligent, well-informed people could not agree on what they knew.

Of the many instances of this difficulty of perceiving the historical field as it is, this chapter takes one from the distant past: the meeting between Pope Leo I and Attila the Hun—who, before they met, could not know what they might reasonably hope to achieve; while they were meeting, did not know what they were in fact achieving; and after they had met, could not be sure whether they had done anything of lasting significance—any more than we can be certain we know in looking back. Their encounter is an impressive memorial to how little we grasp of the world in which we function.

POPE LEO THE GREAT AND ATTILA THE HUN
NEAR SIRMIONE, A.D. 452

When Leo the Great, the bishop of Rome, rode out of the
Eternal City in the year A.D. 452 to meet Attila the Hun, Leo had
no arms, no army, no armor, no bodyguards, no great retinue of
ambassadors and advisors, advance men and area specialists, no
makeup men and publicists, no claque of courtiers, flatterers or
other hangers-on. He went out with only a few fellow churchmen
riding alongside him and a couple of lesser officials of the enfeebled
and fading Roman Empire.

Attila, the man Leo went to meet, came to the encounter
at the head of a large, well-armed, infamously rapacious, battle-
hardened army of Huns on horseback: more than three hundred
thousand of them according to some sources, men who had a reputation—at the time, if not among recent, more skeptical scholars,
who regard him at a comfortable distance—for roasting pregnant
women, cutting out the fetus, putting it in a dish, pouring water
over it, dipping their weapons into the potion, eating the flesh
of children, and drinking the blood of women. They supported
themselves, as they rode through the countryside, with pillage and
extortion. They ate horsemeat and drank vast amounts of wine.
Even the Goths were terrified, according to the Roman historian
Ammianus Marcellinus, when the Hunnish cavalry swept into battle, with dazzling speed, howling and yelling, and dashing in all
directions at once.

The Huns, said Ammianus, were "almost glued to their
horses," which was part of the secret of their success in war. And
if Attila followed his usual custom, he did not dismount when he
met the pope, but instead stayed on his horse, one leg thrown
casually over the horse's neck, surrounded by mounted companions, ready to turn and scatter at any moment.

The two men met because Attila and his followers, having
plundered the northern Italian peninsula, were on their way south,
with the apparent intention of sacking the city of Rome. Leo's task

was to persuade Attila not to move on down the peninsula and plunder and burn the center of Western civilization.

Geographically, the Roman Empire at this time extended from the shores of the Atlantic Ocean across Europe to the Rhine, the Danube, and the Black Sea. To the north, the empire reached as far as Hadrian's Wall in England, and to the south it stretched all the way to Nubia in Africa.

Rome itself was a city of as many as one million inhabitants, who—according to an inventory taken some years before Leo's time—lived in fifty thousand tenement houses and more than seventeen hundred "palaces" of greater or lesser splendor. The city boasted (according to one, suspiciously exact, source) twenty-eight public libraries, eight bridges across the Tiber River, six obelisks, two circuses, two amphitheaters, three theaters, thirty-six marble arches, 290 storehouses and warehouses, 254 public bakehouses, and ten thousand public statues, surrounded by a city wall twelve miles in circumference with thirty-seven gates. Among Rome's greatest distinctions was a lavish supply of fresh mountain spring water, millions of gallons of water a day, that came in over aqueducts or through underground pipes and burst out in fountains or poured down in waterfalls in grottoes decorated with statues. Rome had 856 baths, 1,352 swimming pools, and eleven thermae—places with hot and cold baths, swimming pools, gymnasia, gardens, museums, and libraries where one could meet friends, walk in the gardens, and pass the hours until dinnertime. Rome was a city of many public and private gardens, with walkways paved with mosaics, fenced with pedestals surmounted by statuettes, shaded by laurel, myrtle, plane, and box trees. The walls of private houses and public buildings were painted with murals and other pictures; private houses were filled with bronze and marble statues; markets sold Spanish goods, Chinese silks, tinted glass and fine linen from Alexandria, wine and oysters from Greece, fish from the Black Sea, Arabian spices and scents, emeralds from the Urals; and the buyers and sellers were a cosmopolitan lot, including Parthians, Germans, Egyptians, Nubians, Jews, Dacians, Cappadocians. This was still a great city.

True enough, paganism had already begun to die out, and

although the temples of Cybele and Vesta were still in use, some of the other temples were being used as quarries for new buildings —despite repeated government prohibitions against cannibalizing the temples, and genuine efforts at historic preservation. The festival of Lupercalia and some of the other old pagan games persisted, but by Leo's time, the gladiatorial games in the Colosseum had been brought to an end.

Christianity was gaining the upper hand over paganism. By Leo's time, Rome had twenty-five small parish churches and several quite grand basilicas. Leo's own church, the official cathedral of Rome, was St. John Lateran, erected in A.D. 324. Leo himself lived next door to the cathedral, in the Lateran Palace, the former imperial residence that the emperor Constantine had given to the bishop of Rome.

Well before the time of Leo, the inhabitants of the empire had lived in rough political and military balance with their neighbors on the frontiers of the imperial domains: the *barbari,* as the Romans called them, meaning strangers or foreigners, and referring for the most part to anyone who did not speak Greek or Latin. By the time of Leo, however, it was no longer possible to draw entirely distinct lines between the inhabitants of the empire and the foreigners, to discover a distinct ancient Roman Empire neatly walled off from a distinct array of barbarians. Since the late second century, the Germanic tribes had been providing a good many recruits for the Roman army, and the lines between Romans and barbarians had begun to blur.

Beginning in the late 300s, these already indistinct lines began to shift and break even further. The Huns, who lived with their herds of cattle and sheep somewhere east of the Don River, in what is now southern Russia, became unsettled for some reason. They moved, perhaps in search of better pastures, toward the west. Naturally enough, they encountered the resistance of their neighbors as they went, and they set off a succession of jostling displacements and wars. According to Ammianus, they made their "violent way amid the rapine and slaughter of the neighboring peoples" as far west as the banks of the Don River itself. There they met, "killed and plundered" the Alans, joined in alliance with some of the survivors, and sent others of the Alans fleeing ahead to the west, where these fleeing Alans attacked the Goths, and the Goths, in their turn, fell upon their neighbors.

In the years that followed, the Roman Empire was shaken not only by the migrations or violent incursions of barbarians from all sides but also by rebellions that rose up from among the Romans themselves against the imperial government. These external and internal forces mingled: Roman rebels enlisted the support of barbarian soldiers and generals to fight against the emperors; and the emperors hired German generals to fight the rebels.

By the end of the fourth century, the disintegrating empire had come to be divided between two emperors, one who ruled the eastern empire, one the western. The emperors of the west no longer lived in Rome. They followed their armies from campaign to campaign, or lived now in Milan, now in Treves. As time went on, the emperor himself took to the battlefield less and less, and the conduct of all imperial affairs came increasingly to rest in the hands of the empire's principal general, or *Magister militum.* By the year 395, the Magister militum of the western empire was the barbarian Vandal general Stilicho. Indeed, by the year 400, the year that Leo was born, the rule of the Roman Empire had come to be divided between a Vandal and a Goth: Stilicho in the west, and the Gothic general Gainas in the east. Before Attila the Hun ever set foot in Italy, the Roman Empire had already been conquered by the barbarians within its own bureaucracy.

Then, in the year 401, the Visigoths, with Alaric at their head, invaded Italy, followed by the Alans, Vandals, Alamanni, and others. The Visigoths invaded Italy once again. And by the year 408, Alaric and the Visigoths had descended on Rome and laid siege to the city. The Romans tried frantically to buy off the Visigoths, delivering up to Alaric five thousand pounds of gold, thirty thousand pounds of silver, four thousand silk tunics, and three thousand pounds of pepper. Both public and private treasures were melted down to deliver this ransom, but in 410, the Visigoths invaded Rome anyway.

They came in through the gate at the Via Salaria, one of the main roads from the north. To find their way in the dark, they set fire to the houses as they moved through the streets. And they went on a rampage of raping and plundering and burning for fully six days. The barbarians were joined by forty thousand slaves who rose up against their masters to loot and burn. It was the first time the Eternal City had been entered by an enemy in eight hundred years, when the Celts had come down out of Gaul and sacked Rome.

The sacking of Rome by the Visigoths caused a profound shock throughout the Roman world. It was now clear, if it had not been before, that the empire was in its final days. St. Augustine in Africa wrote in his great work *The City of God* that the destruction of the temporal city of Rome was as nothing compared with the everlasting kingdom of God. In this moment, one can feel the shift in the allegiance of the Western world from the Roman Empire to the Christian church.

The Huns appeared for the first time in Italy at the mountain passes of the Julian Alps above Trieste. It was June of the year 452. According to some sources, an army of three hundred thousand soldiers came over the Alps, according to others as many as five hundred thousand. According to still others, the army numbered seven hundred thousand. Certainly, judging from the terror caused by the appearance of the Huns, they constituted a vast army by the standards of the time—however large it was—living off the land as they went, pillaging and leveling and burning the farms and towns as they made their way along their route of march.

They were like "wolves," one of the Romans said. They were fiendish ogres, said another, "the most infamous offspring of the north," "fiercer than ferocity itself." Or, as Sidonius said, the Huns were "barbarous even in the eyes of the barbarians around them." The Huns stayed on their horses both day and night, said Ammianus, they ate and drank on horseback, and at night, "bowed over the narrow neck of the animal," they relaxed "in a sleep so deep as to be accompanied by many dreams." They were eaters of the roots of wild plants and of raw meat, "which they put between their thighs and the backs of their horses, and thus warm it a little."

Even the dreaded Alans had turned and run, "put to flight," said Priscus of Panium, by the terror of the Huns' looks, "by their awful aspect and by their horribly swarthy appearance. . . . [which] gives evidence of the hardihood of their spirits, for they are cruel even to their children on the first day they are born. They cut the cheeks of the males with a sword so that before they receive the nourishment of milk they are compelled to learn to endure a wound."

Priscus of Panium was not, perhaps, the most reliable witness on the Huns. The Huns in general, said Priscus, "have a sort of shapeless lump, if I may say so, not a face, and pinholes rather than eyes." Nonetheless, because he was sent on a diplomatic mission to the Huns, Priscus did have the advantage—rare among Roman historians—of having met Attila face-to-face, indeed, of having dined with Attila one evening. The house of the leader of the Huns, said Priscus, was built of carved wood planks, "beautifully fitted together"; and inside the house its floors were covered with wool felt mats. Chairs were ranged along the walls. And in the middle of the room sat Attila on a couch. Behind him were steps that led up to his bed, "which was covered with white linens and colored embroideries for ornament." The place of honor, Priscus noted, was to Attila's right. Priscus, an ambassador from the Roman Empire, was put conspicuously to Attila's left.

A cupbearer brought wine to Attila, and a round of toasts was drunk. Then the dinner began. "While sumptuous food had been prepared—served on silver plates—for the other barbarians and for us, for Attila there was nothing but meat on a wooden trencher. He showed himself temperate in all other ways, too, for gold and silver goblets were offered to the men at the feast, but his mug was of wood. His dress too was plain, having care for nothing other than to be clean, nor was the sword by his side, nor the clasps of his barbarian boots, nor the bridle of his horse, like those of other [Huns], adorned with gold or gems or anything of high price."

As the evening went on, said Priscus, pine torches were lit, and two barbarians came in, "advancing in front of Attila," and sang songs they had composed, "chanting his victories and his virtues in war." A court clown entertained as well, a Moor. "On account of the deformity of his body, the lisp of his voice, and his appearance, he was the object of laughter. He was somewhat short, hump-shouldered, with distorted feet, and a nose indicated only by the nostrils, because of its exceeding flatness." The guests at the dinner party were all vastly entertained by the fool. Attila, however, did not find him funny.

Despite Attila's studied simplicity, he allowed himself one mark of distinction: he was the keeper of the sword of Ares, "a sacred object," said Priscus, among the Huns. The sword had been hidden "in ancient times," the Huns told Priscus. But then, "when a herdsman noticed one of his herd limping and found no reason for such a wound, being disturbed, he followed the tracks of blood. At length he came upon a sword which the heifer had heedlessly trodden on while grazing the grass. He dug it up and bore it directly to Attila."

"That magnanimous, or rather that artful prince," Gibbon wrote in an essay called "These Splendid Fighters," "accepted, with pious gratitude, this celestial favor; and, as the rightful possessor of the sword of Mars, asserted his divine and indefeasible claim to the dominion of the earth."

We "may" believe Priscus, says the skeptical Otto Maenchen-Helfen, a recent scholar who spent much of his life gathering every bit of evidence he could find about the Huns for a book he never finished writing. But, to Maenchen-Helfen, this story about the sacred sword sounds suspiciously like a combination of a folktale and a passage from Herodotus ("the Scythians worship Ares in the form of a scimitar"). In other ancient texts, notes Maenchen-Helfen, the Scythians are replaced by other tribes. Ammianus Marcellinus said that the Alans "fix a naked sword in the ground and reverently worship it as Mars." It may be that the Huns had taken over an old Iranian cult. Then, too, the Bulgars swore by their swords. The Franks swore by their swords. Suleiman the Great took an oath on his sword. The knights of Camelot, after all, had Excalibur. Is Attila's sword, then, an object that became encrusted with legend, or a legend for which a sword was created, or simply a legend for which there was never a sword? Under the circumstances, Otto Maenchen-Helfen is inclined to give Attila his sword —but to doubt the story of how he got it.

In any case, all the commentators—the firsthand reporter, the narrative master, and the twentieth-century historian—agree that Attila was a most formidable figure. He had taken over the leadership of the Huns by murdering his brother Bleda, and so, as Priscus said, "he was a man born to shake the races of the world, a terror to all lands, who in some way or other frightened everyone." Or, as Gibbon said, "If a line of separation were drawn between the civilized and the savage climates of the globe; between the inhabitants of cities, who cultivated the earth, and the hunters and shepherds, who dwelt in tents, Attila might aspire to the title of supreme and sole monarch of the barbarians."

The Huns moved first to the north, circled way up around the Alps, and then turned west into the heart of Gaul, cutting swaths through forests to build bridges, plundering without mercy. But then, encountering the Roman legions under the command of Flavius Aetius, and losing thousands of men in a bloody and inconclusive series of battles, the Huns turned abruptly around and retraced their steps back into northern Italy.

Having left the Roman armies behind them, hopelessly out of position back in Gaul, the Huns stormed down out of the mountains and struck at the wealthy city of Aquileia. Poor Aquileia: Alaric had come this way in 401 and again in 408; Aquileia lay at the foot of the Alps, the first Roman city that came to hand, rich and ripe for plunder, as invaders rode down from the mountains. It was sacked again and again in the fifth and sixth centuries.

Aquileia was at that time a considerable city of half a million people, known as *Roma secunda, Maxima Italiae urbs.*

Aquila means eagle, the eagle of the Roman standard, and Aquileia was planted at the top of the Adriatic Sea in 181 B.C., the starting point for roads through the mountain passes of the Alps to north and east, the link between Rome and its neighboring provinces and the Near East. It became the largest city on the Adriatic, its leading naval and commercial port. Augustus had built an imperial residence there in 10 B.C.—and there received Herod the Great. Aquileia became a grand and beautiful city on the water that boasted handsome temples, an amphitheater, a circus, monuments and baths, and a brilliant suburb of palatial villas.

Here, to Aquileia, in the fifth century, refugees came running as the Huns savaged the cities of Spalatro, Salona, Sebenico, Zara, Pola, Parenzo, Capodistria, Trieste. And right behind the refugees came the Huns. The city was assaulted by catapult-fired stones and flaming projectiles, and the walls of the city were attacked with battering rams. But the walls were so solid, and the people so resolved, that they endured the siege of Aquileia for three months, threatening to stop the Huns before they got their invasion of Italy underway.

When at last the frustrated Huns did breach the walls, they were especially furious in the punishment they meted out. And after this punishment, although the residents of the city would successfully labor to rebuild much of it, Aquileia never recovered its lost wealth and power. In fact, many of its citizens fled out into the lagoons at the northern end of the Adriatic and took refuge there among the islands—in particular the Rivus Altus, or Rialto. There, they joined with refugees from Padua and elsewhere who had also fled from the Huns. Because these refugees came from some of the old commercial families of Aquileia and Padua, they founded what would eventually become the greatest sensation ever on the northern Adriatic: the city of Venice.

The Huns, their carts laden down with spoils, turned west then and traveled toward Padua, Verona, and Brescia, and on to Milan, looting and burning. Milan itself was a great prize, and it submitted without resistance, the Milanese having taken to the countryside.

For his own residence in Milan, Attila took possession of the imperial palace. This was, perhaps, his apogee. He was, after all, the ruler of a vast and powerful empire—not as vast as nineteenth-century historian Theodor Mommsen thought (he did not control the British Isles) or as another student of the Huns, Joachim Werner, wrote (reaching fifteen hundred miles from the center of Hunnia into Asia), but vast nonetheless. The Huns ruled the lands from the mouth of the Danube on the Black Sea through much of what is now Bulgaria, some of Romania, Yugoslavia, Hungary, on up into Czechoslovakia, and, in the year 452, was threatening much of the western Roman Empire.

Who were these people who made such an intense impression on the world? They left no writing, no music, no paintings, not even any stories save those that were recorded by Priscus and other Romans. We have only their jeweled, golden belt buckles

and earrings and whip handles and diadems and a few bronze
caldrons from their own hands. The gem-encrusted jewelry is bold
and simple stuff—a band or square of gold, nothing more complex
in shape, covered with as many rough-cut gems, or hunks of gem,
as can be made to fit: sapphires, carnelians, garnets, almandines,
chips of colored glass.

Compared with the jewelry of the Goths—with a gold necklace, for example, of ten multifaceted beads of gold set with garnets
that was made for a Gothic princess—the work of the Huns must
seem crude. Compared with the brooches, or fibulae, being made
along the Rhine at this time—the gold pounded out in swooping
curves, covered with delicate filigree, set with gems in snowflake
patterns—the jewelry of the Huns can only seem brutish. The art
of the Huns, compared with that of their barbarian neighbors,
lacks precision, complexity, suppleness, delicacy, nuance, and
grace.

And yet, not all the world's civilizations have been Apollo-
nian, some have been Dionysian. While some have been complex,
others have been simple, pure, and strong. And neither in their
political strategy, nor in their weapons and tactics of war, were the
Huns simpleminded. It is conceivable that, had the Huns wanted
delicate jewelry, they would have hired a Roman jeweler and had
him make nice things—as the Scythians had used Greek gold-
smiths many centuries before, when they occupied the lands later
taken over by the Huns, to make gorgeous gold-embossed drinking
cups, vases, necklaces, and magnificent ceremonial axes. It may be
that in their jewelry the Huns simply wanted a convenient way to
carry wealth and had no time to waste on designer's niceties. It is
conceivable that the brutal simplicity of the Huns' jewelry was
a political statement, made in purposeful contrast to the useless
refinement of the collapsing Roman Empire.

One other thing besides these few objects was left behind by
the Huns: their names, or at least the names of their leaders. Most
of these names, in the immediate circle around Attila, are Turkish,
as Maenchen-Helfen noted. Attila's father was Mundzuc, a Turkish name. And Attila's sons have Turkish names, Daniziq and
Ellac. Ellac's mother had a Turkish name. The daughter of Eskam,
another Turkish name, is mentioned as one of Attila's wives. Attila

itself is a Germanic name, from the Gothic word *atta*, for father. The same word appears in England in such place names as Attleford and Attleborough. Bleda, the name of Attila's brother, is also Germanic. Ruga, the name of Attila's uncle, is Germanic. Onegesius, his prime minister, is Germanic.

It may be, then, that the greater part of the Huns around Attila were Turkish—this would account for the Romans' insistent description of them as swarthy—and that Attila, because he had some Germans among his ancestors, was especially well placed to create alliances among the Turkish and Germanic tribes that made such a potent combination under his leadership. There is a Persian name among Attila's inner group, too, as well as a number of unidentifiable origins, who may have brought others with them into Attila's camp. In the east—but not in close touch with Attila—were a large number of Huns with Iranian names.

Before the Huns had become professional warriors, robbers, and systematic extortionists, they had been shepherds, and those who were not full-time soldiers still were shepherds. They lived the lives of seminomads, not pure nomads of the bedouin type— that is, not nomads who moved ceaselessly from pastureland to pastureland—but sometime nomads who traveled back and forth between regular summer pastures and winter quarters. Their summer pastures might change slightly from year to year, but their winter quarters stayed the same.

When the Huns were settled in their towns, they lived in houses made of wood. And when they were on the move, they lived in tents of felt and sheepskin. Like the Mongolian yurts that are still in use today, these tents must have been spacious, airy, clean, and with woolen carpets laid down for floors, quite comfortable.

According to Ammianus, they had all sorts of animals, but the basis of their economy was sheep. They ate mutton and cheese and drank milk from their sheep. Their shoes were made of sheep leather, their hats were felt, made from sheep's wool.

They were not enthusiastic farmers. Indeed, Ammianus said, "No one among them plows a field or touches a plow handle." Chelchal, who was himself a Hun, put it more bluntly: the Huns, he said, "despised" agriculture. It is true that archaeologists have discovered the remains of the occasional corn grinder and sickle in the territory of the Huns, but in the time of Attila, only the poorest Huns would have grown much of their own grain. Sheep and cattle, and thievery, were better sources of food for soldiers on the move and those who followed along with them.

The Huns did not, as it was rumored, "warm" their meat by sitting on it as they rode their horses. What they did, as many nomads do—and no doubt the source of the rumor—was use raw meat to prevent and to cure the abrasions that their horses sometimes suffered from having the saddle rub against them on long rides. It may be, too, that they put strips of meat, wrapped in cloth, under their saddles if they wanted a quick meal while they rode; the Tatars of the Golden Horde customarily did that.

What was it that had transformed these presumably peaceful, wandering shepherds into the fiercest band of robbing, murdering, raping warriors in Europe? It may have been nothing more than the weather. In 1907, Ellsworth Huntington advanced the notion —generally scorned—that the barbarian movements into Europe were caused by "a rapid change of climate in Asia and probably all over the world—a change which caused vast areas which were habitable at the time of Christ to become uninhabitable a few centuries later." When Huntington advanced his thesis, he had nothing but guesswork to go on: still, he said, he could not be exaggerating the impact of climate "if we assume that during the great and relatively sudden desiccation" that might have occurred in the early centuries after Christ, the average rainfall decreased in the ratio of two to one. If, say, the rainfall fell from thirteen inches to six or seven, "the nomads would have been able to find pasture for only one sheep where formerly they had found it for fifteen." Or if the rainfall fell from twenty inches to ten, "the number of sheep would decrease from sixty to one"—a change in the economy, a change in the very ability to survive, that might make anyone desperate.

"Manifestly, if such a change took place in the course of a few hundred years, most of the inhabitants would be obliged to migrate. As the nomads pressed outward from the drier central regions of Asia, we can imagine how they were obliged to fight with the neighboring tribes whom they tried to dispossess." Huntington could prove nothing, however, and his argument was based too much on a succession of "ifs" for most scholars. Huntington's work dropped from sight for seventy or eighty years. Recently, however, archaeologists have dated former shoreline levels of the Caspian Sea, and the dates of those shorelines confirm an enormous drought of long duration in about A.D. 300, the time the Huns began to move west.

If they were, by origin, a peaceful group of shepherds, by the fifth century they were the most violent fighters of their time, and the greatest horsemen of Europe. "Scarce had the infant learnt to stand without his mother's aid," said Sidonius, "when a horse takes him on his back. You would think that the limbs of man and horse were born together, so firmly does the rider always stick to the horse; any other folk is carried on horseback, this folk lives there."

To their alarming tactics and their accomplished horsemanship, the Huns added superior military technology. Their weapon was the bow, and they were the best archers in Europe. They fought as the American Plains Indians fought, able to shoot arrows to either side of their horses as they rode full speed at an enemy. The Goths had bows and arrows, too, but they never learned to shoot from horseback.

Moreover, according to Maenchen-Helfen, the bows that the Huns used were the best bows of the time. They were reflexed composite bows, which is to say that when unstrung, they reversed their curvature, and that they were made of a number of layers of different materials, generally of wood, sinew, and horn. The bows were about five feet long, deadly accurate at a distance of 50 yards, and still effective at up to 160 yards.

Such bows required great craftsmanship to make. They had to be tapered with extraordinary precision; the laminations needed to be layered with finesse; all irregularities in the grain of the wood had to be eliminated or incorporated into the design. While the basic work on such a bow might be roughed out in only a few days, it could take several months of intensive labor to finish it properly. To make a good Turkish bow, including the interim periods necessary for drying and seasoning the wood between laminations, required five to ten years.

None of the Germanic tribes were able to make such a bow;

the Romans had nothing in their arsenal that nearly touched the Hunnish bow for long-range accuracy. The Huns must have had professional bow makers who provided them with these weapons, and the bow makers must have been greatly respected—and supported by a social and economic system that allowed them to do their best work. When Japanese artisans made bows of such refinement and precision, they signed them with their names. Evidently, though they did not choose to show it in their jewelry, the Huns could produce work of extraordinary skill and sophistication.

These, then, were the people who turned to the south after they had ripped what they wanted out of the city of Milan and turned their attention on Rome. Certainly they had the requisite motivation, the numbers, the strategic and tactical skills, the social and economic organization of society, the leadership, the training, the experience, the reputation, and the military technology. Who could possibly stop Attila from sacking Rome?

Little is known about Leo's life, but the little that is known suggests a man of enormous personal force, intelligence, and canny political instinct. He was born about A.D. 400 in the town of Volterra, fifty miles south of Pisa. Volterra was an insignificant town by Leo's day, although it had been a large, well-fortified, and important place some centuries before.

In his later years, Leo claimed Rome as his hometown, and it may be that when he was a youngster his family moved to Rome —that they were among the refugees who fled south in the face of the incursions of the barbarians. Nothing is known of his childhood, but it appears that he may have been an archdeacon of the church when he was no more than twenty-two years old, and that he was already, at that age, taking a hand in church politics. His rise in the church was rapid. By the time he was in his late twenties, he was largely responsible for shaping policy for the Bishop of Rome. When the head of the Roman church, Sixtus III, died in 440, apparently no one even mentioned a possible successor other than Leo.

To judge from his sermons and letters, Leo was a man given to simple, straightforward, clear, unequivocal, and politically effective statements.

He assumed office at a time when his world was coming apart —or, it might be said, when a new Germano-Latin civilization was coming into being. And his response to this irresistible change was a firm assertion of his own authority, with the apparent intent of ensuring the establishment of the church as a solid, unified, and centralized institution—the most stable institution of the Western world. It was for his success in this effort that he would become known as Pope Leo the Great.

When he set out to meet Attila, Leo could have headed north out of Rome on the Via Flaminia toward Fano on the Adriatic Coast and then taken the Via Aemilia up in the direction of Lake Garda; or he could have gone north along the west coast of Italy on the Via Aurelia and cut through the Apennines below Parma and so on to Lake Garda. Either way he would have been traveling on one of the famously fine Roman highways. "The roads," as Plutarch wrote, "were carried straight across the countryside without deviation, were paved with hewn stones and bolstered underneath with masses of tight-packed sand; hollows were filled in, torrents or ravines that cut across the route were bridged; the sides were kept parallel and on the same level—all in all, the work presented a vision of smoothness and beauty."

On the great highways leading out of Rome, the surface (put atop a bed of rock and clay, or sand) was made of polygonal paving stones of igneous rock, a foot and a half broad and eight inches deep, which fit together so perfectly that they were very likely taken from the same quarry and put back in place on the road just as they had come out of the quarry, so that they formed a surface nearly as smooth as a billiard table. There is a span of bridge in Spain that rises 245 feet above the water below it that was built by the ancient Romans and is still in use today.

The roads were eight or ten feet wide, enough for two lanes or, in some places, wide enough for three lanes. Just at the gates of Rome, they were thirty feet wide. The well-traveled highways had borders and footpaths for pack animals and pedestrians that added another five feet to the width.

These roads carried the traffic of farm wagons hauled by oxen, and two-wheeled passenger carts, and for the wealthy, large carriages, pulled by a pair of horses or mules. Some of these carriages

—fitted out with silk curtains and silver statuary—made travel elegant, even if the wooden wheels translated every small imperfection in the road into a jolt to the passenger. No one other than cavalry or fast-moving imperial messengers would ride horses on these roads; saddles were uncomfortable, and the stirrup did not come into widespread use in Europe until the ninth century, so that horseback riding was too painful for long distances.

The most comfortable way to travel was by litter—carried by six or eight slaves, or rigged to a pair of mules—but litters moved too slowly for long distances. In a carriage, one could make twenty-five to thirty-five miles a day, so that the trip from Rome to Lake Garda might take ten days or so.

Though Leo might have found accommodations with fellow clergymen as he traveled from town to town, travelers ordinarily stayed at inns along the way. Before setting out, a traveler could get an itinerary that showed what inns and other stopping places might be found along the highway. A parchment copy, made in the Middle Ages, of one of these itineraries has survived; it is thirteen inches wide and twenty-two feet long, and as the twentieth-century historian Lionel Casson has written, it is startlingly similar to a *Guide Michelin*. The parchment rolls out to give a continuous schematic rendering of the Roman road system with the towns and inns along the route, and the distance between them noted in miles. The inns are represented by little symbols: a large, four-sided building with a courtyard signifies a commodious inn; a little house with a twin-peaked roof represents a less luxurious accommodation; a little boxlike cottage is an economy inn. Spots for water or a simple meal are indicated with names and no pictures. The itinerary for the Via Aurelia that Leo probably traveled lists a stopping place (without picture) eighteen miles out of Rome, at Alsium; then a spot with modest facilities ten miles further on at Pyrgi; then a spot six miles further, at Punicum, still with only minimum facilities; but then, just beyond Punicum, comes the first four-star (or four-sided) stopping place: a long day's journey, but not difficult on good roads without too much traffic. In any case, travelers customarily took along food and drink to have on the way.

However simply Leo traveled, he was accompanied by two men who would have been accustomed to some luxury. He had in his delegation two representatives of the Roman government: Avienus, a member of the Roman senate, an ex-consul, a man of wealth; and Trigetius, who had at one time been praetorian prefect of Italy—the second highest ranking civilian office, after the emperor, in the imperial Roman government. Men like this were not beneath bringing an army of attendants with them on such a journey, traveling in carriages upholstered in silk, the seats heaped with soft pillows, accompanied by secretaries who took dictation, servants who brought hot and cold drinks, and companions who were able to wile away the time playing games of chance on an ornate little table set up inside the carriage. For all the wealth and splendor these two imperial representatives brought with them, however, they were the supporting members of the delegation, not the principal members; they had held offices in the past; Leo, the presiding bishop of Rome, held his office in the present. And because the emperor himself was living in Ravenna, Rome was Leo's city.

Leo and Attila met in northern Italy, near the modern town of Peschiera, just south of Lake Garda, then called Lacus Benacus, Italy's largest lake, and one of its most beautiful stretches of waterscape, surrounded by cliffs in the north, and these days, by groves of olives and oranges and lemons and—around the southern part of the lake, in the hills near Bardolino—some excellent vines. Just above Peschiera is the peninsula of Sirmione, where wealthy Romans of antiquity vacationed in their villas among the fig trees, willows, olives, and oleanders, taking the waters at nearby sulphur springs. It is mild here in the winter, and cool in the summer.

Whenever two people meet to speak of business, reality is in some measure a conjunction of performances, a piece of theater. And Leo and Attila were unquestionably great performers. Leo, arriving without entourage, without bodyguard, without an army, dressed in a simple habit, wearing a simple cross: here was the living image of a saint, clothed in the power of Almighty God, with nothing to fear. Attila, at the head of a huge army, matched the pope with his own style of studied simplicity: no jewelry, no courtly manners, a man who took his meals out of wooden cups and bowls. No leaders would ever conceive of more striking icons than these to convey their message of the power of simplicity to their illiterate followers.

It may be that the performance Leo and Attila mounted gave their contemporaries no more authentic a version of what occurred between them than the show that Verdi's nineteenth-century contemporaries perceived when they went to see the opera *Attila* at Teatro La Fenice. In Verdi's *Attila* the prologue opens with the chorus singing:

> Urli, rapine,
> Gemiti, sangue, stupri, rovine,
> E Stragi a fuoco
> D'Attila e gioco.

"Shouts, pillage," the Chorus is singing, "groans, blood, rape, devastation, massacre and fire are Attila's sport." This is the sort of thing the Romans were saying about the Huns, though Priscus of Panium was more subdued in the way he phrased it.

Act 2, scene 5, however, does not seem too unlike the sort of thing Ammianus (or Gibbon) wrote. It is the dark of night. Hunnish and Ostrogothic warriors sing in the flickering light of torches:

> Del ciel l'immensa volta
> Terra, ai nemici tolta,
> Ed aer che fiammeggia
> Son d'Attila la reggia.

> *The universal vault of the sky*
> *the earth, wrested from his foes,*
> *and the air full of flame*
> *are Attila's royal palace.*

And so, the warriors sing on, deliciously:

> *Now let the pleasures of*
> *the drinking vessels be spread around;*
> *let us feast on limbs and severed heads*
> *until the morning!*

Verdi wrote the opera in 1845, in the midst of the risorgimento, when the Italians, led by Mazzini, Victor Emmanuel II, Cavour, and later Garibaldi struggled—against the Austrians primarily—to unify Italy. When at last they succeeded, it was the first time Italy had been united since the collapse of the Roman Empire in the fifth century. The opera—which begins amidst the ruins of Aquileia, and has such great arias as the one in which a Roman commander sings to Attila: "You may have the whole world, just leave Italy to me"—had its premiere at Teatro La Fenice in Venice, the city that had been founded by refugees from the Huns in 452.

Just before Leo arrives at Peschiera, Attila is found onstage with his soldiers, who sing in sepulchral bass: "Glory be to Odin. Your henchmen will always be ready for the blast of the trumpet which calls us to blood." "Speak! Command us!" sing the Huns, and as cymbals and drums and trumpets sound a bloodcurdling cacophony all around, Attila prepares to lead the Huns to war. And then: suddenly, from the far distance, comes surpassingly sweet music, music that immediately brings tears to the eyes, and angelic voices singing, "Come, visit our minds, O spirit of Creation." [*Vieni. Le menti visita. O spirito creator.*]

Attila reels from the sounds of heaven. ("Let the treasures of life shower on us from thy forehead.") He stops, paralyzed.

A chorus of maidens and children enters singing in music that would be translucent if such a thing were possible:

> *Illuminate our errant senses,*
> *breathe love into our breasts.*
> *Subdue the enemy hosts and let*
> *the sweet serenity of peace reign.*

Attila, bewildered and rendered powerless, declaims: "I will defy him!" And then: "Who holds me back?"

And then Leo himself, in an enormous bass voice, sings the only four solo lines Verdi gives him in the entire opera:

> *Thou art appointed as scourge*
> *only against mankind.*
> *Withdraw! The path now is barred;*
> *this is the territory of the gods!*

Attila is overcome with terror and amazement as saints Peter and Paul appear above him in the heavens, and then Huns and

Christians sing together, in a swelling chorus of heaven, praising the eternal God. And as the Huns marvel: "What power is this? The king of the Huns for the first time prostrate on the ground!" the Christians recall "By a shepherd boy Goliath was defeated, by a humble virgin mankind was saved," and so "before a devout and pious array the king of the heathens now withdraws!"

The Renaissance artist Raphael painted this moment in a celebrated fresco that he finished in 1514 for the Vatican: Leo, slightly florid and puffy faced, riding on a white horse, escorted by cardinals in billowing red robes, with a cross held high and saints Peter and Paul hovering above them in the air, comes forward with perfect serenity and confidence; the city Leo defends appears behind him—identifiable by its Colosseum, an aqueduct, the Capitolium. Attila on a black horse, a castle burning fiercely on the hillside behind him, appears in the midst of a barbarian horde that pours down through a mountain gorge like molten lava out of a volcano. Royal banners fly behind the barbarian king; helmet bearers and other soldiers rein in their wild horses; some of these Huns wear a skintight scale armor that makes them look naked and armored at the same time. Trumpeters sound a call. And then, at the center of the picture, Attila reels back suddenly in his saddle as he catches sight of the pope and of saints Peter and Paul; the reins fall from the barbarian's hands as he recoils in wonder and terror. The Vicar of Christ on earth overwhelms the pagan with word and gesture alone.

What really happened at Peschiera, no one knows any better than Verdi or Raphael did. Presumably Leo and Attila spoke directly to each other. And to some extent we may reconstruct something of what must have been said. For Leo, we have the evidence of what he habitually said in his sermons and his pastoral letters. And some years ago, a candidate for a Ph.D. degree at Catholic University did a statistical analysis of the recurrence of certain words in Leo's texts. From this we know that Leo was conservative in his language, not inclined to use neologisms. In fact, except for ten new proper nouns and proper adjectives, Leo used only seventeen new words in all his writings. Two nouns that he *did* use that had not been used before and that were not used again until the

Middle Ages were *cohortator,* meaning one who exhorts, and *sus-picatio,* a suspicion.

Four adjectives evidently unique to Leo were *coartatissimus,* meaning most rigid; *cohortatorius,* meaning exhorting; *presby-teralis,* meaning of a presbyter or elder of the church; and *schisma-ticus,* meaning schismatic. The adverb *pestilenter,* meaning dan-gerously, is quite rare in other texts.

From an older vocabulary, Leo often used words meaning a washing, a cleansing, excommunication, a uniting, a union, a restraining, a binding, creation, contamination, affliction, decep-tion, plundering, charity, a difference, a division, punishment, ex-altation, a hearkening to, destruction, a giving, a sharing, the suffering of men, perdition, tribulation, atonement, restoration, a rising from the dead, sanctification, salvation.

Of course, all these are words that Leo used when he spoke to Christians, not barbarians; and, although they may betray some of his constant anxieties or hopes, they are not the words he would have used with Attila. They may, however, be the general sort of vocabulary he would have used with the Hunnish leader: few new words, traditional language, nothing flashy—above all, a simplicity of speech.

Another scholar at Catholic University did an analysis of the figures of speech Leo preferred. In no sermon, and in no letter, did Leo ever use irony. He avoided almost completely the figures of argumentation, preferring to couch his remarks in simple and posi-tive forms. He used metaphor infrequently; he was not given to picturesque speech. He did not once employ an allegory. He did not often use hyperbole. His speech was direct, clear, concise.

He had some taste for simple alliteration—for twofold allitera-tion rather than for longer repetitions of the same sound. He em-ployed devices of repetition for emphasis, but nearly always the simplest of such devices: anadiplosis and epanaphora. Anadiplosis is the repetition of a word immediately or almost immediately *(Sempiterne enim Filius, Filius est; et sempiterne Pater, Pater est)* and has a pathetic effect that is good for slightly impassioned ora-tory. Epanaphora is the repetition of a word at the beginning of successive phrases *(Quid autem tam aptum fidei, quid tam conveni-ens pietati).* Leo might have used other figures of repetition, such as kuklos, in which the opening and concluding word or words of a sentence are the same, but kuklos is a highly artificial device; Leo used it only six times. Ornament was always subordinated to substance.

Leo asked a rhetorical question from time to time. He would occasionally use polyptoton, in which two or more different cases of the same word are placed next to one another; it is a pleasant enough device, though its frequent use is said to cheapen one's style; that Leo used it sparingly indicates he took care in composing his language. He rarely used exclamatio, a figure that expressed strong emotion in order to elicit a strong emotional response from the listener. He used optatio, the expression of an impassioned wish, only once.

In sum, he was precise, not given to flourishes or displays of vanity, not elliptical or circumlocutory. Leo expressed himself with neither timidity nor aggressiveness. His language expressed patience, modesty, and even good temper.

What then did Leo say? How could he know what might be effective with Attila? Certainly this invader would not have been impressed by Leo's saintliness. Attila knew of Leo, and though he might conceivably have been respectful of the bishop of Rome, no visions of saints Peter and Paul could have danced in his head. Probably Leo did not try to impress Attila with appeals to Christian values (unlike the modern American diplomat who is said to have implored the Arabs and Israelis to settle their differences "in a nice Christian manner"). The Huns could not be threatened, either, by military force, or by the productive economy that stood behind Leo, or by the technology Leo had at his disposal. The big material forces of history that are said by some historians to determine all events were on the side of Attila.

Maenchen-Helfen takes a skeptical view of the sort of thing that might have impressed the Huns. "Roman rhetorics never prevailed with Attila," he said, "unless they were accompanied by the sound of Roman solidi. . . . All treaties the Huns concluded with the East bound the government in Constantinople to pay them tribute." But there is no evidence that gold changed hands at this meeting, or after it—no record, as there was when Alaric was bought off in 408 and 410, of a bribe being paid.

Some historians have conjectured that Leo must have pointed out to Attila that winter was coming on—and that armies customarily retired to their camps during the winter. But it hardly required Leo to make the journey all the way from Rome to Peschiera to inform Attila of the changing season. And it is not clear, either, that the Huns always retired from the battlefield for the winter. They sometimes evidently followed the example of Alaric, who broke through the mountain passes in midwinter when he could be certain the passes would not be guarded.

It could be that, by this time, the Roman army had gathered itself together in Gaul, and that Leo was able to tell Attila that a massive military force was about to come into the field. But Attila would have been better informed by his scouts or by his spies than by a Roman clergyman who was very distant from current information about the Roman army.

What seems most likely, astonishing as it may be, is that Leo told Attila the truth. The truth was that there was a plague raging in Rome and that if Attila brought his soldiers there they might die of the plague. Such a warning would have struck Attila with considerable force: Alaric had died of the plague after he sacked Rome.

To be sure, it may be that Attila had already heard of the plague from others, or as some historians have said, that his army had already been struck by the plague, and his forces were growing weaker moment by moment—and that all Leo did was to add the finishing touch.

But why was it necessary for Leo to make this long trip just to tell Attila what Attila might already have heard from others, or that Avienus or Trigetius could quite as easily have said? Perhaps because Leo was the only credible voice in the empire, the only one Attila, having been lied to repeatedly by emissaries of the empire, could be counted on to believe. This is why diplomats so often insist, odd as it may seem, that truthfulness is the first among the virtues of a successful ambassador. Delivered at precisely the right moment, it can alter the course of history.

Attila turned back from Rome. He took his army and withdrew from Italy. It may be that his intention was to return the following year. That winter, back in camp with the Huns, as Priscus reports, Attila "took in marriage a very beautiful girl, Ildico by name—after numerous other wives according to the custom of his race." Their marriage was celebrated, as Gibbon wrote, "with barbaric pomp and festivity, at his wooden palace beyond the Danube; and the monarch, oppressed with wine and sleep, retired at a late hour from the banquet to the nuptial bed."

And then, in the morning, no sound came from the nuptial chamber. Attila's attendants did not venture to disturb the newly married couple until late in the day when, growing anxious at the unusual silence, they broke into Attila's room, and there, as Gibbon says, they found "the trembling bride sitting by the bedside, hiding her face with her veil, and lamenting her own danger, as well as the death of the king, who had expired during the night."

"Worn out by excessive merriment at his wedding and sodden with sleep and wine," said Priscus, "he lay on his back. In this position a hemorrhage which ordinarily would have flowed from his nose, since it was hindered from its accustomed channels, poured down his throat in deadly passage and killed him."

What this sounds like is sudden and massive gastrointestinal bleeding due to esophageal varices, or varicose veins in the esophagus, which are a common complication of alcoholic cirrhosis of the liver. The swollen veins not infrequently burst and disgorge a vast quantity of blood. If Attila lay in near stupor on his back, his lungs would have filled with blood, which is to say, he drowned in his own blood.

It may be that Attila took his young bride in the first place—or that he had taken a succession of young brides—because he suffered, as half of all men with cirrhosis suffer, from testicular atrophy. Such men, because of damage to both the liver and the pituitary gland, will have a decrease in testosterone levels and an increase in estrogen levels, which causes atrophy of the testicles and often the growth of breasts. This, with the effect of the alcohol itself, will cause impotence. Possibly Attila felt his potency would be restored, as men have often felt, by taking a younger woman to bed. No doubt one of the last emotions of his life was disappointment. And no wonder the young woman, charged with restoring the king's potency, was too frightened to open the door the next morning to Attila's companions. Very likely she feared they would kill her.

With that, the Huns disappeared from European history, never to trouble the empire again.

What difference did this meeting between Leo and Attila finally make? In the years that followed, not even Leo could keep the Roman Empire from final dissolution. By the end of the century, all the remnants of the empire in the west had been incorporated into the Germanic kingdoms, and the great empire of antiquity was gone forever.

As for the places where these events were acted out, the town of Peschiera, near Sirmione, where Leo and Attila met preserves none of the sylvan attractions of its ancient days; it is today an indifferent place of loud motor scooters, small cars, cheap cafes, and a waterskiing school.

As for Aquileia, the second city of the Roman Empire, the great commercial metropolis of the northern Adriatic never entirely recovered from the shock of its sacking by the Huns. With the flight of its merchant families to Venice, and the passage of time, the citizens of Aquileia permitted the silt that came down the river from the mountain ranges of the Alps to fill the city's port so that, eventually, the shoreline moved further and further out into the Adriatic, and Aquileia, having waned to a small, peaceful farming town with a population of three thousand, was left standing finally on a small lagoon fifteen miles inland from the sea.

And as for Rome, it of course still preserves the ruins of many of the ancient monuments that stood in Leo's day. And some of the credit for the survival of some of those monuments may belong to the words spoken by Leo.

Two
THE
ILLUSION
OF POWER

As if it were not already difficult enough to know the truth of things as they are, heads of state and diplomats and even honest citizens labor much of the time to add to the confusion by creating good, or even false, impressions.

In the "theater of power," as it is called by Raymond Cohen, a recent student of the signs and symbols of politics, the skilled politician is not only the performer but also the director and designer of the events in which he participates, and if he can, he contrives a setting for his performance that "removes the performance from the realm of everyday life and transposes it into an artificial universe. . . . Disbelief is suspended; the condensed symbolism of the performance acquires a reality of its own, insulated from the alternative logic of the real world."

Pope Leo I and Attila the Hun were accomplished at this art of theater. In our own time, Charles de Gaulle was one of the great masters. During World War II, as Cohen has written, photographs of de Gaulle as a leader of the French Resistance were "widely distributed by clandestine means . . . to counteract the cult of

Marshal Petain," the leader of the collaborationist Vichy government. One of de Gaulle's most famous wartime portraits, as Cohen
wrote, "shows the General in soaking oilskins and holding binocu-
lars, apparently on active naval patrol. The image was of the energetic and resolute man of action, on duty with his forces off the
coast of France. Actually he was on a brief and quite danger-free
trip off the coast of England." And, after the war, when de Gaulle
became president of France, his press conferences were "set in
plush chandeliered elegance . . . [that] proclaimed a lofty dignity
and sweeping historical vision."

De Gaulle's government, said the British prime minister Harold Macmillan, resembled "a royal court." Or as the historian
Philip Cerny noted, "The dramatic function of grandeur," for de
Gaulle, "was to provide a viable foundation for the development of
a consensus which French society had previously lacked."

President de Gaulle played both to a domestic and an international audience with his grandeur. He wrote of a visit President
Dwight Eisenhower paid him: "Our conversations began at the
Elysée and ended at Rambouillet . . . Housed in the medieval
tower where so many of our kings had stayed, passing through
the apartments once occupied by our Valois, our Bourbons, our
emperors, our presidents, deliberating in the ancient hall of marble
with the French Head of State and his ministers, admiring the
grandeur of the ornamental lakes stretched out before their eyes
. . . our guests were made to feel the nobility behind the geniality,
the permanence behind the vicissitudes, of the nation which was
their host."

If a leader lacks an Elysée palace, a proper stage set can be
built—as Mussolini demonstrated in Rome, Hitler in Berlin, and
the Chinese Communists with Peking's Great Hall of the People.
In the Soviet Union, as Cohen wrote, at the time of World War II,
the Russians built Vnukovo Airport near Moscow, which lacked
many basic technical facilities but was larger than any American or
European airport of the time so that visiting diplomats and other
dignitaries would have a suitable impression of the modernity of
the Soviet Union. And when the Russians were finally able to build
a large airplane, the Tu-104, which came off the production line in
1956, Nikita Khrushchev found occasion to fly to Britain in the

new plane, to offer it to delegations visiting Moscow to take them home, and to get the plane seen in Belgrade, Delhi, Rangoon, Jakarta, and Paris to impress the world with the Soviet Union's technological sophistication and military and economic might, which throughout the Cold War years it never possessed to the degree that outsiders thought.

When it comes to conveying an impression of the secure, comfortable possession of power, less boisterous images are often preferred. Thus, President Jimmy Carter appeared on television in a casual setting wearing a cardigan sweater.

Statements that are made by image or gesture are not only useful because they make delightful photographs, or because they communicate policy to illiterate people; they cut through verbal niceties in a literate society, too; they make declarations that are not easily subject to debate, contradiction, or qualification. How does one debate a sweater or a parade or the color of a suit worn on television? They disarm adversaries. They draw in constituencies that might be excluded by a more exact verbal formulation. They blur distinctions. They are even able to declare two or more contradictory policies at the same time. They may build political coalitions. They may be as benign as Roosevelt's fireside chats, or as malignant as Hitler's rallies, but in either case they may melt differences. They arouse a variety of divergent expectations. And they simplify, which is to say they confound. They encourage us to believe that the spectacle we see is ordained: perfect, eternal, unchangeable, and a comfort to the humble observers.

There are, perhaps, infinite examples of this phenomenon of the persuasive creation of illusions in human history, but the gold standard is the meeting in 1520 between the young King Henry VIII of England and Francis I of France.

HENRY VIII AND FRANCIS I
ON THE FIELD OF THE CLOTH OF GOLD

In June of 1520, Henry VIII of England set sail across the Channel to meet Francis I of France. Henry sailed aboard the ship *Katherine Pleasaunce* with its newly decorated royal cabin, accompanied by the ship *Christopher of Hyde,* carrying the royal jewels, and the *Great Bark,* the *Lesser Bark,* and the *Mary and John.* They made their way across the water, with a cargo of the king's retinue of two dukes, a marquis, ten earls, five bishops, twenty barons, four Knights of the Garter, four counselors of the "long robe," twelve chaplains, twelve sergeants at arms, two hundred of the king's guard, 2,087 horses and 205 grooms—along with the queen's retinue of bishops and barons, knights and chaplains, a duchess, six countesses, sixteen baronesses, eighteen knights' wives —the whole contingent accompanied by 1,175 servants, cooks, heralds, minstrels, butchers, valets, carters, clerks, and others with their own 778 horses as well as cases of armor and garments of damask, velvet, and crimson satin, of cloth of silver, cloth of gold, jeweled collars, gold belts, hats with feathers, doublets covered with gold knots, diamonds, emeralds, rubies, golden chains, pearls, and horse trappings with gold tassels and golden bells the size of eggs.

It was said that England, that June, was stripped of its nobility, its courtiers, its gems, its best cutlery and silver plate and its high-born women—and all of them were hauled across the Channel. Certainly, looking down the lists of those who went or were taken to France, one does have the sense that London must have felt woefully empty to those who were left behind.

The declared reason for transshipping the English royal court to France was the grand opportunity of making a lasting peace with England's long-time enemy, the kingdom of France. The ideal of peace had a strong appeal at that time. Neither the English nor the French had forgotten the Hundred Years' War, in which their two countries had been embroiled in costly hostilities from 1337 to

1453. And in the several decades before 1520, Europe had been
unsettled by more than ten years of serious warfare. It was doubtful that any of the European states had won an advantage in these
recent wars. And as the diplomatic historian Garrett Mattingly has
written, the international conflicts had also created internal ten-
sions in most of the European countries, "and the rumblings of
revolt were audible."

International strains had not disappeared. Charles V of Spain
controlled the import of wool into the Netherlands, and the English
economy was dependent in significant measure on the export of
wool. Francis, for his part, pressed ancient French claims to territories in Italy, which set him, too, in opposition to the interests of
Charles. Moreover, in a recent competition among the electors of
the Holy Roman Empire over whom should be elected to the office
of emperor, Francis had lost to Charles, and so France and Spain
seemed set on a collision course. Francis, therefore, needed some
support from the English. And the English, as had often been their
policy, hoped to balance one continental power against another and
use their influence to obtain their own interests.

Settling these disputes by resort to arms was out of the question. The population of France had been decimated by the years of
war and accompanying famine and plague. And as Mattingly has
written, "the embarrassing fact . . . was that England was in no
position to enter a war." The fleet was unprepared. The English
had few cannon. Powder supplies were low. Trained gunners were
scarce. It was questionable whether a good heavy cavalry could be
put together at all.

Added to this was the fact that Henry and Francis were both
under considerable domestic political pressure—Henry from some
of the leading noble families of England, and Francis from the
Parlement of Paris, which had the power to ratify royal legislation,
or not. In such circumstances, politicians like to be seen as powerful figures on the world stage to buttress their positions at home.

For the time being, peace, or more precisely a convincing
appearance of peace, was the ideal policy. Neither Henry nor Francis had much of anything specific to negotiate, but for both domestic and international purposes, they wanted to be seen in friendly
negotiations. It was under these circumstances that Henry's princi-

pal advisor, Cardinal Wolsey, lord chancellor of England, arranged a conference with the French.

In the party that accompanied Henry VIII was Henry Algernon Percy, the fifth duke of Northumberland, who had something of a reputation for ostentatiousness himself. He liked to be preceded, when he rode out on a journey, by nine servants (including his yeoman of the cellar, his cupbearer, and his carver) and followed by eighteen others (among them his yeomen of the robes, of the pantry, and his clerk of foreign expenses). Also to be seen was the elderly Bishop John Fisher, confessor to Henry VIII's mother and counselor to Henry VII, and a tireless advocate of peace. The good bishop would use the occasion to gather material for a sermon he would later deliver back home: the glories of the world, he would say, are as nothing compared to the glories of heaven, just as Augustine of Hippo had remarked about imperial Rome. And where, in any case, Fisher asked, do these worldly glories originate? The cloth that these great men wear comes from the poor sheeps' backs, the fine and costly furs "from other unreasonable beasts. The sylkes wherwith they couer theyr bodyes, were taken of the intrales of worms." And the gold: what else is it but earth ["what is it els but erthe"]? And so all this glory is only borrowed glory, "taken and begged of other creatures." But take away the precious stones and glistening garments, and then what difference is there between emperor and poor man, both mortal, both destined to return to earth and ashes—and then all their glory, rightly considered, "is but very myserable."

Charles Brandon, the duke of Suffolk, was there in his best apparel, as were the earls of Westmorland, Stafford, Kent, Essex, and Wiltshire. Brandon, the son of one of Henry VII's standard-bearers, still looked down on by many in the court for his "basse condicion," even though he had recently married well to Mary Tudor, the young king's sister. Mary, a beautiful, graceful, and sociable young woman, would often serve as unofficial hostess for the king; she would lead the dances and other festivities at the Field, while her husband Charles would lead the jousts.

Nineteen-year-old Anne Boleyn (the daughter of Sir Thomas Boleyn, Viscount Rochford) was there; it would later be claimed that this was where the twenty-eight-year-old Henry first remarked on Anne's beauty, though that appears to be sheer gossip. Henry's queen, Catherine of Aragon, was also there. Aloof and reserved, she was, at age thirty-four, an attractive, well-educated, and intelligent woman, and still very much the queen.

Thomas More, illustrious author of *Utopia* (a best-seller when it appeared in 1516, in Latin), not to mention his talents as scholar, lawyer, and wit—and one of Henry's favorite young courtiers—was there. It would be another fourteen years before More and Bishop Fisher were both executed for opposing Henry's wish to end his marriage to Catherine and marry Anne Boleyn.

Many of the courtiers had taken themselves to the verge of bankruptcy to purchase suitable clothes and to finance an appropriate entourage to be present at the Field of the Cloth of Gold. The occasion would still be remembered a century later, and Shakespeare, in his *Henry VIII*, would have Lord Abergavenny say:

> *I do know*
> *Kinsmen of Mine, three at the least, that have*
> *By this so sicken'd their estates that never*
> *They shall abound as formerly.*

Lord Buckingham agrees: "O many have broke their backs with laying manors on 'em" (which is to say, by mortgaging their estates and wearing their fortunes on their backs).

Still, says the duke of Norfolk, it was a splendid occasion, this "view of earthly glory" when

> *Each following day*
> *Became the next day's master, till the last*
> *Made former wonders, its. Today the French,*
> *All cliquant in gold, like heathen gods*
> *Shone down the English; and to-morrow they*
> *Made Britain India: every man that stood*
> *Show'd like a mine. Their dwarfish pages were*
> *As cherubims, all gilt: the madams too,*
> *Not us'd to toil, did almost sweat to bear*
> *The pride upon them.*

Strict rules had been drawn up about the clothes these courtiers were required to wear. To make a show was important; to make exactly the right show was critical. According to the recent historian Joycelyne Russell (who has done for this meeting at the Field of the Cloth of Gold what Maenchen-Helfen did for the Huns), it was specified that no mere duke or marquis should be so bold as to wear the costume that rightly belonged to a prince: "All nobles were to come apparelled as belonged to their degree, a duke like a duke, a marquis in his degree, an earl after like pre-eminence . . . grooms and pages ordering themselves accordingly." Silk was specified for gentlemen, cloth for yeomen.

Not all these courtiers were pleased with the rules given out to them, or as far as that goes, with the occasion itself. Raphael Holinshed reported in his *Chronicles* (published in 1587), that the "peeres of the realme receiving letters to prepare themselves to attend the king in this journie, and no apparant necessarie cause expressed . . . seemed to grudge, that such a costlie journie should be taken in hand to their importunate charges and expenses." Buckingham especially "knew not for what cause so much monie should be spent about the sight of a vaine talke to be had, and communication to be ministred of things of no importance." (Given such an attitude, it can come as no surprise that, within twelve months, Buckingham would be executed for treason.)

King Henry VIII was himself a splendid one-man theatrical event. When he came to the thone in 1509, at the age of seventeen, he enjoyed, as the sixteenth-century court chronicler and flatterer Edward Hall said, "exercisyng hym self daily in shotyng, singing, daunsyng, wrastelyng, castyng of the barre, plaiyng at the recorders, flute, virginals, and in setting of songes, makyng of balettes [ballads], & dyd set ii. goodly masses [i.e. composed two masses], euery of them fyue partes, whiche were songe oftentimes in hys chapel, and afterwardes in diuerse other places" (and, indeed, can still be heard today).

The Venetian ambassador Giustinian said Henry could ride until he had tired out eight or ten horses. He could fight toe-to-toe with a heavy two-handed sword, could throw a spear a great distance, and was excellent at archery. He was tall, powerfully built, immensely energetic, handsome, with auburn hair, "combed short and straight in the French fashion," according to another Venetian observer, and a round, pink face so fine "that it would become a pretty woman."

In his early years, he was not yet the coarse, cruel, high-strung, willful monarch he would later become, dispatching wives one after another, referring to his lord chancellor as "my pig," and having his advisors murdered when they disagreed with him. And yet he was already fairly well along in his famous ways of indulging himself in rich velvets and satins, large gem-encrusted rings and diamond pendants as big as walnuts, indulging himself in cards and dice and eating and music and having his own way.

Henry VII had passed to Henry VIII a kingdom prosperous and at peace—but without, perhaps, a certain sense of security: Henry VIII was born just a few years after the end of the Wars of the Roses, the dynastic struggle that went on for thirty years, from 1455 to 1485. Two factions had vied to overthrow the king of England and replace him with someone of their own choice—the House of York on one side and the House of Lancaster on the other, both of them descended from John of Gaunt, the duke of Lancaster and the third son of King Edward III. In those three decades, the crown changed hands six times. Three of the five kings who reigned in that period—Henry VI, Edward V, and Richard III—died violent deaths. And the entire direct male line of both the houses of York and of Lancaster were exterminated.

At the end, Henry VII—the Tudor heir to the House of Lancaster, whose marriage to Elizabeth of York had united the warring sides—was left in possession of the throne of England. But however definitive Henry VII's victory may have been, his son was not raised in a climate that would persuade him to take the throne for granted.

Recent historians view the Wars of the Roses as a struggle among a very few members of the aristocracy which left the country as a whole largely untouched. Few towns were pillaged, few farms were ravaged, few ordinary lives were upset by the wars. In the thirty-two years of the wars, only about thirteen weeks of actual fighting took place. As the English historian Charles Ross has pointed out, the literature of the time does not "reflect any great concern with civil war"; schools were founded, churches were

built, castles were constructed with large open windows on the
ground floor, which showed more interest in light and air than in a
good defense. Nonetheless, if the effects of the wars were not
immediately felt at other levels of society, they had been vast and
swift at the top.

During the Wars of the Roses there had been perhaps a dozen
noble families strong enough to challenge the king directly in
war. By the time Henry VIII came to the throne, only two such
families remained intact, Buckingham and Northumberland. As
for the others, as Ross says, their estates and wealth and influence
among their followers "had come into the firm possession of the
king."

But of course, in politics, nothing is ever permanently fixed.
The nobles, many of them, had not entirely abandoned hope of
recovering their powers and their fortunes, and Henry was sensitive to these challenges. Whereas his father had systematically
stamped out nearly every member of the House of York, Henry
VIII reached out among his erstwhile enemies and hugged them to
his court with endless rounds of hunting and hawking and jousting
and feasting and reveling so that they had no time or opportunity
to be back home raising armies against him.

For his closest counselor, Henry reached outside the ranks of
the nobility and chose Cardinal Wolsey, the son of a butcher, and
allowed him to rise higher than anyone else save the king himself.
The cardinal, nineteen years older than the king, cut a dazzling
figure at court. He lived in quasi-royal style at his Hampton Court
palace, attended by five hundred household servants and hangers-
on, as many as the king himself had. His ceilings were hung with
silks, his walls were gilded, and the eight rooms that led to his
audience chamber were hung with tapestries that were changed
weekly. When he traveled, he was accompanied by fifty gentlemen
dressed in crimson velvet, fifty ushers bearing gold maces, cross-
bearers, a half dozen bishops, lackeys and royal archers attending
him along with bearers of two silver pillars and two gold poleaxes,
while he himself, to show that he was a humble representative of
Christ on earth, rode a mule.

His pretensions did not go unremarked. If Shakespeare has his
character right, Buckingham was capable of referring to Wolsey as

> *This holy fox*
> *or Wolf, or both (for he is equal rav'nous*
> *As he is subtle, and as prone to mischief*
> *As able to perform't).* . . .
> *no man's pie is freed*
> *From his ambitious finger.* . . .
>
> *I wonder*
> *That such a keech can with his very bulk*
> *Take up the rays o'th'beneficial sun,*
> *And keep it from the earth.*

"Keech" is the fat of a slaughtered animal rolled up into a lump —at one and the same time the image of a fat man and of a butcher's son, rolled up together.

This keech was shrewd, vigorous, intelligent, capable of vast amounts of hard work, with an eye both for grand strategy and small detail, and—because of his pretentious ways—he was capable of attracting much of the courtiers' hatred away from the king to himself.

Wolsey was very much the stage manager of the meeting at the Field of the Cloth of Gold, arranging for the conference to begin with, speaking with Francis on nearly equal footing to lay out the matters to be negotiated, and overseeing the details of the conference setting.

Henry's party was met at Calais by an advance guard of English commissioners and their secretaries and lackeys, who helped the arriving English party to get their bags and boxes and horses off the boats and to find their quarters. The commissioners were in charge, too, of security—for having, as Joycelyne Russell says, "scowrers and espies" to "discover vales, woods, towns, villages, castles, passages and other suspect places" where ambushers might be lurking, and also for running a group of spies and counterspies to infiltrate the delegation of the French.

Calais, and a small region of territory around it, was the last remaining English possession on the European continent. Since William, the duke of Normandy, had crossed the Channel in 1066 and conquered England, his descendants had claimed half of France as their hereditary domain. The French had taken it back piece by piece, but Calais remained in English hands and continued to give Henry VIII an excuse to call himself king of France whenever he felt inclined. The English were to establish their headquarters at Guînes, six miles south of the town of Calais, and still within the English pale. Ardres, where the French would stay, was about ten miles southeast of Calais. The three towns formed the points of a small triangle. The countryside between the towns was one of rolling hills.

To accommodate the king and his immediate entourage, the English several weeks earlier had sent over three hundred masons, five hundred carpenters, one hundred joiners, and a crowd of glaziers and plasterers and smiths and painters to put up a vast fake castle made of brick and timber, with a canvas roof painted to look like slate, a moat, and two fountains from which wine flowed continuously. The castle had a gatehouse, brick towers at each of the four corners, an expanse of glass windows that astonished all who saw it, an inner courtyard, first-floor pantries, butteries, cellars, sauceries, spiceries, a jewel house, three rooms each for the king and queen, and a banqueting hall 328 feet long.

But while the king and queen were handsomely accommodated in their toy palace, the others in their party had to make do with lodgings in the towns or with camping in tents, of which 820 were put up near the king's palace, with mess tables nearby.

As the master planner of this conference, Cardinal Wolsey had arranged for himself—alone of all the English dignitaries—to have quarters with the royal family in their palace. (Wolsey had made certain, too, in his detailed specifications of conference arrangements, that his own kitchen would be adequately stocked with capons, herons, geese, bitterns, quails, storks, and others of his favorite delicacies.)

Over in Ardres, few of the French were doing as well as Wolsey either. The king himself, and much of his court, had moved up from the Loire (the king had been hunting there in April), through Paris, to Montreuil, and finally to Ardres.

According to Benvenuto Cellini, the famous Italian sculptor who sometimes traveled with the French court, it took at least twelve thousand horses to move the court from place to place, along with its court pets, dogs and birds, a pet lion and a lynx. (Cellini found the noise, the logistics of feeding, and the odor staggering.) Not only the king but his courtiers too brought along baggage trains jammed with furniture, gold and silver plate, and tapestries, and they moved through one town after another like locusts, consuming the supplies of corn and bread and wine as they went.

To accommodate this horde at Ardres, the French had sent out several hundred tent makers under the command of the French Grand Master of Artillery; and they tossed up a cluster of three or four hundred billowing tents and pavilions. They worked day and night, by torchlight through the night, first planting great wooden masts, then sending sailors up the rigging to hang the tents. They hung the interiors of the tents with ceilings of blue velvet studded with gold stars, the crescent-shaped moon, or walls of azure velvet covered with fleur-de-lis or golden balls or golden apples, or signs of the zodiac that would shimmer in the candlelight at night. And the exteriors of the tents were covered with cloth of gold, woven of threads of gold and silk, so that, during the day, the whole evanescent cluster of tents and pavilions danced in the sunlight.

Among the French diplomats and courtiers, Chancellor Antoine Duprat was to be noticed. A wily, tough, and experienced man of fifty-seven, he was widely despised in his own country. He liked good food and drink and found the wine at this conference wanting. He had been Francis's main advisor when the young king first succeeded to the throne in 1515 at the age of twenty, and he was still a close advisor, but a younger man, Guillaume Gouffier, seigneur de Bonnivet, the admiral of France and a childhood friend of Francis, had recently replaced him as Francis's main advisor. Bonnivet, at age thirty, was already a cardinal; a handsome, suave ladies' man, and an accomplished diplomat. Bonnivet was Wolsey's opposite number.

The duke of Bourbon was there, too, and Francis's brother-in-law Charles, duke of Alençon, and the three marshals of France. The king had made a special point, too, of encouraging his wife to bring the most beautiful women of the court to the conference. Such was the collection of beautiful and accomplished women, and of men who had won battles, managed whole regions of the country, conducted diplomacy and negotiated commercial arrangements that one has the sense, finally, that not simply two leaders, or two sets of courtiers or diplomats were meeting here, but rather that the whole elite—or, as some would say, the most ambitious, ruthless, rapacious, and refined—of two entire nations was being brought together at the Field of the Cloth of Gold.

Francis himself was described by one of the Englishmen as a man of about six feet tall, with a long nose, bloodshot hazel eyes, muscular thighs but thin legs below the knee, and feet both long and flat.

Others of Francis's contemporaries often remarked on his grace in conversation: he was said to be superficial but quite engaging. He wrote poetry (or had poets write poetry for him). He enjoyed archery, ball games, jousts, tournaments, and above all, hunting with his hounds. Although he would come to be regarded as something of a model Renaissance prince—the patron of Cellini, Leonardo da Vinci, Jean Clouet, and many others—he did not receive an education in the "new learning" as a youngster. He had been moderately well educated under the guidance of his mother, Louise of Savoy, who commissioned books especially for her children. He knew Italian and Spanish, some mythology, theology, and Latin.

Cardinal Wolsey had negotiated for four months to get the particulars of the conference worked out to the satisfaction of both parties. Because Henry would cross the channel to France, the English thought it was only right that Francis meet Henry on what was English soil on the Continent. The numbers of attendants and courtiers each king was allowed to bring was worked out in detail.

Finally, negotiations moved into the area in which politics becomes indistinguishable from dramaturgy. The two sides agreed that the two monarchs should meet for the first time midway between Guînes and Ardres in a little valley, the Val d'Or (the valley of gold), exactly on the border of Calais and the Kingdom of France, where a special pavilion would be set up for them. In order that neither king would be higher than the other at the moment they caught their first glimpse of one another as they came over their respective hills and down into the valley, workmen were sent out to level one of the hills, or raise the other—to bring the two hills to exactly the same height.

At five o'clock on the evening of June 7, a cannon was fired three times from Guînes castle—and from Ardres came an answering gun. And so the two processions set out for their meeting place. The English party was led by two thousand foot soldiers, preceded by five hundred of the king's guard. Behind the foot soldiers came archers of the king's and cardinal's guard, then gentlemen, mace bearers, followed by trumpeters, then came the king and his personal attendants. Wolsey was preceded by the bearers of his silver crosses.

From Ardres came the French court, similarly arrayed. It was led by mounted members of the royal household, riding two by two, then the royal guard, the fifers and drummers, the trumpeters and heralds, players of shawms, sackbuts, clarions, and horns, archers, ambassadors, members of the court, the king himself at the center of the most powerful courtiers of France.

Crowds of English and French servants and other onlookers, merchants and provisioners and French vagabonds, covered the hillsides between Guînes and Ardres, and both the French and the English deployed their troops to protect the procession from these crowds—and from each other. The French sent out some of the king's guard, the admiral's guard, the duke of Bourbon's guard, and others. The English were anxious that the French might have more soldiers in the area than they did: one could never discount the possibility that this was a trap, and that the French would pounce on the English troops and kill them all. The French had the same worry.

At one moment, Francis brought his entire procession to a halt, and the French party stood still until the king was reassured that the English were not bringing up threatening numbers of soldiers. Henry, meanwhile, brought the English party to a halt when one of his nobles returned from a scouting expedition with the report that the English were outnumbered two to one. With the English party halted, the earl of Shrewsbury told Henry that the French were more afraid of him than he needed to be of them, and so Henry gave the order to move on.

At last the two parties arrived at the Val d'Or, each one drawn up on its hill, looking across at the other. There was complete silence for a moment. The onlookers were quick to note what the kings were wearing. Henry, said Hall, was dressed in a "garment of Clothe of Silver, of Damaske, ribbed wyth Clothe of Golde, so thicke as might bee." Other observers noted a jeweled collar, a large gold belt, a black hat with black feathers. But compared to the king of France, Henry's outfit seemed understated.

Francis I appeared in "clothe of silver, culpond with clothe of golde, of damaske cantell wise . . . and over that a cloke of broched satten, with gold of purple coloure. . . . this said cloke was richly set with pearles and precious stones; this Frenche kyng had on his hed a koyfe of damaske gold set with diamondes."

And then "trumpetts, sagbuttes, and all other Minstrelles on bothe sides" burst out in a fanfare. Again there was silence.

The two kings moved apart from their courtiers and rode down into the valley toward each other. Henry was accompanied by Wolsey, the marquis of Dorset with the Sword of State, and Sir Henry Guildford, Master of the Horse. Francis rode forward with Bonnivet, Bourbon, and his Master of the Horse, Galeazzo da San Severino. Each king had two running footmen. They rode slowly down the hillside into the valley. At thirty paces, they saluted one another by touching their hats, and then, suddenly, they each spurred their horses and rode at one another full tilt—a moment that must have astonished the crowd of onlookers—and then, at the last moment, the kings reined up and, still mounted, embraced one another, as their horses, still excited from their brief run, pawed and circled round and round.

At last the kings dismounted, and then again, standing on the ground, they embraced. Then once again they embraced. They stood apart, and then once again embraced. They parted, and embraced, parted and embraced, parted, circled, and embraced, and it was said that tears filled the eyes of the onlookers as they thought of the ancient enmity between France and England that had cost so many lives for so many generations, and they thought to see the enmity dissolve before them. They embraced twenty times.

The kings turned, then, arm in arm—Francis, the guest because they were on English soil, in the place of honor on Henry's right—and, with Wolsey and Bonnivet, entered the tent together. The musicians played, and the nobles who had come forward with the two kings stood guard outside. Inside, Francis and Henry signed a treaty that Wolsey had negotiated with the French. France agreed to continue to pay an old war debt, on which, in fact, the French were making payments in any case; England agreed to return the town of Tournai, to the east of Calais, that they had seized in their expedition of 1513, on condition that France pay England six hundred thousand crowns' compensation for the castle the English had built at Tournai; and the kings confirmed an agreement of 1518 whereby Henry's infant daughter Mary would wed Francis's infant son.

This treaty hardly required such an elaborate ritual for its signing. Having negotiated it, Wolsey could easily have taken it back and forth from London to Paris for its signing. Indeed, whatever the excuse, it is clear that this treaty cannot have been the point of the meeting at the Field of the Cloth of Gold. It was the pretext for a display of extraordinary wealth and power and concord for the benefit of the kings' domestic constituents and of the other sovereigns of Europe.

Nonetheless, Henry and Francis delivered speeches to each other. If Edward Hall is to be believed (there was no firsthand report from this meeting in the tent, only gossip), each swore his love for the other. "I neuer sawe Prince with my iyen," Hall says Henry said, "that might of my harte bee more loued." Political rhetoric was more fulsome then than now, protestations of personal love were common: the language of intimacy, spoken in public, was powerful symbolism.

Having spoken their set pieces, the two kings were left alone by Wolsey and Bonnivet for fifteen minutes to talk in private. It may be that there are occasions on which leaders have something private to say to each other, opportunities they long for in order to make a breakthrough in relations that none of their underlings has been able to negotiate over the preceding years.

But neither Henry nor Francis had anything to say to the other in private. What these men had to discuss needed to be said in public, before their respective audiences, and so be relayed to the world at large. The real exchange would take place in the public festivities.

In fact, their conversation must have been banal, consisting perhaps of talk about Francis's pregnant queen, or about his luck at hunting in the Loire, or about Henry's passage across the Channel, or about the weather, whether rain would spoil the scheduled jousting. It was the sort of exchange of niceties at which Francis excelled. Not a shred of gossip, not a hint of a later consequence, survives to suggest their conversation dealt with anything more substantial.

The conversation between the kings lasted half an hour according to some sources, an hour according to others, two hours according to still others. If anything, it signified to the thousands who waited outside the tent that the king of England and the king of France could get along in a friendly way for a long period of time. Eventually, the wine was broken out; the French and English courtiers came down from the hillsides; the nobles on each side were introduced to the kings; toasts were drunk. At nightfall, Wolsey became anxious about getting back to Guînes, but Henry put him off, and the two parties stayed drinking until long after dark.

When Shakespeare declared that "all the world's a stage," he spoke not a poet's sudden insight but a common perception about the court of his day. "We princes, I tell you," said Queen Elizabeth I, "are set on stages, in the sight and view of all the world duly observed." "A king is as one set on a stage," said James I, "whose smallest actions and gestures all the people gazeingly doe behold." No one needed to tell this to Henry.

When the two kings met next, they met in plain sight in the middle of a jousting field. The field was 900 feet long and 320 feet wide, the size of six football fields placed side by side. The area was laid out according to a plan drawn up by Henry, which called for scaffolds along each of the long sides of the field—one side for the queens and lords and ladies, the other side for soldiers and servants. In front of each scaffold, to protect the spectators from unruly horses and unwanted persons, there were barriers and a ditch. At each end there were triumphal arches for entries and "twoo lodgynges . . . for the twoo kynges richely adourned" where their majesties "armed theimselfes and toke their ease: also in the same compasse was two greate Sellers couched full of wyne." Beyond this area were tents and pavilions for the other participants in the tournament and practice fields.

Not only did the kings have wine, but so did the lords and ladies. Indeed, the French thought the English ladies made something of a spectacle of themselves, all of them drinking out of the same flasks and cups, even passing their cups among the lords and back again among the ladies. According to Russell, the favorite wine of the time was the sweet malmsey from Spain, the Canaries, and Madeira. The preferred French wines were those of Beaune and Orleans, and also those of Graves. Presumably one could count on getting the best at occasions of this sort, although at a high-level diplomatic gathering the following year, Duprat said none of the wine was worth drinking.

Of other essential equipment for the tournament, the English ordered up two thousand special blunted lance heads of glazed steel from Flanders, one thousand blunted swords from Milan, six hundred two-handed swords, one hundred heavy swords, thirty-six hundred rivets, one hundred buckles, six hundred feathers with springs; fifteen hundred spear staves were brought out from the Tower of London, and a steel mill and the makings of four forges were shipped over from Greenwich for last-minute reinforcements or repairs.

In the early medieval period, tournaments had a genuine military function: they gave knights training and practice in the use of swords and lances and in fighting together in groups. But the fighting was savage, the waste of useful fighting men insupportable, and with the rise of the Arthurian knightly "Round Tables" in the thirteenth century, some limitations were placed on the tournaments. Blunted weapons were introduced, and strict rules were drawn up to reduce injuries in the encounters. In time, the tournament came to resemble sport more than military exercise.

By the fifteenth century, the form of the tournament had become set. It consisted of three parts: the joust or tilt, in which individual mounted knights, separated by a barrier, ran at each other with lances; the *tournoi* or *mêlée*, in which groups of mounted knights fought with swords; and foot combats, which were fought over a low barricade between groups with short spears, or sometimes axes and swords. It had also become aestheticized, by way of costume and music and other refinements, into pure performance—though still a frequently perilous performance—one of prowess, of display, of entertainment, and even of allegorical statement.

In this blending of sport and spectacle, story line and allegory, set entrances and parades and music and rehearsed speeches, the tournament was, in certain essential respects, simply an outdoor version of a court masque—a thing in which to catch the policy, if not the conscience of the king.

Before the tournament began, Queen Catherine and Henry's sister Mary arrived in litters amid a flourish of crimson satin and cloth of gold and jewels, accompanied by other ladies riding side-saddle and dressed in a style that one observer found frankly "unfit for the chaste." The French ladies came in elegant wagons with another flurry of cloth of gold, velvet, cloth of silver, and jewelry, and they took their places with the English ladies in the galleries which had been hung with tapestries. Certainly Queen Catherine could speak French, and Mary, but some of the others chatted uncomprehendingly with one another, or with the help of transla-tors. (In fact, one of the translators may have been young Anne Boleyn, who was staying at the French court at the time.)

"At the houre assigned, the two kynges armed at all peces mounted on horsebacke, on them attendyng the noble persones [6 knights, 20 esquires and officers, a total party of 120 persons] . . . the French kyng sette hymself on a Courser barded [that is, with a covering over its breast and flanks] covered with Purple sattin, broched with golde, and embraudered with Corbyns fethers."

These "Corbyns fethers," as one might expect of the costumes in a work of dramaturgical art, were not without significance. "Cor-byn," as Hall said, "is a Raven, and the firste silable of Corbyn is *Cor,* whiche is a harte." And the French word for feather is *penne,* signifying pain. The feathers were fastened with buckles which signified "sothfastnes," or steadfastness. And so Hall deciphered this first statement made by the clothes of the French king as he entered the jousting field: "harte fastened in pain endles," or per-haps "pain in harte fastened endles." What could this mean? The political analysts went to work on it at once, but it would not be for several days—when Francis would appear with additional messages on his clothes—that his complete statement could be pieced together.

Henry, meanwhile, made clear, straightforward declarations. His horse's bard was decorated with waves, said Hall, which obviously signified "the Lordeshippe of the narowe sea," that is to say, the English Channel, a source of English security and strength.

The two kings were leaders of their respective opposing teams, and they took part in the jousting along with the others, but they never jousted directly with each other. On this first day of the tournament, Henry came up against Charles de Vendôme, seigneur de Graville, and was lucky enough to give "the sayed Monsire Graundevile such a stroke that the charnell [hinge] of his hedde pece" broke and he could not joust again.

For all the precautions of blunted lances, for all the rules, for all intentions only to score a glancing hit and splinter a lance or occasionally knock an opponent to the ground, despite the fact that, as one recent historian has put it, these sportsmen behind their shields and inside their armor "were half blind, half deaf, half stifled and half cooked, and if they struck their opponents at all, they only gave them a buffet," it could still be a dangerous sport. One French knight died of wounds inflicted by his own brother during this very tournament.

On the first day of tilting, said Hall, all the players acquitted themselves "right valiauntly," and at about seven o'clock in the evening, the heralds shouted "disarmy," and "the trompettes sounded to lodgyng."

The next day, the kings themselves did not joust, and on the following day, the jousting was canceled on account of wind and rain. So the English royal guard staged a wrestling match against the French, and the English won. The wrestling was followed by an archery contest—a sport at which Henry excelled, and at which he clearly outclassed Francis.

Following on the heels of these two triumphs, no doubt feeling buoyant, Henry went up to Francis and challenged him to wrestle, and the French king threw Henry to the ground at once with some sort of special trick called a "tour de Bretagne." As it was reported by a Frenchman who was on the spot, "luy donne ung tour de Bretagne, et le jette par terre et luy donne ung merveilleux sault"; that is to say, Francis gave Henry a marvelous flip and threw him to the ground. (Edward Hall discreetly forbore to mention the incident in his chronicle.)

This might have been a catastrophic political statement to

make. Henry was not without his pride, and his attendants might have been quick to feel that it was England that had been thrown to the ground. Henry asked at once for a rematch, but Francis evidently shrugged it off. It was time for dinner and the moment passed.

The following day the weather had cleared, and the kings resumed their jousting. Francis appeared on the field with an addition to the statement about his heart. He was dressed (as were all the members of his team) all in purple satin and velvet, and all over his clothes were little bits of white satin embroidered with the word *quando* and also many little letters *L,* which in French, as Hall quickly deciphered, "was to be interpreted to be *quando elle,"* which is to say "when she," so that Francis's statement now read: "heart fastened in endless pain, when she . . ."

Henry's statement of the day was, once again, more direct. He and his team were dressed in cloth of silver covered with branches of eglantine, and as Hall said, "this Eglantine tree is swete, plesant and grene, and yf it be kyndely and frendly handeled." But if it is rudely dealt with, "yt wyll pricke."

No doubt the kings and their teams were closely watched, but the team led onto the field by M. de Lescun may conceivably have looked even more striking than the royal bands. M. de Lescun's group of knights were all dressed in black, black damask and black satin, slashed in checkerboard fashion; and when Lescun presented his group to the ladies' gallery, he made his horse curtsy several times and then went around the field repeating his trick. This business of showing off was not unique to Lescun. The tournament was often interrupted for little displays of talent and horsemanship that the crowd loved. The kings themselves would from time to time put their horses through maneuvers of leaping and other tricks.

It was not until Saturday that Francis revealed the conclusion of his fashion statement. On that day he and his men appeared in purple velvet embroidered all over with little books on which was written "a me," and around the borders of his costume was a blue chain. This was no trouble for Hall to decode. The book was, of course, in Latin, *liber,* and so, with the letters, it meant "libera me," or "free me" from the chains. Thus, concluded Hall triumphantly, the full statement of the French king was: "hart fastened in paine endles, when she delivereth me not of bondes." Having deciphered it, however, Hall had no idea what it meant. It seemed to have no political significance. Perhaps it was only a romantic sentiment; certainly the statements made at tournaments were often purely romantic. In such a highly politicized environment, however, to make no statement is to make a statement of sorts. And in particular, to have chosen not to make a bellicose remark was to have made a most significant statement.

Once again, Henry's statement was precise. He wore a costume half cloth of silver and half cloth of gold, its borders decorated with letters in gold (two thousand ounces of gold) set with eleven hundred "great and oriental perles." Henry's statement read, "God willing my realm and I may. . . ." The conclusion—either a threat or a promise—was left blank, reserving to the king, as was his right, complete liberty of action. In effect, Francis and Henry had said the same thing. Two sovereign nations met and kept their options open. And in the midst of a spectacle of the ritual warfare of jousting, with the risk of an outbreak of mayhem at any moment, neither king spoke provocatively; both kept the peace.

The day was one of heavy jousting. Henry broke eighteen lances that day, Francis broke fourteen, the count of Guise broke seven, the duke of Suffolk six. Hall's record of the event registers some confusion about dates, but it may have been on this day that Henry rode so hard, "so freshly and so many courses," that he rode one of his best horses to death. It was on this day that Francis took a hit in the head that gave him a black eye, so that he had to wear a patch for the rest of the meeting.

This day was followed by two days off. There blew "such stormes of wind and wether," said Hall, "that marvaille was to hear, for which hideous tempest some said it was a very prognostication of trouble and hatred to come between princes."

At some point in the midst of all this public posturing, Francis decided to break through and have a private moment with Henry. And so it was that he got up early one morning and rode over to the English castle with only a couple of companions and surprised Henry, who was only just getting out of bed.

Francis's gesture was in fact one of real courage: he might

count it improbable that the English would seize him and take him prisoner, but nothing was certain when he went unarmed into the English camp. (Since he had shown such bravery, Henry felt obliged to ride over to the French camp for breakfast several days later.)

Once again the two kings apparently had nothing to say to each other in private. Indeed, this "spontaneous" moment acted out in public seems simply another instance of appropriating a gesture from private life to make a public statement about trust.

On the last day of the jousting, Francis wore a costume on which one observer said he made out the words *"Cosi l'orso sera,"* or "thus will the bear be." Hall had stopped trying to make sense of the French king's clothes. Henry was apparently wearing his English Channel ocean waves again. On this last day at tilting, Henry ran the courses "fiersly" again and again: "course after course the King lost none." The jousting ended with a total of 327 spears broken.

Then came the *tournoi,* fighting from horseback with swords, two against two. Francis appeared for the *tournoi* in purple satin with bouquets of pansies made of white satin, which signified, according to Hall, "think on Francis," though, as Hall added, "to whom he spake was not knowen." Henry's dress was embroidered with a mountain on which a knight rode toward the top. Out of a cloud came a lady's hand which struck the knight with a deadly arrow, and the motto: "in love whoso mounteth passeth in perill." Hall did not try to interpret this. It would seem that Henry was making some sort of remark about the perils of love and trust; but he was not retracting anything he had previously suggested.

The next day Francis wore purple with embroidered letters with the simple legend *"reciproce,"* reciprocity. Henry had little branches embroidered on his costume which one of the Italian observers said were olive branches but which Hall declared to be branches of basil, with the warning, "Breake not these swete herbes of the riche mounte, doute for dammage." Perhaps it was an olive branch. Conceivably the two monarchs had moved at last to mutual declarations of peace and cooperation. In any event, neither had declared hostility in this silent dialogue, and that alone was a policy worth noting.

On the other hand, in the *tournoi*, said Hall, the two kings "foughte with great randon and force," and as soon as one encounter was finished, "on went swordes and doune went visers, there was litle abidinge," and all the participants fought fervently, battle after battle, "and none ceased."

The *tournoi* was followed by the combat on foot at the barrier, and there the two sides "lashed alwayes one at another," and when their spears were shattered, they beat one another with the stumps of the spears and then threw the butt ends at one another; and then they took up their blunted swords and beat one another with those, and there was no tarrying, said Hall, but they fought with such force "that the fier sprang out of their armure," and then when they had done with those swords they took up the heavy two-handed swords and slammed and hacked at one another some more until their armor was dented and shattered, their swords broken and littering the ground, and their arms hung exhausted at their sides, and so the battle was finally done, as Hall said, "wyth great honor."

The hardest part of a tournament, according to some historians, was getting it to end. Such passions had been aroused, fouls committed, so many scores left uneven, blood sent racing, that the final hand-to-hand fighting sometimes went on even as the groups moved away from the field of encounter and back to their quarters. But on this occasion, when the heralds cried out the end of the tournament, all laid down their arms.

Then Wolsey had one of his finest moments of the conference. That night, a chapel was constructed on the jousting field. It was made so that the congregation could sit in the royal gallery and face the altar across the intervening ditch. Musicians and choirs filled the ditch, and the altar was set out with silver gilt images, gold candlesticks and vases, and a heavily jeweled crucifix. On the right side of the altar there was a canopy for Wolsey himself, who thus took center stage for this closing ceremony of the tournament.

All the church dignitaries who were present for the conference were arranged on the altar in strict order of precedence: Cardinal de Boisy, the pope's legate, had a canopy at a slightly lower level than Wolsey's, and then came the other three French cardinals, twelve French bishops, nine English bishops. The bishops helped Wolsey into his vestments, and at the moment of the ritual washing of his hands, Wolsey had some of the noblemen present to do so. There were trombones, sackbuts, fifes, cornets, and an organ; there were twelve singing priests, sixteen singing men, and twelve singing children. At one moment of the mass there was even a heavenly apparition: a fiery dragon shot across the sky to the amazement of the spectators. (What the dragon was doing was anyone's guess, but the historian Sydney Anglo, who wrote an excellent book about Tudor pageants and spectacles, thinks it was a fireworks device that was meant to be launched that evening after dinner but was set off by mistake, or as a prank, during mass.)

Mass was followed by a banquet, right there on the field, with the musicians continuing to play. By this time perhaps everyone present had lost his grasp on what was real and what was not, or ceased to care, given all the "denties with subtilties" that had been eaten at table in the course of this affair, the swan served in chawdron sauce of liver, entrails, and blood, the porpoise roasted on coals, the cooked pork, pounded in a mortar, as Russell reports, with "raw eggs and then boiled in a bladder with raisins, currants, chopped dates, pepper" and cloves, cut in pieces and served with a sauce of "large raisins, red wine and milk of almonds, flavoured with cinnamon and ginger," the songs of Thomas Farthing ("In May That Lusty Season"), the strident blast of trumpets to announce each course, or trumpets and clarions together as lords and gentlemen entered with dishes with gold covers, accompanied by heralds, cooks, the Grand Master carrying his gold baton, and then the stuffed teal, the partridge with orange sauce, the sauces of raisins, nuts, bread, cloves, and ginger on the young heron or plover or crane, the lark or sparrow or thrush or lapwing with salt and cinnamon, the peacocks served in the medieval manner (their necks broken, throats cut, bodies flayed, skin removed—feathers and head all in one piece—then roasted, allowed to cool, and their bodies dressed once again in their own feathers and heads so that, when the birds came to the table, they looked, like the diners themselves, almost alive), the courses washed down with lashings of ale and beer, or between courses, the palate refreshed with sweet wine spiced with ginger, cinnamon, cardamom, and sugar, and after the third course the herald crying out "largesse" so that money can be distributed in the name of the king of England, new dishes brought in emitting flames and accompanied by eight trumpeters and twelve archers, the sugar sculptures of salamanders and leopards, the great diamond shining on the breast of the queen of France, *"la poincte de Bretagne,"* one of the crown jewels of Brittany, dancing to the music of tabor, pipe and rebec, the Gascony wine served "after mete, and with oysters," and the "chewettes," small pieces of chopped liver of pigs, hens, and capons, fried in grease, mixed with eggs and baked in pastries, the quantity of lard ordered for the kitchens, the second course of soup, capon, wren, sturgeon, peacock, pigeons, quails, apples, baked venison, tarts and fritters, Chancellor Duprat's attempts to popularize the consumption of donkey flesh (herons were in fashion then, and turkeys were just coming in; swans were always in; roasts were going out; venison with white turnips was in, and kid with cheese sauce; quail cooked with bay leaves was in, stuffed teal was in, partridge with orange sauce was in, turbot was in, and salmon from the Loire and the Rhone; porpoises were in, asparagus was in, and apricots, and greengages; raspberries were out, English beer was in, liqueurs were out, Burgundies were in, tasters—for possible poisons—were in), flans and jellies for dessert, stuffed plums and macaroons, the mummeries and charades, maskings and disviserings, these plays within the play, the awarding of prizes for the day's jousting, the jeweled gowns and silver dishes, the song "Pastyme with Good Companye," the fountains even still flowing with wine, the food served so liberally, as Russell remarks, "we are told . . . that people choked," the atmosphere of total unreality created by all this jousting and costumed horses and festooned women and music on all sides, and relentless eating and playing must finally have disarmed everyone—with the possible, though not certain, exception of those at the top who had arranged it all, and maintained some grasp on reality by eating privately beforehand.

In the final celebrations, on Sunday, June 24, Henry and Francis each mounted their horses, and with a clutch of their attendant nobles, set out from their own headquarters to the other's, to have a farewell dinner with each other's queens.

And when they rode home from their respective dinners, the two kings met one last time on the tournament field and there embraced, and got off their horses and went into one of the lodgings at the end of the field to pass three-quarters of an hour in amiable conversation before they parted.

Francis headed back to Paris, to his château at Saint-Germain-en-Laye. Henry headed north, just over the border into the territory of the Holy Roman Empire where, at the little town of Gravelines, he had a quiet, barely noticed meeting with the Holy Roman Emperor, Charles V. In fact, just before Henry had sailed for his meeting with Francis, he had had a brief meeting with Charles—and promised to meet again directly after his conference with Francis, to reassure Charles about his intentions.

The spectacle of friendship between Henry and Francis would put all European powers, and especially Charles, on notice; if any country were to work against the interests of either England or France, that country would have to face the possibility of the combined opposition of these two great nations. Charles had some specific reasons for anxiety on this account, since if England and France entered an alliance against the Holy Roman Empire,* the two of them could close off the English Channel against Charles's ships and cause the empire extreme hardship. And Henry would use the appearance of concord with France to help persuade Charles not to harm England's wool trade with the Netherlands.

When Charles had heard Henry and Francis were to meet, he had rushed up the coast from Spain so that he would just happen to be in the Channel before Henry was to sail for France. They had met in Dover on May 26, and there Henry promised to make no commitments without first informing Charles. Now, after the meeting with Francis, Henry and Charles met for two days at Gravelines and then traveled together to Calais where they spent two more days together. There was some dining, and a bit of masking and dancing; but on the whole, their meeting was businesslike and brief, proving, among other things, that not all meetings in the sixteenth century had to have a lot of foofaraw about feathered hats and pearl-encrusted horse trappings to qualify as important. They covered a good deal of substance with terrific dispatch. Charles tried to break up the marriage alliance between Henry's daughter Mary and the French dauphin, and Henry refused. Charles tried to persuade Henry to enter into a more explicitly proimperial league against France, and Henry refused.

England remained neutral, uncommitted, but friendly—hoping that, by maintaining a balance of power and anxiety on the Continent, England could protect its interests.

In fact, Henry's policy worked—for almost a year. In April 1521, after some months of bickering over French claims to Italian territories, an imperial army took up an ominous position on the northern border of France. In June, Pope Leo X announced that he had made a treaty with Charles, because Charles would help put down the Lutheran rebellion in Germany, would resist the Turkish threat to Italy, and would return some Italian territories to the Holy See. In July, Francis confiscated some funds from the Florentine bankers in France. In August, Charles launched a full-scale attack on France. In April 1522, England entered the war on the side of Charles. English forces marched out of Calais and into the French countryside. By the summer of 1523, Francis had sent an army across the Alps into Italy, and the duke of Bourbon was plotting treason. Europe was back at war. The peace conference on the Field of the Cloth of Gold stood revealed as a spectacular illusion.

Three

THE
INEVITABILITY
OF SURPRISE

Because history is written in retrospect, and reveals to us in hindsight the incidents that brought some event to its apparently inevitable fruition, it prepares us badly for our own lives, in which there are not as many inevitabilities as there are surprises, shocks, accidents, operations of chance, and outright impossibilities that we never took into account when we made our plans, and that alter our lives fundamentally and forever.

"I returned," reads Ecclesiastes 9:11, "and saw under the sun, that the race is not to the swift nor the battle to the strong, neither yet bread to the wise, nor yet riches to men of understanding, nor yet favor to men of skill; but time and chance happeneth to them all."

Which Western government was able to forecast to a degree of certainty in the mid-1980s—and plan its policies accordingly—that the Soviet Union would collapse by the end of the decade, freeing Eastern Europe from its grasp and dissolving the Soviet Empire in a matter of months? Who would have predicted that Premier Mikhail Gorbachev would be thrown out of office? Certainly not Gorbachev himself. Or that a previously little-known mayor of the capital city, Boris Yeltsin, would put down a military coup—bloodlessly? Or that it would soon be rumored that the former apartment of Stalin's chief executioner in the House on the Embankment was now occupied by the senior executive of the Russian branch of McDonald's.

Who could have predicted in 1972 that a night guard at the Watergate apartment complex in Washington would discover a piece of tape holding open a lock on a door? Who could have imagined that piece of tape would lead to the discovery of men breaking into the offices of the Democratic National Committee at the Watergate, ending Richard Nixon's political career and fueling a profound cynicism about politics in the United States for the next twenty years?

If the assassinations of John and Robert Kennedy were the results of plots of whatever scope, they were certainly, too, the result of extraordinary chance, and the starting point of much speculation about how the Vietnam War might have been ended differently had either of them lived, and how the history of the country would have changed as a result.

How could the Japanese have predicted that they had such a short time to negotiate an end to World War II before Hiroshima and Nagasaki would be obliterated? The agent of destruction was a weapon that could not form a part of their calculations because it came from an entirely different era.

Who could have imagined that an earthquake would have occurred in Lisbon in 1755, that would, according to some historians, help put an end to a predominant European attitude of optimism and replace it with a pervasive skepticism that marked the critical rationalism of the late eighteenth century?

For that matter, who could have dreamed that the Black Death would sweep across Europe beginning in the 1340s, reducing the populations of towns by halves and two-thirds, spreading profound grief and wrenching life changes? Who could have predicted that the bacillus in the belly of a flea would have the power to shatter the relationship between agricultural supply and demand across Europe, that the effects of the plague would destroy wage structures, freeing laborers to improve their working conditions, bestowing excess wealth on some of the survivors so that they could indulge in a new trade in luxury goods, and giving the final death-blow to the old feudal political structures that rested on the old financial arrangements? Who would have predicted beforehand that a flea would assist in the rise of new learning to try to under-stand the event that had occurred, and help in some measure to bring about the beginning of the Renaissance?

And how utterly inconceivable it would have been in the six-teenth century to those European masters of the illusion of everlast-ing political stability, Henry VIII and Francis I, that a kingdom as immense and powerful as that of France or of England could be erased entirely from history by a small, unruly band of soldier-adventurers from an unknown and to them unheard-of continent. And yet, at the very time those two monarchs were meeting, this is what happened to the Aztec emperor Moctezuma, another mas-ter of the illusions of political power on a different continent, who ruled an empire of apparently eternal stability.

That Hernando Cortés landed on the shore of Mexico in 1519 was a completely unpredictable surprise to the Aztecs and their leader Moctezuma; and everything that followed from that moment to the destruction of an entire civilization was a succession of stun-ning, seemingly supernatural surprises to everyone involved, both Spaniards and Indians. History offers no more astonishing instance of the part that chance plays in our lives—how shallow is any plan that does not understand its own fragility—than this catastrophic slow-motion coming together of Cortés and Moctezuma.

Cortés and Moctezuma at Tenochtitlán

Even before anyone appeared, there were amazing events: a comet appeared and split into three; the waters of the lake boiled up in a rage; a sign like a tongue of fire burned up into the heavens.

These things began to happen ten years before the Spaniards landed in 1519: omens that foretold the Spaniards' arrival, according to the old men, who drew pictographs of these events some thirty years afterwards for the Franciscan missionary Fray Bernardino de Sahagún—affirming, after the conquest and annihilation of the Aztec civilization, the everlasting power of the Aztecs. The Aztec civilization fell, the pictographs say, not because of the might of the Spanish invaders but because the end of the Aztecs was foreordained. The Spaniards were mere pawns of Aztec cosmology.

The first ship came in the spring of 1519, sailing in along the northern shore of the Yucatán peninsula, according to Sahagún's native informants, who offered a narrative that Sahagún wrote down. The lead ship was followed by eleven others (according to other sources, ten or twelve), carrying ten large bronze cannon, four falconets or light cannon, stores of powder and shot, sixteen horses, a handful of dogs and about 550 soldiers, including thirty-two crossbowmen, and thirteen musketeers, and a hundred sailors, along with two hundred Cuban natives to act as bearers and servants, several blacks, and a few Indian women.

The Spaniards, with their white skin, their suits of armor, weapons, cannon, dogs and horses, were an arresting sight. "They were very white," according to Sahagún. "They had chalky faces." They presented a strange and amazing appearance to the Indians.

Such has been the theme of most historians for the past four centuries, including early indigenous accounts such as Sahagún's, who have described the Spanish ships as "of supernatural size and appearance," crossing "the heavenly water from the east," carrying "men of totally unknown breed" who rode on the backs of extraordinary deerlike beasts, or were perhaps centaurs themselves—or else were gods.

But the natives of the Yucatán and Mexico could hardly have been so naive. A year before, the Indians had seen Spaniards cruise the same coastline in an expedition led by the adventurer Juan de Grijalva. They had met the Spaniards and traded native gold ornaments and vessels, jewels for glass beads, scissors, pins, and other trinkets. And in 1517, Francisco Hernández de Córdoba had sailed into the Gulf of Mexico looking for slaves.

In the spring of 1519, the Spaniards were led by Hernando Cortés. He did not look more godlike than the Spanish traders the Indians had seen before; but his dogs, horses, and weaponry lent an air of exotica not previously seen; and in retrospect, to Sahagún's informants, Cortés's appearance in Mexico, and what followed from it, were astonishing enough to earn the most extravagant reports.

Cortés was a soldier of fortune whose parents had destined him for the law until he had quit school at the age of sixteen, which "vexed his parents exceedingly . . . He was a source of trouble to his parents as well as to himself, for he was restless, haughty, mischievous, and given to quarreling, for which reason he decided to seek his fortune." This account is the best that can be said of Cortés as a young man. It was written years later by his private secretary and chaplain, Francisco López de Gómara, no doubt relying greatly on what Cortés had told him. Cortés had set his sights on shaping a career in the New World. He arrived at Hispaniola, in 1504, and seven years later took part in the conquest of Cuba. There he was eventually chosen by Diego Velásquez, the governor, to command an expedition to Mexico.

The men who sailed with Cortés were mostly in their twenties and thirties. They had signed up for this voyage in the hope of getting rich. They received no salary for joining the expedition: they would be paid in spoils. They were marginal young men, their prospects at home not good enough to keep them there. They talked of converting the Indians to Christianity, and they meant what they said; they were devout Christians. But one did not fight for God and king without pay. They talked of trade, but if the Indians were unwilling to trade, armed robbery. They were a nervous, sometimes panicky band who might become uncommonly rich or be left for dead on an unknown continent.

Along the journey, dropping anchor from time to trade with the Indians, they picked up Jerónimo de Aguilar, who had been among those shipwrecked on a voyage of 1511, and who had lived among the Mayans and learned their language. They also picked up a woman who had been sold into captivity to the Mayans, whom they called Doña Marina. Doña Marina spoke Nahuatl, the language of the Aztecs, as well as Maya. As the Spaniards moved into Aztec territory, Doña Marina translated from Nahuatl into Maya, and Aguilar translated from Maya into Spanish.

The fleet found safe harbor just before Easter at Chalchiuh-cuecan—the island of San Juan de Ulúa as the Spaniards called it —set in a beautiful landscape of meadows and streams with broad sandy beaches. As they dropped anchor two large canoes came out filled with Aztec ambassadors. The Indians brought some gifts, and they were taken aboard the flagship and given food and wine and some blue beads.

"They said that their lord," wrote the twenty-seven-year-old Bernal Díaz, "a servant of the great Moctezuma, had sent them to find out what kind of men we were and what we were seeking." According to Gómara, the Indians also inquired, with diplomatic tact, "whether they intended to stop or continue on beyond." Cortés responded that the Spaniards had come to speak to the lord of the Aztecs.

On the next day, Good Friday, the Spaniards went ashore on the mainland and set up a rude camp. On Easter Sunday, the local Aztec governor arrived. His name was Tentlil, and as Gómara wrote, he was accompanied by more than four thousand men, unarmed and handsomely dressed, and loaded down with presents. Díaz noted that Tentlil had also brought along some Aztec artists who made portraits of Cortés and his captains and soldiers, his ships and sails and horses and guns—a detailed intelligence report to send back to Moctezuma, the lord of the Aztecs. When Cortés asked to see Moctezuma, saying that the Spaniards came as ambassadors from the greatest king on earth, Tentlil replied that word would be sent to Moctezuma, and they would see what he would do.

Cortés asked whether Moctezuma had any gold. Tentlil replied that he did. Cortés asked, "Send me some of it, because I and my companions suffer from a disease of the heart which can be cured only with gold."

The emperor Moctezuma, as Cortés would learn, ruled over a vast imperial domain from his capital city of Tenochtitlán, the site of present-day Mexico City. The Aztec empire in central Mexico stretched from the Gulf coast, where the Spaniards had landed, to the Pacific Ocean, which had not yet been explored by the Spaniards; and south to present-day Guatemala. The creation of an oligarchy, the Aztec emperors were chosen by a group of about a hundred of the richest and most powerful lords. Moctezuma ruled by means of subtle, skillful, and constant maneuvering. Central Mexico at the time had a population of perhaps twenty-five million, with two million or so in the region about Tenochtitlán. Of these, perhaps a total of five hundred thousand could be mustered as soldiers, though the offensive force comprised, on average, probably about fifty thousand men. Just how the Spaniards might seem impressive enough to earn a meeting with a ruler of such power remained to be seen.

Moctezuma's reply came back in just seven or eight days, accompanied by more gifts, and the word that the emperor "rejoiced to learn about" Cortés's great king, and that Cortés should determine what he needed for himself and "the cure of his sickness," as well as whatever supplies he needed for his men and his ships. But as for a meeting, that would be "impossible."

Cortés gathered a sample of his own wealth to send to the emperor, asked again for a meeting, and inquired about the possibility of trade. As he awaited a reply, he got to know some of the local Indians, whom he found quite civilized, and who identified themselves as being from the city of Zempoala—a city, they said, that had to maintain its independence from Moctezuma "by force of arms."

This piece of unforeseeable luck electrified the Spaniard. As Díaz reported, Cortés had thus learned "that Moctezuma had opponents and enemies, which greatly delighted him." Cortés would come to learn that Moctezuma's great empire was fragmented and fragile. Mexico was composed of a loose collection of city-states, of hundreds of small villages, united and divided by more than twenty different languages and hundreds of different dialects. The empire was based upon the conquest and subjugation of many diverse peoples, and the conquered peoples were bitter and resentful. As Gómara put it, "Cortés was well pleased to find the lords of that country at war with each other, which would allow him the better to carry out his plans and intentions."

When Moctezuma's reply came to Cortés the second time, it

was brief. Cortés might have whatever he needed but he must take his fleet and leave.

Cortés replied that it was not possible for the Spaniards to leave without seeing Moctezuma. And with that the Spaniards retired to their temporary huts; the Indians retired to theirs. The following morning, the Indians' huts were empty. And Cortés called his captains together, according to Gómara, and "prepared for battle."

When at last the Spaniards set out for Tenochtitlán, the route they took was circuitous. They went first toward the north, to Zempoala, where they knew they would find people ready to join them in an uprising against Moctezuma. Indeed, according to Gómara, the chief there told the Spaniard that "if Cortés so desired, he would make a league with all of [the neighboring provinces] that would be so strong that Moctezuma would not be able to stand against it." From Zempoala, gathering allies as they went, the Spaniards moved on to Quiahuitzlán, where they came across some of Moctezuma's tax collectors and had them arrested. As soon as the chiefs of the neighboring towns of the Totonacs heard that the Spaniards had arrested Moctezuma's tax collectors, they drew up a treaty of alliance with Cortés against Moctezuma, bringing with them thousands of warriors. According to Gómara, "They finally decided to rebel and . . . they begged Hernán Cortés to approve their decision and act as their captain and leader. . . . God knows how delighted Cortés was at this turn of events, for he thought by this means" of leading a revolution "to reach Mexico."

With their new allies, the Spaniards ventured into the territory of Tlaxcala, where they were met by a force of several thousand warriors in several small skirmishes and two major battles. Both sides rushed forward, the Indians fighting with clubs, arrows, javelins, and fire-hardened darts, the Spaniards with artillery, muskets, crossbows, lances, and double-bladed swords. These were days of nearly continuous hand-to-hand fighting. Stones came "like hail" from the Indians' slings, and their "barbed and fire-hardened darts fell like corn on the threshing-floor," as Díaz wrote. The Spaniards fought them in a confused melee. At night a cold wind blew off the snowcapped mountains, and the Spaniards suffered from the chill.

Soon enough, they were suffering, too, from wounds (some had two or three wounds) and footsoreness, from rips and tears in clothes and boots, from a hailstorm, from the exhaustion of continuous fighting, and from the paucity of oxygen in the atmosphere in the seven-thousand-foot-high mountains. The report of Díaz is a chronicle of human endurance beyond the limits of endurance; at the moment it seems he must finally conclude that here, at last, the Spaniards gave up and collapsed, Díaz only goes on to recount another and yet another extraordinary ordeal.

The Spaniards woke, fought to exhaustion, and dropped back to sleep, and as Díaz said, after some days of this, "weary and wounded . . . ragged and sick . . . [we] wondered what would happen to us when we had to fight Moctezuma if we were reduced to such straits by the Tlaxcalans, whom our Zempoalan allies described as a peaceful people."

How was it possible for this little band of Spaniards to march ever deeper into unknown territory, to decimate the vast armies brought against them and, as Díaz recorded, lose only a relative handful of Spanish lives in such encounters?

Not too much faith should be placed in the numbers Díaz and the other Spaniards used to describe the size of the enemy. Though the Spanish accounts are filled with references to 30,000 or 150,000 warriors, it is clear that if these numbers are to be taken literally, nothing save a miracle would account for a Spanish survival. The numbers must have been grossly exaggerated.

Nor can much credit be given the Spanish crossbows. Although they outclassed Indian bows, as Norman Davies has written, they were not especially good weapons. And the Spanish pikes were not enormously impressive either. Neither can too much credit be given to the purely material effects of gunpowder. Spanish powder was often wet, the guns were cumbersome over the mountains and difficult to bring effectively to bear on the enemy. The rate of fire of cannon and muskets could not compare with the rate of fire of the Indians' bows.

The psychological effect of gunpowder and horses and glistening armor, however, was incalculable. In some way, the Spaniards must have impressed the Indians in the way that unarmed demonstrators are impressed when heavily armed riot police wade into the midst of a crowd.

The weapons the Indians fought back with were hardly impressive. Indian bows were not often lethal, even when arrows rained on the Spaniards. It is significant that the Spaniards, when they complained about their wounds, complained more about the wounds received from stones than arrows. At close quarters, the Indians used wooden clubs tipped and ridged with sharpened obsidian, a vicious weapon when used against other Indians, but one that often shattered against Spanish helmets, or was cut apart by the blow of a Spanish sword.

In close combat, the swords were effective. Pointed and double bladed, the Spaniards could stab and slash left and right. The obsidian club had to be hoisted above the head and brought down with force against an enemy to be most effective, but the Spanish sword worked well with fast, repeated slashes and jabs at waist level. Driving directly at the clusters of Indian warriors surrounding their chief, the Spaniards would often capture or kill the local chiefs. Once their leader was captured or killed, the warriors often retired from battle. This fierce superiority of the sword gave the Spaniards their real material advantage.

But even more than these differences in weapons, the difference in the rules of warfare by which each side fought determined the outcome of the battles: the Spaniards fought to kill; the Indians, in accord with their custom, fought only to capture.

Finally, the Spaniards had their Totonac allies with them— and as they penetrated farther and farther into Mexico, to their good fortune they recruited more and more allies. When they at last reached Moctezuma's capital city, the odds would be more favorable to Cortés's army.

Eventually, in any case, the Tlaxcalans surrendered—and agreed to join Cortés against the Aztecs. Meanwhile, in his capital city, Moctezuma did nothing.

How is it that Moctezuma could have been so resigned? Sahagún's informants offer an explanation that has endured ever since: Moctezuma and the Aztecs thought that Cortés was the ancient king-god Quetzalcóatl, the Feathered Serpent, who, the legend goes, had been driven from his kingdom and had vowed to one day return to reclaim his rule over their empire. Some historians have claimed that Moctezuma was, therefore, the prisoner of his own mythology. The myth is a wonderful explanation; but it will not do. By the time the Spaniards had reached Tenochtitlán, the Aztecs no longer believed the invaders to be divine.

Aficionados of diplomacy prefer the explanation that Moctezuma waited for Cortés to arrive at Tenochtitlán because it was the Aztec custom that an ambassador was immune from harm. Still others claim that Moctezuma's strategy of lavish gift giving and of permitting Cortés's entry into Tenochtitlán was aimed at impressing the Spaniards with Aztec superiority or dominance.

Or it may be that, as the Spaniards brought off one military and diplomatic victory after another, Moctezuma came to understand to his surprise that this insignificant stranger was being transformed into an unprecedented and puzzling threat that needed to be handled with great care. This appears to have been Cortés's view. As Gómara explained: Moctezuma "did not wish to stir up trouble for himself (and this was the truest reason)" by appearing to resist Cortés and so encouraging other provinces to join him in an uprising that would develop into a revolution. He would pursue the strategy of the spider and the fly; he would bring Cortés into Tenochtitlán and hold him hostage, as, in fact, he ordinarily held as many as six hundred Aztec chieftains in permanent hostage.

As the Spaniards advanced, they laid waste to the town of Cholula. As they approached closer and closer to the capital city, their reputation for savagery and invincibility was widespread, and their march, as they drew in allies along the way, came unexpectedly to resemble a triumphal procession.

When the Spaniards reached the city of Cuitlahuac, they entered the lake country in the Valley of Mexico, where the towns were sometimes half in the water and half on land or sometimes built entirely in the water and connected to the land by broad causeways. They entered the world of the "floating garden people," whose towns and buildings, "all made of stone," said Díaz, "seemed like an enchanted vision. . . . Indeed, some of our soldiers asked whether it was not all a dream."

Past Iztapalapa, on November 8, 1519, they set foot on a broad causeway—wide enough, said Cortés, so that eight horsemen could ride abreast. And partway along the causeway, the Spaniards came to a large stone bastion with towers and a gateway—and there were met by four thousand "gentlemen of the court" of Tenochtitlán, according to Gómara, "richly dressed after their fashion, all in the same style," and as a sign of peace each one in turn touched the ground with his right hand and kissed it and bowed and passed along.

Then, just across a little bridge, the Spaniards saw Moctezuma. "He walked," said Gómara, "under a pallium of gold and green feathers, strung about with silver hangings, and carried by four gentlemen." He was supported on the arms of two royal princes, the great princes Cuitlahuac and Cacama. "All three were dressed alike, save that Moctezuma wore golden shoes set with precious stones."

Servants walked ahead of Moctezuma, laying mantles down on the ground so that he would not touch the earth. Then came two hundred lords, all barefoot, but wearing exceptionally rich cloaks and carrying gourd vases of popcorn flowers, yellow tobacco flowers, and cacao blossoms. Moctezuma walked in the middle of the causeway, and all the rest followed him, "hugging the walls, their eyes downcast."

Cortés dismounted and stepped forward to embrace the emperor, Gómara wrote; but the two princes put out their hands at once to keep Cortés from touching Moctezuma. Moctezuma spoke a few words of welcome, and Cortés replied with wishes for the emperor's good health. At that Cortés was permitted to step forward and put a necklace of pearls and diamonds around the neck of Moctezuma.

The emperor ordered one of his nephews to take Cortés by the hand, and Moctezuma turned and walked back up the causeway, while his followers turned their faces to the walls, and his nephews brought Cortés and the Spaniards and several thousand of their Indian allies along behind.

They came almost immediately to a large and beautiful palace that had once belonged to Moctezuma's father, and there Moctezuma himself took Cortés by the hand and led him into the palace, "and bade me," as Cortés said, to "sit on a very rich throne . . . and then left saying that I should wait for him."

The Spaniards and several thousand of their native warriors were ensconced in the very center of the Aztec capital, surrounded by the Aztecs. The Aztecs, however, were surrounded, Díaz noted, by more of Cortés's allies outside the city. Frozen in this balance of forces, Cortés and Moctezuma commenced a singular dialogue whose end was entirely unpredictable.

After the Spaniards had eaten, Moctezuma returned and beckoned his aides to bring in presents. Moctezuma was about forty years old, said Díaz, "of good height, well proportioned, spare and slight." He bathed every afternoon, said Díaz—twice a day, said Gómara. The Spaniards, still sleeping in their armor, were impressed by the frequency of Moctezuma's bathing. Moctezuma and Cortés exchanged brief, polite speeches, and Moctezuma took his leave once more.

For the next six days, the Spaniards were left alone. The city in which they found themselves would have impressed anyone, and must have seemed glamorous to this lot of rough soldiers, most of whom had never in their lives seen any large city, except perhaps for a few days they might have spent in a Spanish port before their departure to the New World.

Tenochtitlán lay at the center of a vast bowl formed by high hills. At the bottom of the bowl were a large plain and many shallow lakes. Tenochtitlán had been built up atop a bit of rocky ground and a network of sandbanks and mudbanks and marshes in the very midst of a large saltwater lake, until, like Venice, it was a marvel of human artifice, laced with canals, connected by bridges and little causeways. Four long and wide causeways connected it to the mainland. An aqueduct brought fresh water into the middle of the city from a mountain spring.

Near the center of this complex of little man-made islands, Cortés remarked, was a marketplace "twice as big as that of Salamanca, with arcades all around, where more than sixty thousand people come each day to buy and sell," where one could find chickens, partridges, quail, wild ducks, turtledoves, pigeons, parrots, eagles, sparrow hawks, falcons—some of these birds used for food, some for feathers, some for hunting. Or one could get gold or featherwork in the forms of butterflies, trees, flowers, herbs, rocks. Or one could get a silver fish with silver scales, a silver monkey that moved its feet and head, a parrot that moved its wings and head and tongue, carved turquoise and emeralds, stuff made of conches, periwinkles, bones, sponges, pebbles, toys for children, herbs and roots, leaves and seeds, ointments, syrups and waters, culinary delicacies such as snakes without head or tail, little barkless dogs that had been castrated and fattened, moles, mice, worms, and lice. One could get beans, leeks, onions, garlic, artichokes, sorrel, borage, watercress. One could even get a sort of scum that was skimmed from the ooze that could be found atop the lake at certain times during the year and that was spread out on the floor, dried, made into cakes and eaten like cheese: "delicious," Gómara remarked.

All around the city, said Cortés, there were many temples, "beautiful buildings," and among them all, the principal one "whose great size and magnificence no human tongue could describe." The main temple occupied a site seventy by eighty yards at its base, with two staircases leading up nearly two hundred feet to a terrace and twin shrines. There the stones were splattered black with the blood of human sacrifices.

Most often, the victim would be led to the top of the temple steps and stretched out over a block of stone by five priests. And a priest would cut him open with an obsidian-bladed knife, reach in, and pluck out his heart while it was still beating. The heart would be offered up to the sun, to keep it moving in its course. The body was often then thrown down the temple steps and flayed and cut up. Its skull went to a great skull rack (where, according to Gómara, there were 136,000 skulls, in rows, teeth outward), and the remainder was distributed among the warriors who had captured the victim and ceremonially consumed by the victors.

In the days following, Cortés and Moctezuma met from time to time. In all of Spain, said Cortés, there was "nothing to compare" with Moctezuma's palace, with its hundred rooms and hundred baths with walls of marble, jasper, alabaster, porphyry, black stone shot with veins of ruby red and ceilings of cedar, palm, and cypress, set amidst gardens of medicinal and aromatic herbs, flowers, and sweet-smelling trees with walkways and ponds and baths and summerhouses and fountains and bowers of small songbirds, parrots, and quetzal birds. Cortés mentioned his wish to convert Moctezuma to Christianity, and this topic of conversation must have struck Moctezuma as outrageous, and irrelevant to the negotiations about trade, if negotiations were what they were conducting.

The Spaniards evidently became increasingly aware, too, of the absurdity and perilousness of their position. Cortés had come to feel "beset with misgivings," and to have a dreadful sense that they were caught in a web. It had begun to dawn on the Spaniards that there was no reason for Moctezuma to allow them to leave Tenochtitlán alive. The Spaniards were as much surrounded as the Aztecs were and came to see no way out of this dilemma except, extraordinarily, to kidnap Moctezuma and hold him hostage in their palace.

Cortés took thirty armed men with him to pay a call on Moctezuma, Cortés greeting the emperor, according to Díaz, "as usual, and then began to jest and banter with him, as he had done before." But soon he moved to the point. The emperor would need to come and stay with the Spaniards.

Moctezuma was "profoundly shaken," said Gómara. "My person is not such as can be taken prisoner, and even if I should consent to it, my people would not suffer it."

According to Díaz, Cortés and Moctezuma spent half an hour "discussing" the question. As the "discussion" went on, some of Cortés's soldiers grew jittery. "What is the use of all these words?" one of the Spaniards burst out. "Either we take him or we knife him. If we do not look after ourselves now we shall be dead men."

In the end, perhaps calculating that resistance would not only cause his own death but that of many others and the destruction of his city, Moctezuma did not resist.

As the Spaniards kept Moctezuma captive, sometimes in manacles, they maintained the myth of his rule. Each day they would ask Moctezuma what his orders were, and each day those orders would be relayed to the city. Sometimes Cortés and Moctezuma would sit together and play a game called Totoloque, as Díaz said, "with small, very smooth gold pellets specially made for [the game].

They would throw these pellets a considerable distance, and some little slabs as well which were also of gold, and in five throws they either gained or lost certain pieces of gold or rich jewels that they had staked."

Nonetheless, for all the courtesy between Moctezuma and the Spaniards, the Spaniards slept in their armor and kept their horses saddled and bridled.

Eventually, perhaps understanding that he had lost this curious game and must now purchase his freedom and that of his city, Moctezuma opened up his personal treasure and gave it to Cortés and bid his chiefs to bring gifts, too: all the gold and silver Moctezuma possessed, along with garments of cotton and magnificent featherwork, golden nose crescents, golden discs and necklaces, blowguns inlaid with wood and silver, jewels and precious stones and pearls, silver plates and cups, pitchers, and saucers: more than the Spaniards could ever have desired—so much treasure from Moctezuma's gifts alone, said Díaz, that it took the Spaniards three days just to examine it all and remove all the little embellishments from the hunks of solid gold that were of most interest to the conquerors.

Just at this moment, in May 1520, Moctezuma's messengers brought the startling news that another Spanish fleet had been sighted at the very place where Cortés and his men had landed. A picture painted on cloth had been brought to the emperor. There were eighteen ships, eighty horses, nine hundred soldiers. This force was led by a captain named Pánfilo de Narváez, who had been sent by Diego Velásquez to stop Cortés from operating in defiance of his commission.

Cortés greeted the news of the Spanish fleet with a show of relief and even joy. However, out of Moctezuma's presence, Cortés grew "very thoughtful," as Díaz said, suspecting Narváez's true mission, and presenting a situation the Aztecs would take advantage of. Messages to and from Pánfilo de Narváez confirmed his suspicions, and so Cortés left at once for the coast, taking about 120 of his best soldiers with him and leaving about 80 at Tenochtitlán, under the command of Pedro de Alvarado, who had a reputation for both bravery and cruelty.

After several days' march, Cortés located Narváez's army at

Zempoala and took them by surprise at night, so quickly that only
one cannon was fired against Cortés's troops. Narváez himself took
a pike thrust which cost him an eye and was dragged down the
steps and taken off and put into irons. Thus Cortés augmented his
forces with a sizable and fresh lot of soldiers, including, as Gómara
remarked, "a Negro man sick with the smallpox"—who would, in
fact, turn out to be a very significant figure.

In Tenochtitlán, the whole city had exploded in violence. The
Indians had been celebrating the annual festival of Toxcatl in the
sacred temple courtyard. Hundreds had come, as Gómara wrote,
with drums, conchs, trumpets, bone fifes and other instruments.
Covered with necklaces and jewels, feathers and pearls, they
danced in rings, accompanied by singers.

Then, in the midst of the dancing—for some reason, from
sudden fear that the Indians meant harm, or else from a precon-
certed plan—the Spaniards abruptly closed off all the exits from
the temple courtyard and, with swords drawn, waded into the
midst of the dancers.

"They attacked the man who was drumming," according to
Sahagún's native informants, "and cut off his arms. Then they cut
off his head, and it rolled across the ground. They attacked all the
celebrants, stabbing them, spearing them . . . some of them from
behind, and these fell instantly to the ground with their entrails
hanging out. Others they beheaded . . . or split their heads to
pieces. . . . Some attempted to run away, but . . . they seemed
to tangle their feet in their own entrails . . . they could find no
escape."

The next day those Aztecs who had not been trapped in the
temple courtyard attacked the Spaniards with javelins and arrows.
The initial fighting saw several Spaniards killed and many on both
sides wounded. The Aztecs closed off the causeways, tore up some
of the bridges over which the Spaniards might have escaped, and
threw up barricades and roadblocks across the streets.

Cortés, hearing the news of the Aztec uprising, set out at
once to return to Tenochtitlán but as he passed back through the
countryside discovered "all the land was in revolt and almost uninhabited." And when he reentered the city of Tenochtitlán, at midday in late June 1520, he found the streets and squares almost

entirely deserted, some broken bridges and barricades; "all the houses were empty," said Díaz. And there was quiet as the Aztecs let the Spaniards back into the trap.

The roads around Tenochtitlán were filled with warriors, enemies of the Spaniards. The thousands of Cortés's "faithful" native allies now disappear entirely from the accounts, all except the few thousand Tlaxcalans trapped inside the city with the Spanish troops. The revolution had evaporated. Those who now surrounded Tenochtitlán were supporters of Moctezuma or of other rival chiefs.

Such "a multitude" of Aztec warriors now rushed to surround the Spaniards' quarters, said Cortés, "that neither the streets nor the roofs of the houses could be seen for them." And soon so many stones were "hurled at us from their slings into the fortress that it seemed they were raining from the sky, and the arrows and spears were so many that all the walls and courtyards were so full we could hardly move for them."

At the end, the Spanish force was overwhelmed by superior numbers. Still, the Aztecs repeatedly tried to scale the walls of the palace, reluctantly running headlong into Spanish cannon and swords. At last they shot burning arrows into the fortress, hoping to burn the Spaniards out.

Cortés summoned Moctezuma and asked him to go up to the roof of the palace and tell his people to stop the fighting. According to Díaz, Moctezuma mounted to the roof, and a great silence fell over the thousands who swarmed over the streets and nearby rooftops. The emperor begged his people to put down their arms and let the Spaniards go. But a few of the Aztec chiefs replied to Moctezuma "in tears," as Díaz said, that they no longer recognized him as their leader, and they would not stop now until all the Spaniards were dead "and they begged for his forgiveness."

And then, said Díaz, the Aztec warriors began to throw rocks at Moctezuma. The Spanish soldiers rushed the emperor back inside the palace where they discovered he had been wounded. He refused to have his wounds tended or to eat anything and soon died.

Other sources, including some native ones, indicate that Moctezuma was not struck but that he was murdered by the Spaniards back in their palace quarters. Some of the native sources say that not only Moctezuma but other lords who were kept as hostages by the Spaniards in their palace were murdered. One, it is said, fought so hard at the end that he had to be stabbed forty-seven times to kill him. Which of all these stories is true, we cannot know. But it would not seem to have been in the interests of the Spaniards to kill Moctezuma at that moment.

In the middle of the night, the Spaniards brought the gold and jewels and silver out into the middle of a hall in the palace. Those who wanted some took it and stuffed it into their packs and clothes. Narváez's men and "some of our people" took most, Díaz thought. In the dark, a night of mist and drizzle, they made a run for it.

The horsemen went out first to charge and scatter any Aztecs who might block the way. The horsemen were followed by soldiers carrying a large makeshift wooden bridge to be thrown down over water where the Aztecs had removed the usual bridges along the causeway. Another group lugged the heavy cannon. Musketeers and crossbowmen and swordsmen followed in an increasingly panicky disarray. They managed to slam the bridge down across the first break they came to. They had caught the Aztecs by surprise, and so a good many Spaniards slipped past the main mass of Indians in their headlong dash down the causeway; but then the Aztecs came awake with cries and whistles, and the Spaniards broke in a stampede out onto the causeway. Such a mass of canoes closed on them from the lake on either side, and so many Aztec warriors threw stones and spears from the rooftops, that the soldiers left the bridge behind at that first crossing, and as their horses slipped and fell into the lake, they plunged on ahead, crossing over the next water gap by stepping on the cannon and bundles and boxes that had fallen in along with the dead troops, servants, and horses. As they rushed from water gap to water gap, just ahead of the warriors behind them, chancing the improvised gauntlet of warrior-filled canoes on either side, those who had stuffed much gold into their clothes were among the first to sink into the water gaps, and become stepping-stones for their fleeing comrades. "So those who died," said Díaz, "died rich," though they had not been rich for long.

The remnants of the Spaniards had reached the mainland by dawn. According to Díaz, there had been 1,300 Spanish soldiers in Tenochtitlán in those last days as well as 2,000 native, mostly Tlaxcalan warriors. In the siege and flight more than 850 Spaniards and 1,000 allies were killed. (Others put the figures at 450 Spaniards and more than 4,000 Indian allies.)

The remaining Spaniards fled all the way to the city of Tlaxcala, where their strongest allies gave them refuge. For the Tlaxcalans, however, there was no quitting the civil war that they had begun with Cortés. And so, with their urging and support, the Spanish troops pulled themselves together.

Since he would have to attack the city from both the causeways and the surrounding water, Cortés had thirteen brigantines that could operate in the shallow lake waters constructed. In late December 1520, Cortés and his men, along with thousands of Indian warriors, crossed the mountains and reentered the valley. Securing the shores of the lake, they cut the city off from the support of the countryside. Then they destroyed the great aqueduct that brought the main supply of fresh water to the city.

Finally, in late April 1521, the siege began. Ordering his brigantines across the water and his foot soldiers down the causeways, Cortés attacked the capital. The Aztecs had prepared their defenses by planting sharpened stakes just under the water at the gaps in the causeway. The Spanish lost both men and horses on the stakes, and in short order the water gaps were flush with stones, spears, and dead horses and men. A group of Spaniards were caught out ahead of their companions and the Indians took them prisoner, beheaded some, and bowled their heads along the causeways toward their mates.

After several weeks of stalemate, Cortés instructed his men to remove every barricade more slowly and deliberately and destroy every Aztec wall, to demolish every Aztec tower and house along the way. As they advanced, they filled in the gaps of the causeway with rubble, leaving the landscape level behind them.

The slow destruction of Tenochtitlán went on for eighty days, and toward the end the stench of the bodies rotting in the water was overwhelming. As the city began its final collapse, old men, women, and children flooded out toward the causeways in such panic, said Gómara, "that they pushed each other into the water, where many drowned."

The end came on August 13, 1521. The few Aztec warriors still alive gathered on the rooftops of the few houses that still stood and "stared at the ruins of their city in a dazed silence, . . . the women and children and old men . . . all weeping." The conquerors walked down the streets of the city, white handkerchiefs over their noses. They could see stagnant and briny water that had served as the drinking water in the last days, and what had served for food: lizards and salt grasses from the lake, corncobs, water lilies, twigs, pieces of leather, weeds, and dirt. And everywhere, piles of dead bodies. They had died mostly of starvation and smallpox—the virus that had been brought ashore by the man in Pánfilo de Narváez's crew which had made its way across Mexico with Cortés and had even run ahead of his army, decimating the population even before the Spaniards arrived.

The pestilence did not end with the death of Tenochtitlán; the smallpox—along with outbreaks of influenza, measles, and typhus —spread throughout the countryside, subsided and recurred, subsided and recurred, until by 1600, of a total population of perhaps twenty-five million, an estimated eighteen to twenty-two million were dead.

In some regions of Mexico, the mortality rate was so great that the living could not bury the dead. According to Fray Toribio de Benavente, the Indians, overwhelmed by the task, simply "pulled down the houses" on top of the dead, "so that their homes became their tombs."

A civilization died, not simply a city or a government or an empire, but the accumulated knowledge of life and art and skill. Here and there, fragments of the civilization would persist with remarkable hardiness. But the civilization as a whole was gone. And all that would remain of it were its artifacts and its story of a succession of stunning and devastating surprises that brought about its end, the surprise to Moctezuma that Cortés should have arrived at all in the Aztec empire, the surprise to Cortés that he would step into a land where so many wanted to rise in revolt against the central government, the fact amazing to both Cortés and Moctezuma that the Spaniards could overcome the enormous military odds against them, that Cortés could take Moctezuma captive in his own capital, that the Spaniards could level the entire city of Tenochtitlán, that illness could annihilate tens of millions of people, that the backbone of an entire civilization could be broken in a matter of only a few decades. It is a humbling story to anyone who neglects to take into account the inevitability of the unpredictable in human affairs, of what the Romans called Fortuna.

Four

THE
PRINCIPLE
OF CONTINGENCY

There are no laws of history. Instead, there is the principle of contingency: everything depends on everything else. The biologist Stephen Jay Gould, writing about the evolution of the human species, puts it this way: "A historical explanation does not rest on direct deductions from laws of nature, but on an unpredictable sequence of antecedent states, where any major change in any step of the sequence would have altered the final result. This final result is therefore dependent, or contingent, upon everything that came before—the unerasable and determining signature of history."

The historical field, as the Greeks knew, includes the world as it is given—what the Greeks called nature—as well as chance, or fortune, as Cortés and Moctezuma came to know so well; it includes also the "forces" of history that are constituted of men and women working as groups—economic forces, military forces, political forces. It includes the structures that men and women have made and that remain—structures of production, technology, social organization. It includes an additional "resistance of reality," which, as Paul Veyne wrote, does not come from "infrastructures" but from the resistance of "all other men for each of them." It includes the mental substructures that people bring to bear on their perceptions of the world.

Each and all of these figure among the contingencies that operate in the production of historical events, and yet they do not form a complete set of causes. Even if we were to identify all the classes of cause of historical events, we could not construct a complete causal explanation of any given moment. Because each cause has a previous cause, if we were to attempt to explain the complete causes of events, we should soon become trapped in an infinite regression of explanation. Customarily, we draw an arbitrary line across this infinite regression of explanations and declare: here are the necessary and sufficient causes of this event. But even then, "to have noted once," as Veyne says, "that the system of taxation made a king unpopular is to expect the process to be repeated. . . . But that does not at all mean that it becomes constant; indeed, that is why we never know what tomorrow may bring. . . . Futures are contingent, the tax system may make a government unpopular, but it may also not have that effect." It is for this reason that there can be no laws of history, that each individual moment is singular, a constellation of causes and effects that never recurs in exactly the same way.

A leader who leads a nation through a victorious war will be immensely popular and be rewarded by reelection for another term of office, unless the leader is Winston Churchill at the end of World War II, or George Bush after the war in the Persian Gulf.

Bombing will break the will of an adversary in war, except when that adversary is Vietnam, or the people of London or Coventry in England during World War II.

Rewards for private savings—the creation of tax shelter retirement plans, IRAs and 401K plans—will increase a nation's private savings for investment, except, as in recent years in the United States, when they don't. The lack of such savings can be blamed on lack of resources among the poor and middle class, except, as has been the case in the United States, when the rich don't save either. Savings will increase when the rich are given a tax cut, except when, as in the United States recently, they don't. The lack of such savings can be blamed on an increasing deficit that siphons off funds, except, as has been the case in the United States, when private savings began to decline before the deficit had that effect. The reason for this lack of private savings can be explained by economists, except when it can't.

If history were a work of art, it would be what Umberto Eco called an *opera aperta,* an open work. The poetics of an open work, as Eco says, tend to encourage "acts of conscious freedom" on the part of the performer and place him at the focal point of a network of limitless interrelations, among which he chooses to set up his own form without being influenced by an external necessity which definitively prescribes the organization of the work in hand.

If there are many instances of the principle of contingency, in art and politics and in life, none is more exemplary than the Congress of Vienna in 1815.

CZAR ALEXANDER I OF RUSSIA, EMPEROR FRANCIS I OF AUSTRIA, KING FRIEDRICH WILHELM III OF PRUSSIA, VISCOUNT CASTLEREAGH OF ENGLAND, PRINCE CHARLES MAURICE DE TALLEYRAND-PERIGORD OF FRANCE, PRINCE KLEMENS VON METTERNICH OF AUSTRIA, PRINCE KARL AUGUST VON HARDENBERG OF PRUSSIA, THE DUCHESS OF SAGAN, THE DUKE OF WELLINGTON, BARON VON STEIN, SIR CHARLES STEWART, COUNT NESSELRODE, AND FRIEDRICH VON GENTZ—AMONG OTHERS—AT THE CONGRESS OF VIENNA

Announced by cannon fire that startled the late-rising Viennese, Czar Alexander arrived in Vienna at midday on Sunday, September 25, 1814. He was accompanied by his host Emperor Francis I of Austria, round-shouldered, shy, unprepossessing, but popular with the crowds that lined the route, and King Friedrich Wilhelm of Prussia (stiff, the Austrians said, so like a northerner, unhappy, cold, and suspicious). They were preceded by an honor guard of resplendent Hungarian cavalrymen who made their gorgeous, clattering way along the broad, tree-lined boulevard, through the vast rolling meadows of the Prater Park where deer and stags roamed freely. They passed the Sunday strollers with their children, come to spend the day at the bandstands, the merry-go-round, the circus, the cafes and shops. They proceeded through the streets of the imperial city to the gardens and courtyard of the Hofburg Palace where they were greeted by Prince Klemens von Metternich, the foreign minister of Austria, King Friedrich I of Württemberg and Friedrich VI of Denmark. Thereafter they plunged into a crush of monarchs and princes and eighty-seven plenipotentiaries of large and small powers. These included the various Germanic states, the cities of Danzig and Bad Kreuznach and of Mainz, the Jewish community of Frankfurt, the subjects of the count of Solms-Braunfels represented by Baron Franz von Gärtner, whose calling card read: "Plenipotentiary Extraordinary of 42 Princes and Counts." They were assisted by their secretaries, servants, physicians, cooks, valets, and hairdressers. Seeking to aid them was a local swarm of clerks, milliners, grooms, coachmen, portrait painters, singers, swindlers, pocket pickers and personal confessors. In addition, there were those who had come to Vienna in hopes of employment. In all, 16,000 guests to the city of a quarter million filled the boardinghouses and rooms, drove up the price of firewood, soap, candles and kerchiefs. The imperial kitchens worked through the night to roast ox and geese and boars' heads, setting out scraps for the rabble who scuttled around the edges of the palace.

Czar Alexander was "rather handsome," and rather conscious of the impression he made, according to the Viennese countess Lulu Thurheim. His eyes are "deep-set, yet display wit and liveliness." He favored trim, tailored military tunics (and enjoyed beginning his sentences with "we soldiers . . . ," perhaps to annoy the diplomats, who had never set foot on a battlefield), tight knee breeches, high patent-leather boots with pointed toes. It was said that Alexander washed his face in the morning with ice to tone his skin. Slightly hard of hearing in his left ear, he had a way of inclining his head slightly and gracefully. He was thirty-eight years old, and he created an immediate stir among the women of Vienna, as well as among the men.

Alexander and the other heads of state and diplomats had come together to consider the restoration of Europe after Napoleon's defeat and the dissolution of his empire. Because Napoleon, retreating from his invasion of Russia in 1812, had been followed back west by the Russian army, the Russians now occupied Poland, and Alexander declined to withdraw his troops from the heart of Europe.

Napoleon had been finally defeated and forced to abdicate on April 11, 1814, by the combined might of a Quadruple Alliance of Russia, Prussia, Britain, and Austria, with the help, finally, of most of the lesser European powers. His empire, which had at one time encompassed most of Europe, had collapsed in a rush that left physical destruction and enormous political turmoil in its wake. The political disarray was a matter not only of order among states but also of internal order within states. The French were without a ruler, until the coalition of powers who had brought down Napoleon restored the brother of Louis XVI to the French throne: Louis XVIII.

Whole nations and governments had vanished. For Germany as a whole, as the historian Enno Kraehe has recently written, "It is no exaggeration to say that more people than not were unsure of who their future rulers would be or what kind of government they would have."

Moreover, Napoleon had arrived on the heels of the French Revolution, and the heritage of that revolution was alive throughout Europe. "The French Revolution," as Alexis de Tocqueville wrote, "had no territory of its own; indeed, its effect was to efface, in a way, all older frontiers. . . . It formed, above all particular nationalities, an intellectual common country of which men of all nations might become citizens . . . [and it] is still destroying (for it still goes on) everything which in the old society arose from feudal and aristocratic institutions."

The aristocrats—the monarchs, the princes, and their plenipotentiaries who still held their positions after the defeat of Napoleon, or resumed them—were frightened of what the revolution had loosed. They were intent upon restoring not only order among nations but among classes. They meant to restore a concerted and collaborative aristocracy to the rule of Europe.

The treaty that ended the war included Article 22 that called for a congress to be held in Vienna, beginning October 1, 1814, to engage in a general settlement of European affairs. That article struck the Europeans with riveting force. As one Austrian diplomat said: "All eyes are turned on the congress, and everybody expects of it the redress of his grievances, the fulfillment of his desires, and the triumph of his projects."

"I found all Europe in my anteroom," Metternich wrote to his wife Eleonore, who was at home with the children in Baden, seventeen miles or two hours by carriage, south of Vienna. And the emperor's houseguests included King Friedrich of Württemberg, King Friedrich of Denmark, King Friedrich Wilhelm of Prussia, King Maximilian of Bavaria, and the czar of Russia, two empresses, a queen, two crown princes, two grand duchesses and three reigning princes, all of them busily gossiping about one another.

Friedrich I of Württemberg, at sixty-one, was the oldest of the monarchs. He enjoyed presenting himself as a ferocious conservative, and he rode around the city in an old-fashioned coach just large enough for himself. He was known as the "Württemberg monster," and Lulu Thurheim was pleased to note that he had such a large paunch that a semicircular piece needed to be cut out of the dining table to permit him to sit.

Maximilian of Bavaria was accounted "the most bourgeois of the kings," according to the Prussian count Karl von Nostitz. Because the king enjoyed the use of a common expression from time to time, popular opinion relegated him to the "pig's corner," but he presided anxiously over the largest of the German central states.

Friedrich VI of Denmark, said Countess Thurheim, was on the other hand "noble, openhanded, kind, witty, and forever concerned over the welfare of his people. He was probably the most beloved and popular of the monarchs in Vienna." It was said that he left no street beggar empty-handed, and so he was quickly dubbed the "King of the Rag Fair." Best of all, his interests threatened no one in Vienna.

The Russians, meanwhile, the gossips said, were not house-trained, and performed their natural functions in the parlors of the palace.

The lesser dignitaries and their gossiping chamberlains, equerries, and ladies-in-waiting were scattered all over Vienna—though they gathered from time to time for dinner with Emperor Francis, who had forty tables set for dinner every evening, and three hundred carriages to whisk his guests from place to place around the city. All the carriages were identical so as to avoid unpleasant scenes over grandeur and precedence. In a gathering such as this, intricacies of precedence might stop traffic permanently.

The people of Vienna were at first charmed to see the royal celebrities strolling about the city like ordinary people. The exhilaration of false egalitarianism swept the city. In the parks, one might see the emperor "like any ordinary burgher" ride past in a plain coach so that any coach for hire felt perfectly free to cut him off, "only soon to be overtaken himself by a Bohemian magnate or a Polish palatine, driving his own coach-and-four. Light gigs appear, drawn by speedy horses . . . and containing ladies in red and white, like flowers in a basket."

Away from the crowds, on the evening of September 16 and for the next several days, in the quiet of Prince Metternich's study in the foreign ministry in the Ballhausplatz, the ministers of Russia, Prussia, and Britain had gathered with him to discuss the procedures that would govern the work of the conference.

It was these ministers who would conduct the vexing daily negotiations of the conference—although they would never be allowed to forget that this was a summit meeting, not a meeting of ministers. The heads of state hovered and conferred constantly in the background, prepared at any moment to step into the negotiations—contradict, or dismiss a minister, announce a decision, then retreat to a dinner table or royal reception. Czar Alexander could not resist functioning as his own foreign minister, plunging constantly into the daily negotiations, and Emperor Francis and King Friedrich Wilhelm were apt to make occasional forays into the discussion at what were sometimes the most inopportune moments. The ministers were given the power to talk, but not to decide.

Article 22 had provided that "all the Powers engaged on either side in the present war" should be invited to attend the Congress of Vienna. Eight powers had signed this treaty: Russia, Prussia, Austria, Britain, France, Spain, Portugal, and Sweden. But a secret article specified that the disposition of the territories surrendered by France would be decided by the four Great Powers of the Quadruple Alliance, Russia, Austria, Prussia, and Great Britain.

This secret article had not been communicated to the minor powers, or to anyone else, and so many delegations who had come to Vienna at great trouble and expense to represent their interests and plead their claims and lend their influence to the shaping of a new Europe were not exactly invited to participate in any real business, or certainly not initially. Just how to inform these eager thousands that they were not wanted, and would be strictly excluded, was the excruciatingly nice problem that the ministers of the Big Four now faced.

Present for Great Britain was Robert Stewart, second viscount Castlereagh, age forty-six, an Irish landowner. Castlereagh, said Harold Nicolson, who wrote a perceptive history of the Congress of Vienna, "possessed a solitary soul and derived but little pleasure from the amenities of society. He had little gift of intimacy and the only two people whom he really loved, his wife and his half brother Charles Stewart, never shared with him the lonelier recesses of his mind. . . . The social shyness which had tormented Castlereagh since his boyhood in county Down had induced him to hide himself behind a screen of glacial good manners. Handsome and seemingly imperturbable . . . he would in his uncertain French exchange conventional but icy compliments with those who addressed him."

For Russia, Count Karl von Nesselrode, age thirty-five, was, according to one in Castlereagh's delegation, "not quite clever enough for the emperor." Nesselrode was already a man on the way down, even before the congress began. It may be that he was falling from the confidence of the czar because one of his own diplomatic aides, Johan von Anstett, who was jealous of his immediate superior, was spreading gossip that Nesselrode had "sold his soul to the Austrians," and that in exchange for "services rendered," Nesselrode had received from the Austrians "five gifts in the form of snuffboxes, each worth 100,000 rubles." In any case, since Alexander intended to be his own foreign minister at this congress, whomever he sent to sit in with the other ministers was destined to be undercut.

For Prussia, Prince Karl August von Hardenberg, the sixty-five-year-old chancellor of Prussia, was, according to the reports of spies in the employ of the Austrian secret service, "the most diligent statesman at the congress." The spy reports also say that he received a hundred thousand ducats from the nephew of Napoleon, and that a bag filled with money was taken by two of Alexander's "court Jews" to one of Hardenberg's associates—though these rumors did not serve to harm his career. Hardenberg was nearly deaf and so he was accompanied always by Baron Wilhelm von Humboldt.

Representing Austria was Prince Klemens Wenzel Nepomuk Lothar von Metternich-Winneburg-Ochsenhausen, age forty-two, "an opportunist pure and simple," according to Charles Webster, a young King's College Cambridge historian who was commissioned to write a history of the congress for the edification of the British delegation to the Paris Peace Conference of 1919. "He was a rococo figure," wrote Henry Kissinger, in his history of the congress, who deeply admired the Austrian minister. Kissinger described him as "complex, finely carved, all surface, like an intricately cut prism. His face was delicate but without depth, his conversation brilliant but without ultimate seriousness. Equally at home in the salon and in the cabinet, graceful and facile, he was the *beau-ideal* of the eighteenth-century aristocracy which justified itself not by its truth but by its existence. And if he never came to terms with the new age it was not because he failed to understand its seriousness but because he disdained it." His diplomacy, Kissinger wrote, was marked by that "circuitousness which is a symbol of certainty." He excelled "at manipulation, not construction. Trained in the school of eighteenth-century cabinet diplomacy, he preferred the subtle manoeuvre to the frontal attack." He opposed revolution and liberalism, "not because they were wicked, but because they were unnatural. . . . Revolution was an assertion of will and of power, but the essence of existence was proportion, its expression was law, and its mechanism an equilibrium." He considered himself a realist. "I am," Metternich said of himself, "a man of prose, and not of poetry." And though he would be widely despised for his "smug self-satisfaction and rigid conservatism," Kissinger concluded that he "came to dominate every coalition in which he participated" for more than a quarter of a century.

It had been Castlereagh's notion that the Congress of Vienna should open with a grand assembly of all the plenipotentiaries in Vienna, who would, on this occasion, give their sanction to the four Great Powers to direct the work of the congress, and to prepare a settlement to be submitted for the consideration of all the delegates. It would be suggested to the assembled diplomats that it was self-evident that, with a group as numerous as the one gathered in Vienna and the issues to be settled so complex, no progress toward a settlement could "be expected to originate in the body at large." Thus "a limited body of plenipotentiaries must be charged to prepare and bring forward" a recommendation for a general European settlement. Clearly, such a limited body could only be constituted from "among those who have borne the principal share in the councils and conduct of the war," that is to say, the major powers. And so, until the major powers had completed their preparatory duty, the congress, scheduled for October 1, was adjourned.

The other diplomats in Metternich's study were horrified by Castlereagh's idea. The worst prospect, of course, was that the assembled representatives of the many would simply decline to surrender their fates to the hands of the few. But this disastrous possibility was not the only obstacle. Before anyone might even issue invitations to this assembly, or receive them, some would have to constitute themselves the authority for reviewing credentials and issuing the invitations. And the fight over credentials constituted a fight over the very matters of substance the Prussians, Russians, Austrians, and British were interested in.

The Russians, for instance, were unable to recognize the right of the Saxon count Friedrich Albrecht von der Schulenberg to occupy any official position lest it compromise precisely what they wished to negotiate; nor, for the same reason, could Castlereagh recognize the emissary of Joachim Murat, the king of Naples. Nor would any German sovereign be able to recognize Baron Gärtner, who was claiming to represent forty-two different rulers.

But above and beyond all these details, Castlereagh now suggested that the inner steering committee of four Great Powers should be expanded to six, to include the two other big continental powers, France and Spain. Castlereagh calculated that France could be used as leverage against Russia. But the Russians let it be known at once that they would not tolerate having France on the committee. And as for Spain, the Prussians could not see what entitled the Spanish to a voice in the settlement of German affairs.

Metternich evidently thought he might like to keep the French out of the inner group but hold them in reserve for possible use later on. He tried to slip around these nasty difficulties by suggesting that the six powers be constituted as a committee to be consulted, but that the four would first reach agreement among themselves and only then consult the other two. In addition, Metternich suggested separating Germany out of general European affairs. The Congress would thus be composed of two committees: one made up of Austria, Prussia, Bavaria, Württemberg, and Hanover that would prepare a plan for all the German states; and a second committee to be made up of the six powers to settle general European affairs. The six would approve the German settlement and also the agreements of the four, and then the work of both committees would be presented to the whole congress with the invitation to the other states to sign as accessories to the general agreement.

Castlereagh liked this plan, but he was troubled at the thought that the four would do business with no approval or recognition from all the plenipotentiaries assembled in Vienna. Never before in diplomatic circles had a distinction been made between great and small powers (though, once made in Vienna, it has been ever since). To make the distinction and then simply assume the right of the few to speak for the many struck Castlereagh as dubious, even though he was himself eager to do it. The advantage of having some sort of assembly of all the delegates to commence the congress, said Castlereagh, "is that you treat the plenipotentiaries as a body with early and becoming respect, you keep the power by concert and management in your own hand, but without openly assuming authority to their exclusion. You obtain a sort of sanction from them for what you are determined at all events to do, which they cannot well withhold."

Castlereagh suggested, rather weakly, that if it was thought too risky to issue invitations to a formal opening ceremony, then an *informal* convocation of delegates could be arranged. The invitation could simply be printed in the newspaper. Then, when the delegates happened to gather, Metternich could explain the need for the committee of six to prepare work in an orderly way for the congress as a whole, and assure the others that they would be consulted, as needed, by the six. France and Spain would then be told separately, and privately, that the four would prepare matters first and then call them in for consultation.

The Prussians were upset that Castlereagh clung to his notion of bringing Spain and France into a committee of six. Humboldt drafted a protocol stating that the four would not consult France until a final agreement had been reached and that, in the meantime, France and Spain were not to sit in discussions with the four, even as observers. Castlereagh thought this was too harsh. Several contradictory proposals were put forward by the diplomats, but they could agree on none of them. And so, in lieu of an agreement, they simply turned to Metternich's principal aide, Friedrich von Gentz, and instructed him to draw up something for them to look at.

Gentz, as Nicolson wrote, was "one of those rare men who are universally mistrusted and yet esteemed." A man much criticized for his voluptuary tendencies, his excessive makeup, his chasing after young ballerinas, his propensity to take a bribe, he was also a man of considerable knowledge and political astuteness. He also worked tirelessly at his tasks even while, in his leisure hours, he wrote a cynical account of the congress in his diary ("Dinner for eight at my house . . . Prince Metternich . . . Prince Louis Rohan . . . I was struck more forcibly than ever with the futility of human affairs, the weakness of the individuals who hold the world's fate in their hands, even with my own feelings of superiority, but all this only in a semiconscious state and as if in a fog in which the inane twaddle of my dinner guests had warped my brain . . . I enjoy the whole spectacle as if it were given for my private pleasure.")

Gentz, because of his intimacy with Metternich and his position at the center of negotiations, was to become the informal "secretary of the conference." At this moment he was sent away to do his best at bringing into a single harmonious piece of prose all the contradictory positions that had been stated by the ministers—or, short of that, framing something so vague and elusive that no one could find in it any grounds for objection.

It was while Gentz was busy at this task that Czar Alexander arrived in Vienna. As his first order of business, he elbowed the other heads of state and diplomats aside and invited Metternich to lunch. Afterward, Metternich reported the lunch this way in a letter to his mistress, the duchess of Sagan: "I have had my first skirmish with the emperor. He sent for me and I saw that he wanted to reconnoiter the terrain . . . and the result of the emperor's attempt is that he knows nothing of what I want but I see clearly everything that he wants. I have chosen my outposts—my main guards are in position, and I can sleep easily—the army corps will not be taken by surprise."

In fact, the situation was this: Alexander's erstwhile allies had taken as their first order of business—as soon as they could get the business of procedure settled—to frustrate Alexander's ambition to take over Poland. A Russian takeover of Poland, as Alexander and the others knew, would force the Poles west to seek compensatory territory in Prussia, and so force Prussia to move west seeking compensatory territory in the smaller German states. The smaller German states could seek compensation elsewhere or seethe.

Perhaps, from the Russian point of view, this desire to take hold of Poland was seen as defensive, not aggressive. Having been invaded by the French army, the Russians were intent upon securing their western border. They were determined to control the strategically placed strongholds of Cracow, in the south of Poland, and Thorn, in the north—between which any invading army would have to pass on its way to Russia. The Russians wanted Poland as a buffer in the center of Europe, Prussia as a buffer to the north, and Austria as a buffer to the south.

In elaboration of this strategy, Alexander wished to give Saxony to Prussia, in order to strengthen Prussia. He would concede the north of Italy to Austria to compensate Austria for its concessions in Poland and to strengthen Austria—though not too much —as a counterweight to Prussia in central Europe.

The others were not convinced that Russia's interests were

merely defensive. There was a fear among some of the Prussian diplomats "that we may exchange the yoke of Napoleon for the yoke of Alexander." But if the Russians' intentions were self-aggrandizing, they were not the only ones who had designs on the world. The British, though they represented themselves as disinterested mediators, refused to negotiate any issue that touched on their mastery of the seas. Britain had emerged from the Napoleonic Wars whole, undamaged, financially strong. Indeed, now that the Napoleonic Empire was destroyed, Britain, with Russia, was the other great power of the moment.

In fact, the British were resolved on some rearrangements on the Continent. Napoleon had at one time threatened to take over Holland and cut the British off from any continental port. They insisted now upon forming a strong Netherlands, incorporating Antwerp, and placing between this new Netherlands and France a buffer state, preferably controlled by Prussia, to make certain that England would always have an opening to the Continent.

Prussia was not eager to take over the slice of territory that Britain had in mind to give it—a slice of territory on the Rhine that was not contiguous to Prussia, and therefore awkward to defend. Instead of territory on the Rhine, the Prussians wanted a slice of Poland and the whole of Saxony, the richest and most industrious state in central Germany.

The Austrian negotiators were acutely sensitive to the weakness and delicacy of their position. From the beginning of the Napoleonic Wars in 1792, Austria had suffered a string of defeats. When the wars began, Francis I was the Holy Roman Emperor, a title that had been passed down in his Hapsburg family since the fifteenth century. By the end of the Napoleonic Wars, the Holy Roman Empire had ceased to exist. The Hapsburgs ruled over a vastly reduced Austria which was in severe financial straits, and Francis bore the much-diminished title emperor of Austria. The task for the Austrians, then, was to conserve what they had and to look south to Italy, to the territories of the extinguished Venetian Republic and the receding Ottoman Empire for new opportunities.

The German states, some without governments, most without clear policies, were gathered to address the vague notion of forming a German confederation. Some of these smaller states depended upon dynastic ties with the czar to protect their interests; some looked to Prussia for protection, some to Austria. Some advocated two great German states, a northern and a southern German state, one under the leadership of Prussia, the other under Austria. In short, the future of thirty-five monarchical states and four city republics would provide irresistible ground for negotiation, for ever-shifting loyalties, competition, arrangements, and alliances. Each time Prussia or Austria would make a move in negotiating their own primary interests, ripples of hope and anxiety would flow through all the German states—not to mention the delegations of Italians, of the Frankfurt Jews, the spokesmen of the chamber of commerce of the city of Mainz, the envoy from the Vatican, and the representatives of the German book trade.

Since none of these powers was strong enough to impose its will on the others, the situation was ideal for the practice of diplomacy—in which the success of each negotiator would be contingent upon, among other things, the position, strength, will, perceptiveness, persuasiveness, dexterity, and deviousness of all. This was the ground for personal diplomacy that diplomats relish.

It may well be that the initial luncheon between Metternich and Alexander was an agreeable one for both, but a few days later, the czar summoned Metternich to another audience and for several hours delivered a strict lecture on Russian foreign policy that made it clear that Russia would settle for nothing less than a Polish kingdom under Alexander's sway. However suave and poetical Metternich might be, the Russian armies were unmovable, and the prince came away from that meeting chastened.

The borderlines the czar mentioned provoked a flurry of gloomy and anxious discussions among the other heads of state and their ministers. The Prussian delegates were prepared to desert Alexander at once, and would have—except that their king Friedrich Wilhelm undercut them instantly and completely and insisted on remaining loyal to his Russian friend. And so now the gossips set upon Friedrich Wilhelm, calling him "weak" and "cowardly." Even Hardenberg, in his logbook for the day, described his own monarch as "the pusillanimous king" ("Pusillan. regis," as he wrote tersely)—although it may simply be that

Friedrich Wilhelm was understandably determined to stand firm with the only power that stood firm with him in his wish to have Saxony.

The first meeting of the committee of six had been set for September 30—even though, strictly speaking, the committee of six had not been established and there were still those who hoped it never would be. The ministers of the four were already in session when, at about two o'clock in the afternoon, they received the ministers of the other two—Don Pedro Labrador of Spain, and Talleyrand of France. The illustriousness of Talleyrand has become a legend in the histories of the Congress of Vienna—perhaps not so much because Talleyrand was more important than the others as because he kept excellent notes of events in which he managed to show himself in a favorable light.

At one end of a long table, as Talleyrand reported to Louis XVIII, was Castlereagh, at the other end Gentz. "I was then shown to a vacant chair between Lord Castlereagh and Prince Metternich. I immediately asked why I, alone of your majesty's embassy, had been invited."

"It was wished to bring together only the heads of the cabinets at the preliminary conferences," said Castlereagh.

"But Count de Labrador is not a head of cabinet, and he has also been invited."

"That is because the secretary of state of Spain is not in Vienna," said Metternich.

"Even so," Talleyrand replied, "I see that Herr von Humboldt is here, in addition to Prince von Hardenberg, and he is not a secretary of state."

"This is an exception to the rule, made necessary by the infirmity [of deafness] with which, as you know, Prince Hardenberg is afflicted."

"Well, then," said the clubfooted Talleyrand, "if it is a question of infirmities, each of us has one of his own, and we can all claim an exception on that basis."

Napoleon, whose foreign minister Talleyrand had once been, described Talleyrand as "filth in silk stockings." He was, as the English historian Arthur Bryant said, "a politician perfectly adapted to the prevailing moral climate of his country and a disordered Europe . . . There were few crimes, including incest, of which he was not believed guilty. No one who saw his dirty, crafty, powdered face, with its half-closed eyes, villainous mouth, and slobbering, darting tongue, was left in any doubt as to the manner of man he was." He had an excellent head, said the emperor Francis's brother Archduke Johann, but "a worm-eaten heart."

He liked a lilac coat, or something in a dove-gray silk brocade; he favored black silk stockings with a touch of gold, and pumps with red heels and diamond buckles. He was sixty years old. Talleyrand had sidestepped the Revolution, going into exile in England and America; he had survived to serve Napoleon, as he now served the restored French monarchy. He had arrived in Paris with his lovely twenty-one-year-old niece, Dorothea, duchess of Talleyrand-Périgord (the sister of Metternich's mistress the duchess of Sagan). The gossips naturally assumed the worst about Talleyrand's relationship with the young woman, and while he conducted himself with circumspection, his wife of twelve years left him at once, never to return.

"The object of today's conference," Castlereagh said, once Talleyrand had settled himself in at the long table, "is to acquaint you with what the four courts have done since we have been here." And then (according still to Talleyrand's report to his king) Castlereagh turned to Metternich, saying, "You have the protocol."

Talleyrand was handed a copy of Metternich's original plan that specified the way in which the Big Four of the former allies against Napoleon, working by themselves, would reach agreement on matters, then consult with France and Spain, and finally present their conclusions to the full congress.

And Talleyrand reacted with surprise. "In this document," as he wrote to Louis XVIII, "the word 'allies' occurred in every paragraph. I objected to that expression. I said it had become necessary for me to ask where we were . . . If we had not made peace, then had there been a declaration of war? And, if so, against whom?"

The ministers of the four hastened to assure Talleyrand that the expression had been used only for the sake of brevity.

"However important it may be to be brief," said Talleyrand, "that importance cannot be such as to justify inaccuracy."

He read on. And after a few moments, he looked up again, puzzled.

"I do not understand," he said.

He read on further.

"I do not understand any better. To me, there are but two dates: that of May 30 [when the Treaty of Paris was signed and the congress called for] . . . and that of October 1, when this Congress was to meet. Between those two dates, there is only a vacuum. Nothing that has been done in that interval exists, so far as I am concerned, and I will ignore it."

What had been done, of course, was an understanding about excluding France from the congress. Talleyrand simply assumed, since he recognized nothing that had been done, that he had not been excluded.

Talleyrand had not much to gain by being admitted to the conference. France had already agreed to accept its pre-Napoleonic borders as its proper borders in 1815, and such overseas colonies as it possessed were not threatened by any of the other powers. But as Talleyrand knew, it was dangerous, simply as a matter of principle, to be excluded from conversations affecting any international arrangements.

The protocol that Talleyrand found so offensive was withdrawn; and Metternich now introduced the document that Gentz had been instructed to craft.

Gentz's declaration skirted by all the arguments over including or excluding France from the committee of six by specifying that there should be such a committee—but by tactfully refraining from naming any of its members. This was a slippery document, and Talleyrand was appropriately on his guard. He would want time, he said, to consider this proposal, he was not entirely comfortable with Gentz's paper.

"We have assembled to consecrate and secure the rights of each of the powers," said Talleyrand, "and how unfortunate it would be if we started out by violating them." Altogether, it seemed to him, "the idea of arranging everything before the congress assembles is quite new to me. You are proposing that we begin by doing what, in my opinion, we should finish by doing." On the whole, he thought the congress should be assembled "here and now."

As the other ministers gave their reasons why it was impossible to convene the congress just yet, one of them happened to mention the complexities surrounding the throne of Naples. France, for example, refused to recognize King Joachim Murat as the rightful ruler of Naples. Indeed. Talleyrand refused even to mention Murat's name, but rather insisted on speaking of "he who reigns at Naples." When, in the heat of discussion Labrador referred to the king of Naples, Talleyrand asked: "Of what king of Naples are you speaking? We do not know who he is."

Nonetheless, whatever Talleyrand's objections, as Baron von Humboldt said, some way must be found to keep such small powers as Liechtenstein and Leiden from interfering in the general settlement of European affairs. On that note, the ministers adjourned for two days to give Talleyrand time to study the Gentz declaration.

And then Talleyrand did something extraordinary: rather than wait for the scheduled meeting he sat down at once and wrote a memorandum in which he argued that the eight signatories to the Treaty of Paris had the right only to draw up an agenda for the congress and propose the formation of committees, but that the ultimate power of decision lay with the congress as a whole. Thus the powers of the Big Four were nonexistent, and even the German committee, once its formation was referred to the whole congress, would doubtless be constituted with an enlarged membership.

Talleyrand signed the memo, making it official and therefore subject to publication. Since its arguments incorporated an exposition of the plans of the Big Four, the deliberations of the four were now exposed. And so, on the day the congress was scheduled to begin, only Talleyrand was calling for its opening—and he was issuing his call as the champion of the small powers against the great, of the many against the few. "The intervention of Talleyrand," said Gentz, "hopelessly upset our plans. It was a scene I shall never forget."

The next day, extremely vexed, the ministers of the four met in Metternich's study to decide how to respond to Talleyrand's memo. By now they felt they had to abandon the idea of the six altogether and to embrace instead the idea that the eight signatories to the Treaty of Paris should be constituted as those who would prepare whatever was to be submitted to the whole congress. This decision was drawn up in a revised declaration.

But the ministers were unhappy with the thought that, in this way, they would be replying formally to Talleyrand. A formal reply would acknowledge Talleyrand's standing and his right to have had his thoughts considered by the four. In order to make their revised declaration something other than official, they decided that Metternich should hand the document to Talleyrand that evening, casually, at a social gathering at the duchess of Sagan's.

Talleyrand reacted by calling a meeting of the small powers of Germany, and convinced their delegates that he—the representative of the country that had only recently overrun them—was the champion of the small powers. He wrote a letter to Castlereagh, rejecting the four's revised declaration and insisting that the congress be convened at once.

The following day, the four ministers invited Talleyrand to a meeting to give him the opportunity to withdraw his letter. Talleyrand refused. Metternich retorted that Austria might be forced to announce that there would be no congress at all. With that threat, Talleyrand agreed to have the convening of the congress postponed for several more weeks. He had one condition: "Any prince may send plenipotentiaries to the congress who had universally recognized sovereignty over a state that took part in the recent war, who has not ceded that sovereignty, and whose sovereignty is uncontested. The same holds true for any state which was independent before the recent war and which . . . is now independent again."

This was Talleyrand's famous principle of legitimacy, and it struck with force. Certainly no one could say that he wished to base his government on a principle of illegitimacy. At the same time, none could help but notice that this principle, as Talleyrand formulated it, firmly established the right of Talleyrand to be a delegate to the congress, ruled out France's enemy Joachim Murat in Naples, and ruled in the king of Saxony who would give immediate trouble to Prussia and therefore Russia. Like Alexander, Talleyrand defined as principle what suited his interests. It was a stunning formulation: simple, complex, self-serving, irrefutable. No one had a ready reply; and so the session was adjourned.

Within a few days, the four ministers were meeting with Talleyrand again, contemplating another revised declaration from Gentz. This one stated simply that the eight signatories would do their best to confer with all the powers assembled in Vienna and then convene the congress on November 1. There was no mention of the four or the six, of committees or of rules of admission to the congress. To this, at last, Talleyrand gave his approval.

And so, Talleyrand, who had feared he would be excluded from the official steering committee of the congress, had forced the committee to abolish itself. He had not, strictly speaking, succeeded in making himself included, but there was no longer anything, formally speaking, from which he could be excluded.

He could not prevent the others from speaking to one another informally on social occasions. And that is what they did. Talleyrand had forced into being the practice of a style of diplomacy that came particularly to distinguish the Congress of Vienna. The congress did not take place in official meetings in formal settings since Talleyrand had dislodged it from such settings, forcing it into "informal" sessions in Metternich's study, and into the ballrooms and salons and boudoirs of Vienna, whispered conversations in the corners of the rooms at the duchess of Sagan's. If Metternich lured Nesselrode into a corner to talk of social matters, and happened to mention Poland, neither Talleyrand nor anyone else could complain of being left out. In this way, the small powers were entirely excluded from any participation in the Congress of Vienna, though Talleyrand himself, a master at this sort of diplomacy, would never be eliminated.

In truth, because of the difficulty in finding a satisfactory way to exclude the small powers from their deliberations, there never was a Congress of Vienna. The congress was postponed until November 1, and then postponed again and then again until it simply never occurred. The congress convened on only one day—its last —and then only, and truly, as a mere formality to approve what had been arranged in the salons and ballrooms and private meetings in Vienna.

The most famous remark ever made about the Congress of Vienna, by the Prince de Ligné, was not only clever but also true. *"Le congrès ne marche pas,"* said the prince; *"il danse."* The congress doesn't work; it dances. Dancing became its business—the hard work of keeping the small powers—of whom Metternich referred to as "the other powers"—excluded from the real business of the conference, and so entertained that they would not notice. "The dances and the waltzes played by the orchestras never stopped throughout the night," the count de la Garde-Chambonas reported. "The spectacle of happiness and splendor never broke off."

The emperor Francis appeared with his empress Maria Ludovica for a performance at the Imperial Theatre. "Everything brightly lit," as one diarist recorded the scene, ". . . the entire court present. First the Dane, applause,—then the Swabian [the king of Württemberg], little clapping. At last, the imperial pair, great noise. She . . . looks pale. Being close, I watch them carefully. They look bored." Francis liked to present himself as a genial patriarch. His sister, Maria Theresa of Saxony, said, "Waiting for his interminable stories to end, one often doesn't eat for days, which leads to stomach trouble that, with me, always causes excessive sweating."

There were concerts. One night there was a dreadful "Evening of the Hundred Pianos." Another evening there was the premier of a new Beethoven symphony (the Seventh). According to the Weimar book dealer Carl Bertuch, "Beethoven is excelling himself. The known world is too small for him. . . . Both high and low are putty in his hands." Others disagreed, finding Beethoven too loud, too aggressive. Haydn was the darling of the musical world just then, and Salieri; Mozart was not yet at his most popular. One spy reported, "There are actually anti- and pro-Beethoven factions forming."

"Four thousand guests were invited," Friedrich Anton von Schonholz wrote of one dress ball, ". . . the ladies in white, light blue, or pink dresses, the gentlemen in blue or black tailcoats with blue or white breeches, silk stockings . . . plumed hats. . . . Opera hats had become so rare that their procurement was a problem . . . hat shops were mobbed like bakeries in a famine. . . . Toward midnight the number of guests crowding the buffets had increased. . . . A man in black court dress, girt in dress sword, his powdered coiffure caught up in a dignified hairnet, hat under arm, betokened a ruler, thankful if only for a glass of water."

"I am deadly tired of all this partying," said Baron von Humboldt. The dancing, said Count von Nostitz—no waltzes, all polonaises—"is boring."

"If this goes on," said the emperor Francis, "I shall abdicate. I can't stand this life much longer."

Meanwhile, Countess Flora Wrbna-Kageneck was surprised by a wager proposed by Czar Alexander. Men, the czar happened to remark, were able to change for dinner so much more rapidly than women. When the countess demurred, the czar bet he could take off all his clothes and put on court attire more quickly than she could. The czar and the countess withdrew to separate dressing rooms, stripped, and dressed again. The czar came out first, fully dressed, with all his decorations in place, and went into the countess's dressing room to show he had won. The witnesses, it was said, "were silent about the state of his partner's dress when he went to collect his bet."

At a ball given by Franz Palffy, Czar Alexander said to Countess Szechenyi-Guilford, "Your husband is not present. It would be pleasant to occupy his place temporarily."

To which the countess replied, "Does Your Majesty take me for a province?"

The duchess Gabriele Auersperg-Lobkowitz, age twenty, had been a widow for two years when the czar arrived in Vienna. So far as the gossips knew, the two never had an affair, although they had a very close and intense friendship, and when the czar left Vienna at the end of the conference, a lady friend found the duchess "on her knees in her boudoir, drowned in tears."

"It isn't always conscience that bothers one," as the prince de Ligné's daughter Fifi put it, "sometimes it is regret."

"The decisions of the Congress of Vienna," as Charles Webster wrote, ". . . depended almost entirely on the settlement of the Polish-Saxon question." And so it was to that issue that the diplomats first addressed themselves after their tussle over procedure.

In 1750 Poland had possessed a large territory. But the Poles were unable to preserve their independence against the expansive designs of their three more powerful neighbors, Russia, Austria, and Prussia. Under a partition of 1772, Russia took a slice of Poland that included a large part of Lithuania; Austria took a slice that included Galicia; and Prussia took a smaller, but more prosperous, slice in the north. Poland was reduced from a population of ten and a half million to about eight and a half million. Then, in 1793, Poland was repartitioned, and lost another five million in population. Finally, in 1795–1796, Poland disappeared into Russia, Austria, and Prussia.

In 1807, when Napoleon defeated Prussia, the French emperor reconstituted a miniature Poland, calling it the Duchy of Warsaw, and placed it under the rule of the king of Saxony. And in 1809, after Napoleon defeated Austria, he added back a piece of Galicia and other territory to the new duchy. It was this Poland that Russia meant to absorb entirely—and that the other powers wanted to see secured as an independent nation.

It was Castlereagh's view that a "just equilibrium" needed to be established in Europe with a strong center holding back both east and west. The notion of equilibrium was not new. As the diplomatic historian James Der Derian has written, the idea of balance-of-power politics had become altogether the norm by the late seventeenth century.

Still, not everyone conceived of a balance of power in precisely the same way. As Metternich saw it, Castlereagh's idea of equilibrium was too mechanical, too focused on a balance of the external relations among nations. Metternich believed a balance of power must exist not only externally among nations but also internally among factions and classes. The external and internal equilibria buttressed each other; they could not be separated without threatening the survival of the whole society.

He believed, too, that the only acceptable outcome for the congress would be a "legitimate" settlement. By legitimate, how-

ever, Metternich meant something different than Talleyrand did
by the word. He meant a settlement in which all the powers felt
they had a vested interest, and so would commit themselves to
maintain the settlement out of conviction, not force. Legitimacy
was what the powers would agree was legitimate.

Thus, while each state had selfish interests to pursue, they
also had common interests. "Isolated states," said Metternich,
"exist only as the abstractions of so-called philosophers. In the
society of states each state has interests . . . which connect it with
the others. The great axioms of political science derive from the
recognition of the true interests of *all* states; it is in the general
interests that the guarantee of existence is to be found." It was not
enough to satisfy the most powerful few; one must, in some degree,
satisfy all. Metternich understood that he must seek the well-being
of Austria as a constituent of the well-being of Europe as a whole.

To Alexander's occupation of Poland and his championship of
liberalism, Talleyrand countered with the principle of legitimacy.
Castlereagh countered with the idea of a just equilibrium with
buffer states. Metternich countered with a balance of power that
encompassed both nations and classes, internally and externally,
and an idea of "Europe."

Some would make of these ideals and principles eternal truths
or maxims of political relations. Certainly each of the diplomats
presented his formulation as a universal verity, not as a truth that
merely suited his selfish convenience, not as a truth he made up,
but as a truth he found already existing that happened to apply to
the present case. And yet, in fact, there was no right or inevitable
principle to which the diplomats were all constrained to repair, any
more than there was any right or inevitable structure to which they
could return as the ordained size and shape and relationship of the
states of Europe. There were no "natural" borders to be discovered
in Europe, no universally and eternally accepted notion of the true
or the good to be shared, not even any immutable reality to which
they must bow. There was only what was to be agreed on, or
created.

This world of undefined relations is one of immense complexity. Since a settlement on Poland and Saxony would necessarily
affect the balance of power between Austria and Prussia and among

the German states, any moves on the Polish and Saxon questions would have to affect the disposition, for example, of Mainz, whether it would be given to Prussia or Bavaria, which could be seen as dependent in Austrian eyes on keeping Hesse-Darmstadt from going to Prussia and on ensuring that Austria have a free hand to encourage Württemberg's designs in Swabia, and all this was dependent on making a confederation for all the German states— and all these issues might well be affected by agreements on Naples and Tuscany and Parma and Piacenza and the needs and wishes of others far distant from the diplomats in Vienna.

The complexities involved in these calculations can only barely be suggested. The diplomats worked with hundreds of dependent variables that changed from day to day, all of them contingent upon all the others.

At the same time, the delegates had to struggle, as Metternich understood so well, with the calculations of domestic politics. While Metternich might be prepared to sacrifice Saxony, he would have to do it with extreme care, and without anyone crying out, since his biggest political antagonists in Austria were opposed to sacrificing Saxony and might defeat his entire policy if he were to expose this one element of it prematurely. Before long, Metternich would be complaining that the negotiations were giving him "the most painful year of my life," saying "I am completely ill, my body is wracked." Hardenberg, worn out, would fall asleep at his desk, or be found in tears of exhaustion and frustration. All of them, finally, were forced to an awareness of the immense web of contingencies that characterized the negotiations in which they were caught.

First, Castlereagh proposed that England, Austria, and Prussia undertake a "joint approach" to Russia. But then Hardenberg hesitated to join England and Austria for fear that Prussia might lose Saxony if the Prussians antagonized the czar. So the Prussians refused to join the others until they were guaranteed Saxony. Metternich hesitated at that—not wanting to strengthen Prussia in central Germany. And Russia would not back down until all three of the other powers joined together.

Caught in this trap of logic, unable to make a move, Metternich, as Kissinger has said, "adopted a policy of procrastination in order to exploit Austria's only bargaining weapon, that the other powers required Austrian acquiescence to make their annexations 'legitimate.' "

"For several weeks," Kissinger wrote, "he was unavailable because of 'illness.' After he 'recovered,' festivities succeeded each other in endless profusion and his love affairs and abstractedness became notorious."

In this diplomatic atmosphere, Castlereagh tried to maneuver Hardenberg and Metternich into a partnership and could not entirely understand why he encountered repeated delays and quibbles, changes of mind, waverings, mutual distrust, and backbiting.

Finally, on October 22, Metternich allowed himself to be persuaded to agree to Prussia's possession of Saxony, but only in the event that the united front against Russia was successful. On this basis, the three ministers were able to present a joint plan to Alexander for the establishment of an independent Poland.

Metternich was designated to carry this message to the czar. When he delivered the message, he provoked a terrifying outburst from Alexander. The czar was absolutely immovable. He immediately dubbed the "joint approach" a "conspiracy" on the part of his former allies, and let loose a tirade, Talleyrand said, that "would have been thought extraordinary even toward one's own servants."

Metternich apparently threatened the czar with a resort to the full congress, telling him that Britain, Austria, and Prussia were quite as capable of restoring Poland as Russia was, a sentiment so insolent, Alexander charged, that no one else in Austria could have spoken it. If Metternich doubted Russia's ability to hold onto Poland, the czar screamed, let him send someone to inspect the two hundred thousand soldiers he had there.

Metternich had trouble finding the door on the way out. It was a scene that became instantly famous in the salons of Vienna, and in the annals of diplomacy.

As it happened, the monarchs had scheduled a pleasure trip just then to Buda, and Alexander went from his meeting with Metternich to the royal round of balls and concerts and parades and theatrical performances in Hungary, where he spoke contemptuously of Hardenberg to King Friedrich Wilhelm and savaged Metternich to emperor Francis, trying to get the emperor to cut

Metternich out of the negotiations and permit the monarchs to deal directly with one another.

Friedrich Wilhelm, aware that his interests lay in remaining loyal to Alexander until he had Saxony firmly in hand, didn't hesitate for a moment to sacrifice his minister. He disowned the joint approach instantly and, in that moment, destroyed it.

The monarchs no sooner returned from Buda to Vienna than Hardenberg was summoned into the presence of the king and the czar together. The czar delivered a tongue-lashing to Hardenberg in the presence of his own monarch. Prussia and Russia, Alexander informed Hardenberg, had arrived at a "definite and unshakable" agreement on Poland. He insisted that Hardenberg say at that moment whether or not he intended to follow the commands of his king. Hardenberg had no choice but to consent.

Talleyrand now had an opportunity to insinuate himself, and now Metternich and Hardenberg were more inclined to include France in combination against the czar.

The czar now tried to corner Talleyrand in one salon or another to bring Talleyrand around on Russia's side against Metternich. Delighted at the attention, Talleyrand tried to avoid the czar in the Viennese salons, since the French were not (yet) (definitively) prepared to abandon the English and the Austrians for the Russians.

Talleyrand succeeded in avoiding Alexander for almost a week, until a reception one evening at Julie Zichy's, which he was obliged to attend even though he knew the czar would be there. He spent the evening slipping from one room to another, just out of the czar's reach until, when he was about to leave as the other guests sat down to dinner, he felt the czar's hand on his shoulder. Alexander invited Talleyrand for an informal visit, "in ordinary clothes rather than court dress, as a friend." It was an invitation Talleyrand could not refuse.

At this informal session, Alexander suggested that Talleyrand support Russia on Saxony, in exchange for which he would support France on Naples.

"Your majesty knows," Talleyrand replied, "that such a bargain is impossible. . . . It is not possible for your majesty to differ from us with respect to Naples."

The conversation meandered and ended without any bargain, but at last both sides were courting Talleyrand.

Still, no problems were being decided, no firm agreements being reached. The variables had become so numerous, so complex, and so fluid in their possible relationships that the committee charged with working out a German confederation stumbled among the contingencies, floundered, and when they found they no longer knew how to keep their discussions going, stopped meeting.

Having failed to force a Russian retreat from Poland, the ministers of Britain, Austria, and Prussia decided now to ask the czar precisely what borders he wanted in Poland and what influence he wanted to have there. If the three began by recognizing Russia's rights in Poland, then they harbored at least a hope that Alexander would define those rights with a sense of moderation. The ministers sent Hardenberg to clarify these issues.

Hardenberg's opportunity to speak with the czar came on the evening of November 23, while most of the delegates were attending a huge masked ball at the Spanish Riding School. "Some 8,000 people," reported the bookseller Carl Bertuch. "Not a leaf could drop to the ground, and to move was nearly as impossible as it was to get to the refreshments."

As the ball continued through the night, Hardenberg went to the czar's rooms in the imperial palace to tell Alexander that, in return for recognition of Russia's right to establish a kingdom of Poland, Austria would want to edge its border south and east, taking in Thorn and Cracow. Prussia was willing to leave the king of Saxony a nucleus of territory around Dresden, in order to placate Austria. Alexander listened cordially and promised an answer in a few days.

Several days later, Alexander gave his answer: Russia would not insist on having Thorn and Cracow as part of a Kingdom of Poland, but rather would consent to having them be free, neutralized cities. As for the other principal point of negotiation: Prussia must have the whole of Saxony.

With this reply, Hardenberg's attempt at making Talleyrand a deal had failed—not because he had gotten what he wanted, but because he had been offered more than he wanted. So long as

Alexander insisted on having Poland for himself and on giving all of Saxony to Prussia—despite a Prussian readiness to compromise —Austria could not agree.

Metternich, seeing the complete failure of the Hardenberg maneuver, decided to stab Hardenberg in the back. He went directly to the czar and proposed that Austria and Russia combine against Prussia. Austria, he said, would agree to Russian claims in Poland for three small concessions: that Alexander give Cracow and its environs to Austria, that the czar adopt a constitution that would limit Russian influence in Poland, and that the czar help to persuade the Prussians to lessen their demands in Saxony, or that the czar at least remain neutral on the question of Saxony.

Betrayed by Metternich, Hardenberg went directly to Alexander and brought with him some of the private correspondence he had shared with Metternich over the past few months which he laid before the czar—a "very incorrect act," as Castlereagh remarked.

Alexander was particularly enraged by a letter of Metternich's in which the Austrian denied the czar's charge that he, Metternich, was a liar and implied that it was the czar who was a liar. The czar went at once to Emperor Francis and challenged Metternich to a duel.

Metternich showed the czar a letter from Hardenberg in which Hardenberg suggested that Prussia, Austria, and Britain give in to Alexander for the time being and then double-cross him.

With that, Alexander confessed that he no longer knew whom he could trust.

At last it was clear that what had finally occurred, as Talleyrand reported to King Louis, was "the rupture of the coalition" of the four major allies against Napoleon. The congress was in shambles, Europe was on the verge of war, and Talleyrand understood that his moment had arrived.

"As from another, possibly hellish, world," said Count Nostitz, "this old curmudgeon gazes into the arena and does nothing except send notes to everyone, pointing out to the recipient the advantages to be gained by this or that action."

In the evenings, it was said, when no diversion called him out, Talleyrand could often be found at home, sunk deep into an armchair, silent and motionless, thinking. One of his aides would sit nearby, quietly playing Haydn and Mozart. Another aide kept a set of files organized and placed on the table next to Talleyrand's chair so that, from time to time, he could page through them.

Hardenberg tried frantically now to work his way back into the game. He drafted another proposal with a new set of suggested compromises. But by this time, he was no longer taken entirely seriously as a player. It had become clear to Metternich and Castlereagh that Austria, Britain, and France together could ignore Prussia and bring their combined strength to bear against Russia.

When Hardenberg's proposal was delivered to Metternich, as Kraehe says, Metternich left the paper "unread for half a day while correcting the proofs of satirical pieces to be recited at the next fete," and Hardenberg had to write him the following day to beg him "in the name of friendship" to look over the proposal and consider it seriously.

At the same time, Alexander himself turned his charm on Emperor Francis. Evidently having sensed that he needed to reach a settlement before the momentum turned too far against him, Alexander apologized for the rigid Russian position on Cracow (he was forced to be so rigid, said Alexander, because Cracow was the ancient burial place of Polish kings)—and offered the District of Tarnopol to Austria in place of Cracow.

As the alignments shifted with dizzying speed, Talleyrand wrote a note to Metternich saying that, while France had no selfish interest to press, the French did have a general interest that they shared with all Europe—an interest in equilibrium and in legitimacy. The dethronement of the king of Saxony, Talleyrand explained, violated both those principles. And yet, while Talleyrand ostensibly threatened bad behavior on Saxony, his note took for granted that the Polish question had been settled. Thus, when the note inevitably found its way to Alexander, the czar could only find it reassuring. A certain agreeableness began to ease the differences between Alexander and the three powers of Austria, Britain, and France.

Hardenberg then called on Castlereagh to beg the British ambassador to mediate on Saxony. And Castlereagh agreed, after a fashion. Perhaps, he suggested, a statistical commission could be formed to demonstrate precisely what might be given to the Prussians in return for Prussia giving up a portion of Saxony. Hardenberg hastened to agree.

Castlereagh moved through this opening. Talleyrand, he said, would need to be given a seat on the statistical commission. Hardenberg objected. But then, persuaded that the statistical commission would be nothing but a fact-finding operation, he relented. And so Talleyrand took his place as a member of a minor, but nonetheless official, conference body.

But in the next session with the Russian negotiators, Castlereagh placidly suggested that if Saxony were to be discussed, a representative of France would have to be present. France was required, said Castlereagh, because the matter was one of general European interest. And for that matter, said Castlereagh, the French were necessary so that they could help persuade the king of Saxony to agree to the settlement, since his consent was necessary, too.

Hardenberg, stunned, lost all control. He would rather break up the conference, he shouted, than grant the king of Saxony the right to accept or reject a plan for his own displacement. If Austria and Britain refused to recognize Prussia's rights in Saxony, said Hardenberg, then Prussia and Russia would have to consider such a refusal "as tantamount to a declaration of war!"

This was, noted the imperturbable Castlereagh, a "most alarming and unheard of menace." Such "an insinuation might operate upon a power trembling for its existence but must have the contrary effect upon all alive to their own dignity." If such a "temper" were really to prevail, the diplomats could no longer be said to be "deliberating in a state of independence, and it were better to break up the congress." Tempers were cooled. A compromise was suggested. The assent of Saxony was to be considered "desirable," but not as essential as the assent of France.

On New Year's Day, 1815, acting in direct violation of the written instructions of his cabinet, Castlereagh sat down and drafted a military treaty among Britain, Austria, and France. The three would finally bring their combined force against Prussia and Russia—or at least allow rumors to suggest that they were prepared to back their common negotiating position with force. The three powers agreed to establish a military commission to prepare plans in the event of an invasion of Europe by Russia.

"The general outlook is sad indeed," Gentz wrote in his diary on New Year's Day. "As concerns politics, I am fully aware of the futility of believing it capable of fulfilling the hopes the enthusiasts put in it, hopes I have forever abandoned."

Castlereagh, Metternich, and Talleyrand pledged themselves to keep their treaty a secret. Given the general level of gossip, that must be considered to have been a ploy. Whether as a result of the threat, or because events were moving toward a settlement in any case, two days later Hardenberg announced that Prussia would accept Talleyrand at the conference table.

The import of Hardenberg's remark was not lost on the diplomats. Henceforth France was to be reckoned again as a major power, entitled to participate in any European settlement; henceforth the weight of Prussia was diminished in the European balance of power: Saxony would not go whole to the Prussians. At a stroke, several contingencies fell into place.

"The alarm of war," Castlereagh reported to a cabinet that had not known that there was one, or that their own minister had raised it, "is over."

Talleyrand, now that his position among the new Big Five was secure, stopped referring to the rights of the small powers. Castlereagh went to work with his statistical commission to tally up the souls of Saxony and Hesse-Darmstadt and Saxe-Weimar and Hanover and others of the small states to reckon where Prussia could be suitably compensated. The Russians suggested the appointment of a technical committee—so peripheral had the issue of Saxony now become in their calculations—to work out the details.

The Prussian count Nostitz was stunned by the suddenness of it all. "At first, the woods are not seen for all the trees," he wrote in his diary, "and then, both woods and trees are gone. Poor, dear Congress! One hardly knows, has it begun?"

The work on Poland and Saxony was not finished; there were details to settle. But because a constellation of powers and interests had been recognized as having the standing to direct the major negotiations, the lesser issues began to fall into place.

Castlereagh was recalled, now that the main lines of agreement had been established, to attend to business in London. He was replaced, to the delight of most of those in Vienna, by the illustrious Englishman, the duke of Wellington, the hero of the Napoleonic Wars, a man who impressed Nostitz as one who "lets people talk and listens attentively. His answers are to the point, his objections couched in courteous terms. His whole being exudes calmness rather than pouncing forcefulness and shows a soberness that is most attractive."

The diplomats now turned to some of the secondary issues. The problems of Italy, and in particular of Naples, were complicated by the fact that there were two delegations from Naples in Vienna, both claiming to represent the legitimate government. Metternich had once been, possibly still was, the lover of Caroline Bonaparte, the wife of King Joachim Murat of Naples.

Murat had the support of none of the big powers. Because he was given to making appeals to the ideals of Italian nationalism, Metternich considered him dangerous to Austrian interests in Italy. The British, because of their interests in the Mediterranean, did not desire the undependable Murat on the throne of Naples—and, in any case, the British looked on Italy as a place to compensate Austria for sacrifices Austria would make elsewhere. The Prussians had consistently said that Murat must go. The Russians declined to defend him. All that saved Murat was the rivalry between Austria and France. Talleyrand, too, wished to remove Murat—but only in order to replace him with the Bourbon king Ferdinand, and restore French influence in Italy. If Murat were removed, it would be difficult for Metternich to resist the claims of Ferdinand, since he had the most "legitimate" claim to the throne. It was another logic trap for the diplomats, and while Talleyrand urged its resolution, Metternich insisted they postpone discussion—hoping that something would turn up.

Closer to home, Metternich was still grappling with the Prussians and the smaller German states over just what their relationship was to be. Napoleon had created a confederation of the Rhine out of his conquered German territories; with his defeat, the confederation had dissolved, but many Germans felt that it had been German disunity that had allowed Napoleon's conquest.

Baron von Stein, a Prussian who had joined the circle of the czar's advisors, was one of the leading advocates of a Germany united under a strong constitution. There were many liberals who argued that this constitution should be the foundation for representative government, and that the sovereignties of the many German states should be subordinated to the common welfare of Germany. But neither the Prussians nor the Austrians nor the smaller princes wanted to surrender sovereignty to a central government, and none was prepared to surrender power to their peoples. In the event, there was infinite room for bargaining, for the combining and recombining of different clusters of powers, for the adamant exercise of vetoes, for threats of war, for offers to yield on one point or another for the sake of the realignment of a border or the acquisition of a fortress—but very little room indeed for agreement.

At last, the outline of a confederation was drawn up and agreed to. It was not a detailed constitution—that was too difficult to achieve—but a general design calling for a federal diet, with thirty-five states and four city republics as members, dedicated to "the preservation of the external and internal security of Germany and of the independence and inviolability of the individual German states." No provision was made for popular representation. And the diet was designed, as the United Nations a century and a half later, to possess almost no authority at all.

Far more difficult to quiet was the clamor to redraw borders to compensate states for losses caused by the redrawing of others' borders.

Prussia was finally to be given Posen and the city of Thorn in Poland, along with two-fifths of Saxony (but not Leipzig), Swedish Pomerania, and a large share of the left bank of the Rhine and the duchy of Westphalia, among other things. These possessions on the Rhine and in Westphalia gave the protective buffer to the Netherlands that Britain wanted. Evidently no one foresaw that they were creating in Prussia what would become, by the end of the nineteenth century, a vastly powerful northern German state that would come to possess the resources and industry, and to feel the need, to try to dominate the Continent. With all the possibilities the diplomats considered, this one never occurred to them.

Denmark, to whom Pomerania had been promised, had to make do instead with Lauenburg and a financial settlement.

With the strong support of Britain, Hanover got pieces of Westphalia, East Friesland, Goslar, and the bishopric of Hildesheim—to build up Hanover as a buffer for the northern Netherlands.

The new Kingdom of the Netherlands itself—Holland and Belgium from the seacoast to the river Meuse—was augmented with a sliver more of land beyond the Meuse. The British held back from augmenting the Netherlands even more, in order to make sure Prussia had a large enough territory on the Rhine.

Austria, having given up the Austrian Netherlands, got Galicia and the district of Tarnopol from Poland along with Lombardy-Venetia directly to the south, Istria and Dalmatia on the Adriatic coast, and Tyrol and Salzburg (without Berchtesgaden) from Bavaria.

Bavaria was given the Lower Palatinate, but deprived of Mainz.

Mainz was given to Hesse-Darmstadt.

And so it went as the territorial settlements cascaded across Europe and down into Italy. Count Nostitz, still brooding perhaps over the treatment of Prussia, was not impressed. "The big results of the bighearted congress," Nostitz wrote in his diary, "will be nought but bartering of souls. . . . everyone is caught in the . . . dilemma of self-service, narrow-mindedness, and stupidity. Rotten, mediocre ministers who conduct demoralized politics and who override the needs of their peoples with their own worm-eaten personalities."

Then, on March 1, Metternich was awakened at six in the morning by his valet, who handed him a letter from the Austrian consulate general at Livorno. Metternich, glancing at the point of origin written on the envelope, put it on his bedside table and tried to get back to sleep. Unable to return to sleep, he got up and opened the envelope and read that Napoleon had escaped from Elba. "I was dressed in a few minutes," Metternich wrote in his memoirs, "and was with the emperor before eight o'clock."

The emperor read the dispatch calmly and said to Metternich,

"Go at once to the czar and to the Prussian king and tell them I am ready to order my army back into France. I do not doubt the two monarchs are of a mind with me. . . . In this way," Metternich concluded, "war was decided on in less than an hour."

"The news hit the social world," said de la Garde-Chambonas, "like a bolt out of the blue, and the thousands of taper candles seemed suddenly dimmed. The news spread with lightning speed. The waltz stopped; in vain the orchestra played on; one gazed in disbelief; questions were asked." It was not difficult, said Lord Clancarty, of the British delegation, "to perceive that fear was predominant in all the Imperial and Royal personages."

By March 10, Napoleon had been received in triumph in the city of Lyons, by crowds who had been remembering in the recent days of Louis XVIII's reign how much they despised the Bourbons. The government in Paris counted on the troops of Marshal Ney to arrest Napoleon; on March 17, the news came that Marshal Ney had gone over to Bonaparte. On March 18, Louis XVIII, in his bedroom slippers, scurried out of the Tuileries palace and climbed into his carriage to set out for a safe haven in Ghent. In the middle of the night of March 20, Napoleon entered Paris, accompanied by cavalry, soldiers, and by crowds cheering *Vive l'empereur!* and installed himself once more in the Tuileries. "The congress," Napoleon had declared when he first landed in France from Elba, "is dissolved." He was wrong.

Despite Napoleon's best efforts to insinuate his representatives into the negotiations at Vienna, and to divide and confuse the powers there, in fact his reappearance caused the diplomats in Vienna to unite. And just two weeks after Napoleon arrived in Paris, the duke of Wellington was in Brussels to take command of a new allied army there.

While the diplomats in Vienna argued over who ought to direct the campaign against Napoleon, and over who ought now to be supported for the throne of France, and over whether and how harshly Napoleon ought to be punished when he was again defeated, and while the czar insisted he would prefer even a republic to another restoration of the Bourbons, the army of British, Dutch, and Hanoverians under the duke of Wellington, and the Prussians under Blücher and Gneisenau, defeated Napoleon at the Battle of

Waterloo on June 18. On June 22, Napoleon once again abdicated; and before debate started up again, Wellington restored Louis XVIII to his throne.

Napoleon's reappearance had invigorated the diplomats in Vienna. The issues that they had been nudging were now expeditiously settled. The problem of Naples, as Metternich had hoped, settled itself. Murat had joined Napoleon and launched his own offensive against the Papal States. He was defeated and forced to give up his crown and so, as Talleyrand had wanted, Ferdinand was restored to Naples—having given a promise, in return for Metternich's support, not to grant his subjects a constitution, and so to hold the line against liberalism. With the question of Naples settled, the status of the other states—of Tuscany and Modena, Parma, Piacenza, Lucca, Ravenna, Bologna, Ferrara, and others—easily fell into place, and largely to Metternich's satisfaction.

Even the tertiary issues were now promptly settled. A Swiss confederation of twenty-two cantons was formed; its neutrality, and the inviolability of its territory, was guaranteed.

A treaty of 110 articles was drawn up. Not all the agreements were incorporated in the articles; some were attached as appendices to the treaty. Then Metternich insisted that the outline of the German confederation be included in the treaty, which brought the number of articles up to 121. The question arose: who was to sign the treaty? Just the job of making copies was by itself so forbidding (it took twenty-six secretaries a full day from morning to night to prepare a single copy) as to discourage the notion of having all the sovereign states be given their own copies and be made parties to it. Many of the powers no longer had plenipotentiaries in Vienna. Some of the powers were likely to raise objections to the completed treaty. Thus it was decided to have the eight powers sign the treaty and to invite all the other powers to sign the treaty as accessories. The date was set for the plenary session at which the congress would assemble, the treaty would be signed, and the congress would be adjourned. The day came. But the Russians, given the treaty to sign, said they could not put their signatures to it until Alexander had read it in its completed form. The delegate from the Vatican lodged a protest that the treaty did not take into account the pope's temporal interests. Several of the smaller powers refused to sign. Sweden agreed to sign, while protesting certain articles. And so the congress met, and adjourned, on June 9, without actually signing the Treaty of Vienna.

Days later, when another sitting was scheduled for the formal signing, the Russians did not yet have permission to affix their signatures (they would sign a week later), and Lord Clancarty insisted on rereading the whole document before signing it—forcing those who attended this session to sit by until midnight.

What had been achieved? The Congress of Vienna confirmed the leaders of Europe in the belief that no one power could be allowed to dominate the Continent and that all powers, certainly all the major powers, must work together to preserve the peace and the status quo—seeing themselves as contingent parts of a larger balance of powers on the continent.

Unfortunately, as Nicolson pointed out, there was an underlying fallacy to the Vienna settlement, for in the end the "existing order could not preserve its unity in a Europe in which interests and ambitions were in a state of constant flux."

The "spirit of unrest," as Nicolson called it, "which was the spirit of the first half of the nineteenth century, was seething in every country"—not only from discontent on the left, but also from discontent on the right. Or, as Arthur Bryant was to write, "the static dream of centuries had been broken. The old Order could never again be accepted without question where men had seen the overthrow of the thrones and altars they had believed eternal. . . . They tried to eliminate everything that had happened since 1789. Instead of making provision for the ideas of the young, they assumed that these had been discredited forever by the crimes of Napoleon and the Jacobins. By refusing to compromise with the new, they made its ultimate rebellion certain. They thus undermined the world order they so carefully restored."

Metternich had been right to insist that the enduring success of the settlement would rest on the willing assent of all. He was wrong in how he defined "all." This too-limited conception of "others" who needed to be accommodated tore the Vienna settlement apart, and set the stage for the catastrophe of the Great War.

Five

THE
FALSE LESSONS
OF HISTORY

When he won the presidential election of 1976, as Ernest May and Richard Neustadt have written, President Jimmy Carter—having learned from the experience of Franklin Roosevelt and Lyndon Johnson that he needed to "hit the ground running" and push through his agenda in his first Hundred Days, set a goal he could not achieve. And so, by the end of his first few months in office, he looked incompetent.

"The underappreciated Gerald R. Ford," according to Fred Greenstein of Princeton, "took office in a glow of approval. Jettisoning the hierarchical Nixon staff system of Watergate infamy, he looked back to Harry S Truman and attempted to be his own chief of staff. Promptly and without adequate staffing, he pardoned his predecessor, and his support plummeted."

The lessons of history as they apply to American political campaigns are: be a fountain of facts in a television debate, as John Kennedy was in his winning debates with Richard Nixon; do not be belligerently ideological, as Barry Goldwater was in 1964; do

not be too specific, as George McGovern was in promising $1,000
to every taxpayer; do not get too emotional, as Edmund Muskie
did, bursting into tears in his primary campaign in New Hamp-
shire. "Never mind," say May and Neustadt, "that Ronald Reagan
won two gubernatorial and one presidential election being vague or
wrong on facts, highly ideological, and very specific in promises;
or that John Glenn became a senator and briefly a presidential
prospect because an opponent said he had never held a job and he
replied by recounting in a choked voice what it was to be a career
military officer."

In 1938, when British Prime Minister Neville Chamberlain
returned from his meeting at Munich with Adolf Hitler, the prime
minister triumphantly predicted that he had negotiated "peace in
our time." Yet within a year, Europe was at war, the very word
"Munich" had become a synonym for cowardly surrender to a
tyrant, Chamberlain was turned out of office, and the "lesson of
Munich" took its place as the premier lesson of twentieth-century
diplomatic history: dictators only understand raw power; compromise with them is seen as a sign of weakness and will be taken
advantage of.

The lesson of Munich was invoked repeatedly by the Western
powers when the status quo was challenged after World War II, in
Korea, in Vietnam, in Cuba. Indeed, most recently, it was invoked
by President Bush in the war in the Persian Gulf. None of these
countries was Germany, none was led by Hitler, none presented
a similar historical situation to that of Europe in the thirties, and
the lesson of Munich was not ultimately the most instructive insight a leader might have had about any one of them as they
developed.

(Hitler, incidentally, learned an entirely different lesson from
Munich. According to transcripts found in the führer's bunker in
Berlin after the war, Hitler railed against Chamberlain to the very
end, convinced that the British prime minister had tricked him into
delaying the war for a year, certain that, had Germany started
earlier, he would have won the war.)

Even if everyone might agree on what lesson a given historical
event teaches, there are probably no true lessons of history, if

what is meant by that is a mine of specific lessons to be applied to specific events. Because all historical moments are unique, because history does not repeat itself, the wisdom of history is an elusive quality.

As Paul Veyne has written, if effects have causes, not all causes have effects. And the causes necessary to produce a certain effect are unknown before the effect occurs: "Louis XIV became unpopular because of fiscal matters, but, when the nation's territory is invaded, the peasants are more patriotic, or if he had been taller and his figure more majestic, perhaps he would not have become unpopular. So let us beware of stating that all kings become unpopular just because Louis XIV was."

The best use of history, its true lesson, may simply be, as May and Neustadt have suggested, that it reminds us always to think of events not as isolated phenomena, like mathematical problems with universal rules of solution, but as part of a flow of time, each event with its own set of unique antecedents and possibilities.

When we draw on history for more specific lessons, we run the risk of dreadful consequences. Perhaps the most awful instance of this irresistible urge to apply the lessons of the past to the incomparable circumstances of the present occurred at the Paris Peace Conference of 1919. There, President Woodrow Wilson drew, for his guidance, on the democratic ethos of America, which persuaded him that his Fourteen Points and Four Principles of democratic justice would ensure peace in the world. Premier Georges Clemenceau drew on his experiences as a Frenchman who had seen German troops march into Paris in the Franco-Prussian War of 1870–71, and was certain that the way to prevent future trouble from the Germans was to be unforgiving with them. Prime Minister David Lloyd George drew on the experience of a lifetime in British parliamentary politics, in which survival depended on compromise. Each one acted from (to him) persuasive lessons of history. In another time or place, the lessons might have been reliable guides to behavior; but in this instance, the remembered past contained the wrong lessons, or at least the wrong combination of lessons. In Paris, in 1919, the memories of the past helped to create the nightmare of the future.

WILSON, CLEMENCEAU, AND LLOYD GEORGE IN PARIS, 1919

May 7, 1919: Count Ulrich von Brockdorff-Rantzau, pale, perspiring, wearing a black frock coat, and using a slender walking stick, led his delegation slowly down the narrow corridor from the rear entrance of the Trianon Palace Hotel at Versailles, past half-opened doors from which servants peered, past the cloakroom, bar, and smoking rooms, to the conference room. He paused at the entrance, dazzled by the explosion of sunlight in the vast mirrors and chandeliers, white walls, great glass door, and large windows.

A French officer, Colonel Henri, announced in sharp, ringing tones: *"Messieurs les délégués allemands!"*

There were sounds of scraping chair legs and of leather soles on the wooden floor. The representatives of the Allied powers— President Woodrow Wilson of the United States, Prime Minister David Lloyd George of the United Kingdom, Premier Georges Clemenceau of France, and their staffs, about two hundred people, rose. The German foreign minister bowed. The Allied plenipotentiaries were arranged at the tables around three sides of the room. On the fourth side, a small table was set for the Germans.

Brockdorff-Rantzau moved stiffly to the table. He looked ill, the English Lord Riddell thought. "He walks with a slight limp. His complexion is yellowish, and there are black rings under his eyes which are sunk deep in his head."

The German could not be certain, even as he took his seat, whether this meeting was the beginning of a peace conference in which victors and vanquished bargained over final terms—as at the Congress of Vienna when Talleyrand had taken his place at the table with the victors—or a dictated peace. The Germans had had a feverish discussion just before they had come to the meeting. Their doubts were resolved immediately.

"Gentlemen," said Clemenceau, "plenipotentiaries of the German Empire, it is neither the time nor the place for superfluous words. . . . The time has come when we must settle our accounts. You have asked for peace. We are ready to give you peace."

And with that, Clemenceau presented to the German delegation a bound book of some two hundred pages, containing 75,000 words, or 440 articles, of a finished treaty. Should the Germans have any questions or "observations," they might submit them, "in writing," within fifteen days, and the Allies would be happy to explain any passages that the Germans did not understand, although, as Clemenceau stated, the Allies were resolved to obtain "every justifiable satisfaction that is our due."

Brockdorff-Rantzau had brought two speeches. He chose the more defiant one, and raised his hand for recognition.

The Allied delegates were shocked that he did not stand. But the German minister had seen in a French newspaper that morning a diagram for the arrangement of the tables and remarked that the German table was labeled *"banc des accusés."* The count had sensed, as one of his colleagues said, "the words 'the prisoner will stand up,' and it was for this reason that he kept his seat."*

It is demanded of the Germans, said Brockdorff-Rantzau, who had had some advance briefing on the treaty, "that we shall confess ourselves to be the only ones guilty of the war."

Clemenceau tapped slowly on the table with an ivory paper knife.

"Such a confession in my mouth will be a lie."

A stir passed through the Allied delegations.

"We are," the German continued, "far from declining any responsibility for this great world war having come to pass . . . but we energetically deny that Germany and its people, who were convinced that they were making a war of defense, were alone guilty."

---

* Later, when Harold Nicolson asked his superior, the British foreign minister Arthur Balfour, whether he shared the general sense of indignation, Balfour replied, "What indignation?"

"Oh, about Brockdorff-Rantzau's conduct."

"What conduct?"

"His not standing up when replying to Clemenceau."

"Didn't he stand up? I failed to notice. I make it a rule never to stare at people when they are in obvious distress."

Balfour, said Nicolson, "makes the whole of Paris seem vulgar."

It was, Wilson said later, "the most tactless speech I have ever heard." Lloyd George thought, as he later said, that the Germans were extraordinarily "arrogant and insolent." By the time Brock-dorff-Rantzau had finished, the whole room was murmuring. And when he finished, Clemenceau simply declared that the meeting was ended and brought down his gavel with a sharp crack.

When the Germans got back to the Hotel des Reservoirs, they had an opportunity to examine more closely the treaty they had been given. Because they had only one copy, they tore open the binding and handed out sections to twenty translators. And by midnight, with a rough translation, they were stunned at what they read.

And not only the Germans were stunned. The treaty was so large and complex, the product of innumerable subcommittees, subject to compromises and revisions to the last moment, that not even the Allies had read the finished treaty before it was presented. Many of them were also horrified.

"I am not enamored of our so-called peace terms," said Jan Smuts of South Africa. "Sometimes they appear to have been conceived more in a spirit of making war than of making peace." Herbert Hoover, America's head of postwar relief for Europe, had been unable to sleep the night before after reading an advance copy. Secretary of State Robert Lansing was filled with "disappointment . . . regret . . . depression." John Maynard Keynes, the young economist in the British delegation, thought that the demilitarization and disarmament clauses alone "go beyond what any self-respecting country could submit to." The Germans, said Winston Churchill (who, at age forty-five, was in Paris as Lloyd George's secretary for war and air) would be traitors to their country if they accepted the peace terms. "If I was in the Germans' place," said Harold Nicolson, a young member of the British Foreign Office, "I'd rather die than sign such a peace." The terms were, Nicolson went on, "not stern merely, but actually punitive." It was, said another English delegate, "a peace with a vengeance."

The treaty provided that Germany should return Alsace and Lorraine to France. Germany would keep the Saar itself, but its mines and its coal belonged to France for fifteen years. A demilitarized zone was established along the Rhine River as a buffer between Germany and France and Belgium. British, American, and French troops were to be stationed along its course to guarantee its security. Little bits of territory—Eupen and Malmédy and Moresnet—went to Belgium. A large slice of Prussia was given to Poland to give that landlocked country access to the Baltic Sea through Danzig. Unfortunately, this piece of land, the Polish Corridor as it was called, cut through Germany, dividing the mass of western Germany from German East Prussia. Other, smaller pieces of territory in the south were given to Poland, too. A popular vote was to be arranged for the northern provinces of Schleswig and Holstein. (In the event, the people in the farther north voted to join Denmark, those in the south voted to stay with Germany.)

Altogether, Germany lost slightly more than 13 percent of its territory. Not a great loss, it rankled. More dramatic was its loss of all its colonies. And beyond that, Germany was to reduce its army to a force of 100,000, barely enough to ensure internal order, and its navy to a handful of ships. It was to surrender all its largest merchant ships, to deliver coal free to France, Belgium, and Italy for ten years, and to "make compensation for all damage done to the civilian population of the Allied and Associated powers and to their property." This last provision made Germany liable for a reparations bill that the French estimated might run as high as 200 billion dollars, and the British 120 billion. Some payments would be accepted in kind, so that the Germans might compensate the French in part by delivering five hundred stallions, thirty thousand fillies and mares, two thousand bulls, ninety thousand milch cows, one hundred thousand sheep, ten thousand goats. Belgium would accept a quarter of Germany's fishing boats, as partial payment.

Germany was to return to France the flags and war trophies that it had taken in the Franco-Prussian war of 1870–71. The skull of the sultan Mkwawa, which had been removed from the Protectorate of German East Africa, was to be given to Britain. The astronomical instruments Germany had taken from China during the Boxer Rebellion of 1900–1901 were to be restored. The treaty detailed a list of small demands from one country after another. And finally, Article 231 required the Germans to accept responsibility for imposing war on the Allies.

The Germans considered the territorial concessions painful,

and in the case of the Polish Corridor, intolerable, the demand for reparations economically ruinous, the interminable list of small demands insulting and provocative, the war guilt clause humiliating.

According to the most recent scholarship, the economic effects of reparations were negligible. The Germans paid thirty-six billion gold marks in reparations, but they took thirty-three billion marks in loans from foreign sources that were largely never repaid. But the Germans of the 1920s did not have the benefit of this hindsight. The reparations were seen as disastrous. They caused resentment among the Germans, and misgivings among economists and politicians of other countries. A good many economists and politicians, and not Germans alone, blamed the Great Depression of the 1930s on reparations.

Hitler would rise to power making the same speech over and over again, expressing the Germans' deep resentment of the Treaty of Versailles. The Nazi party was first fueled by bitterness over the Polish Corridor, the reparations, and the imposition by the Allies of German guilt. Nazis rode the wave of anger over Versailles right on into World War II. And so, having waged the war to end war, the Allies had made the peace to end peace.

How had this happened?

The conference opened on January 18, 1919, in Paris, at the French Ministry of Foreign Affairs on the Quai d'Orsay. The British delegation filled five hotels. The opening session was attended by representatives of thirty-two nations, but the war had loosed a plethora of new nations, or aspiring nations, that clamored for attention. Also seeking attention was a large and permanent class of bureaucrats, legal experts, and political specialists. They clogged the hotel lobbies.

The Germans had laid down their arms on November 11, 1918, relying on Wilson's Fourteen Points to ensure a just peace. Four empires had fallen in the war—the German, the Austro-Hungarian, the Turkish or Ottoman, and the Russian. The collapse of these vast nineteenth-century empires gave rise to the great political drama of the twentieth century: the revolutionary movements that churned through Europe and Russia, the efforts of the

European powers to hold their old imperial possessions, the struggle of the colonies to free themselves, and the emergence of the United States as the world's predominant power.

Seventy million men had been mobilized to fight in World War I. Nine million were dead, twenty million more were injured, ill, or spitting blood from the gas attacks. The war had swept in soldiers from the French colonies of Indochina, Algeria, and French West Africa, from the British colonies of India, Australia, New Zealand, South Africa, Canada; the war had spread to take in even the territories of China and Japan. Twenty-two million civilians were killed or wounded, and many survivors were living in rubble, on farms churned to mud, their cattle dead.

In Berlin and Belgrade and Petrograd, the survivors still fought among themselves—fourteen wars, great or small, civil or revolutionary, flickered or raged about the world. Thirteen million tons of shipping had been sunk; ten thousand square miles of northern France ruined; twelve hundred churches and 250,000 other buildings destroyed. Hundreds of square miles of central and eastern Europe were devastated. In parts of central Europe, a member of a relief commission reported that "children were dying for want of milk and adults were unable to obtain bread or fats. In eastern districts . . . the population was living on roots, grass, acorns, and heather." A pandemic of influenza that struck in the last year of the war killed another twenty million people worldwide.

People looked to the diplomats to relieve this dreadful carnage and suffering, and in particular to Wilson, whose arrival in Europe had been greeted by ecstatic crowds. His Fourteen Points were widely embraced as the basis of a just and enduring peace—that international arrangements should not be subject to the sort of secret agreements that had dragged so many powers into World War I, but that:

• first, agreements among nations must be made by "open covenants openly arrived at";

• second, that there must be "absolute freedom of navigation upon the seas";

• third, that damaging economic competitions should be avoided by "the removal, as far as possible, of all economic barriers";

• fourth, that "national armaments will be reduced to the lowest point consistent with domestic safety";

• fifth, that all colonial claims be adjusted based on "the interests of the populations concerned" as well as any "equitable" claim of a government;

• sixth, that all foreign troops be withdrawn from Russia, and the Russians be given "unhampered and unembarrassed opportunity" to determine their own "political development and national policy";

• seventh, that Belgium be evacuated and restored;

• eighth, that France be evacuated and restored, and Alsace-Lorraine returned;

• ninth, that the frontiers of Italy be drawn along lines of nationality;

• tenth, that the many peoples once under the sway of the Austro-Hungarian Empire be given the freest opportunity for autonomy;

• eleventh, that Romania, Serbia, and Montenegro be evacuated and restored;

• twelfth, that the Turkish portions of the Ottoman Empire be assured "a secure sovereignty";

• thirteenth, that an independent Polish state be established; and,

• finally, that a democratic world government, a League of Nations, be established to guarantee "political independence and territorial integrity to great and small states alike."

To these, Wilson added his Four Principles: l) that each part of the final settlement must be based on the justice of that particular case; 2) that "peoples and provinces must not be bartered about from sovereignty to sovereignty as if they were chattels or pawns in a game; 3) that "every territorial settlement must be in the interests of the populations concerned; and 4) that "all well-defined national elements shall be accorded the utmost satisfaction that can be accorded them without introducing new, or perpetuating old, elements of discord and antagonism."

"Not only," said Harold Nicolson, "did I believe profoundly in these principles, I took it for granted that on them alone would the treaties of peace be based. Apart from their inherent moral compulsion, apart from the fact that they formed the sole agreed basis of our negotiation, I knew that the president possessed unlimited physical power to enforce his views." If Wilson's values were indeed the values for which people yearn, his reading of American history may have misled him to believe that they were easy to attain once they had been pointed out to people of good will.

Wilson looked and dressed like a clergyman: three-piece suit firmly buttoned and silver-rimmed pince-nez. He had a very broad toothy smile and a courtly, Virginia charm. He loved familiar things—old southern songs, such hymns as "The Son of God Goes Forth to War" and "How Firm a Foundation," and he liked to read the same books over and over, take the same automobile rides, vacation in the same places in the English Lake Country, wearing his old cape and an old gray sweater bought on a bicycle trip in Scotland some years earlier.

Wilson was born in Virginia in 1856, the only son of a strict Presbyterian minister. He had been an indifferent student, but he worked hard, tutored by his father, and had risen by the powers of his eloquence as lawyer, professor of history at Johns Hopkins and Bryn Mawr and Princeton, president of Princeton, governor of New Jersey, to president.

Georges Clemenceau, seventy-eight years old in 1919, a short, powerful man with a solid, square body, short legs, a barrel chest, was a natural antagonist for a man such as Wilson. He was a ferocious infighter, sarcastic and cutting. His nickname was "the Tiger." He had no close friends. He wore at all times indoors and out, morning and night, at work or at the dinner table, a pair of gray suede gloves.

Clemenceau came from the Vendée, rugged farmland facing the Atlantic, a country of hedgerows, stone cottages. It was conservative and Catholic. In that context, the Clemenceaus were unconventional—rationalists, anticlerical, supporters of the Revolution, republicans, antimonarchists. "At Nantes," said Clemenceau, "my father used to go to a reading room . . . where people came to read and gossip—old folk, who had seen the Revolution and Napoleon. My father pointed one of them out to me and said, 'Do you see that man over there? He's an old friend of Marat.' "

Clemenceau went to Paris to study medicine, took up with

republican circles, and began to write for a small radical journal. But his real introduction to politics occurred during the Franco-Prussian war, when the Germans invaded France in 1870, the French government fell, the radical left swept into power, and Clemenceau was appointed mayor of one of the arrondissements of Paris. As the Germans inflicted military defeats on the French, and the French broke into factions among themselves, the more radical of them declared a socialist commune in Paris, and Clemenceau was constrained to resign his office and witness the defeat of France as an anguished spectator. He never forgot the date the French capitulated and agreed to accept an army of occupation, to pay reparations of a billion dollars, to surrender Alsace and Lorraine, and signed a treaty at the palace of Versailles. (It was January 18, 1871, forty-eight years later to the day that Clemenceau set for the opening of the 1919 conference.)

When the Great War broke out, Clemenceau used the newspaper he wrote for to whip up war fever. When there was talk in 1917 about a negotiated peace, he castigated the "defeatists." "The winner is the one who can believe for a quarter of an hour longer than his enemy that he is not beaten," he wrote. Because no war ministry could hold up under Clemenceau's attacks, he was finally asked to take over as premier. He explained his policy to the chamber of deputies: "I wage war! In domestic politics, I wage war. In foreign politics, I wage war. Always, everywhere, I wage war. . . . And I shall continue to wage war until the last quarter of an hour!"

Now Clemenceau had a single idea and that was that the Germans be subjected to the treatment they had meted out to the defeated French in 1871. Wilson found this notion inconceivable. "Pray, Monsieur Clemenceau," the president asked him, "have you ever been to Germany?"

"No, sir!" replied Clemenceau. "But twice in my lifetime the Germans have been to France."

Germany had not been invaded and wasted during the war as France had been; its fields and factories were intact. And now forty million French faced seventy million Germans. Under such circumstances, the French felt that their victory would be rendered hollow unless their powerful neighbor were disarmed, any possibility of its union with Austria thwarted, its economy harnessed to helping France rebuild, and the borders between them strictly secured. If Clemenceau seemed hard, he was not nearly so adamant as others of the French, led by Marshal Ferdinand Foch, the commander in chief of the Allied armies, who insisted that the French would never be safe unless they established their border right on the Rhine River. Some Frenchmen wanted to divide Germany into many small states, as they had existed before Bismarck. A former French foreign minister tried to cloak this notion in Wilsonian rhetoric, calling for German "federalization." The new Germany, according to Gabriel Hanotaux, would be composed of six to eight small states, without the Rhineland. Clemenceau preferred three autonomous German states, bound together in a customs union, its market regulated by France.

If what was wanted was a compromise between Wilson's view and Clemenceau's, David Lloyd George was perfectly suited to the task, too perfectly suited, according to some of his colleagues. Lloyd George, said Sir Colin Coote, "had really no principles at all, only emotions," and Lord Northcliffe called him, "a chameleon . . . oblique, evasive, and Welsh. . . . You never know what he is up to."

Born on January 17, 1863, the son of a schoolmaster who died when the boy was one year old, he was raised by his mother and uncle, a shoemaker in Wales. The shoemaker learned Latin in order to teach the boy, and David became a lawyer at the age of twenty-one and was elected to Parliament at twenty-seven, where he sat as a member for fifty-four years. "His ruling passion," as the historian A. Lentin has written, "was a passion for brilliant improvisation. It was not simply that the ends justified the means: the means justified themselves." He was the acknowledged master of the House of Commons.

He was a short, stocky man, with a large head and a great shock of white hair that he wore in a flowing mane that fell below his collar. A champion of the weak and the poor, the author of much of the legislation that established the modern welfare state, fearless opponent of the landlords, a resourceful, tenacious, and naturally crafty parliamentarian, he was not always able to harness his skills to his convictions and his convictions often fell to the sheer play of his skill. With women, as with politics, he could not resist temptation and was constantly in the midst of an affair, including one of many years with his secretary Frances Stevenson. Obliged for decades to choose between Frances and his wife Margaret, as he was often forced in politics to choose between one loyalty and another—he chose them both.

Still, for all Lloyd George's dangerous attraction to compromise, he went into the conference with interests to defend. He wanted some spoils for Britain and to neutralize the German high seas fleet, ensuring continued British supremacy. He wanted a share of reparations money, not only because he had promised it to British voters in the general election called immediately after the end of the war (and that gave him a great electoral victory), but because he needed it to pay off British debts. He wanted to break up the German colonial empire in order to reduce competition with the British Commonwealth. In reducing German power, however, he wanted to be sure that France was not left so strong as to dominate the Continent and get the upper hand in the ancient Anglo-French rivalry. Finally, Lloyd George wanted to avoid a peace so harsh on Germany that its resentment would result in the rise of bolshevism within Germany, or a desire for revenge that would end in another war.

Determined not to repeat the errors of the Congress of Vienna, the major powers—Britain, France, Italy, and the United States, who had constituted the Allied Supreme War Council—took as their first order of business a thorough hearing of the representatives of the small powers who had come to Paris, as Wilson's Fourteen Points had promised they would. They added Japan and established a Council of Ten, composed of the premier and foreign minister of each of the five: Clemenceau and Stephen Pichon for France, Lloyd George and Arthur Balfour for Britain, Wilson and Robert Lansing for the United States, Orlando and Sonnino for Italy, and Saionji and Makino for Japan. (Russia might have been on the committee had it not been in the midst of revolution and so lacking any representation in Paris.)

It was tactfully explained to the representatives of the small powers that, while they could not expect to take part in all the negotiations of the conference, the major powers would call upon them to present their cases when their interests were under discussion. Once the large formal opening session was out of the way, the Council of Ten sat down to listen to a parade of the small powers.

"A high room: domed ceiling: heavy chandelier," Nicolson recorded in his diary, "dado of modern oak: doric panelling: electric light: Catherine de Medici tapestries all round the room: fine Aubusson carpet with a magnificent swan border: regence table at which Clemenceau sits . . . secretaries and experts on little gilt chairs: about twenty-two people in all. The lights are turned on one by one as the day fades behind the green silk curtains. . . . Silence—very warm—people walking about with muffled feet—secretaries handing maps gingerly. . . . President Wilson gets pins and needles and paces up and down upon the soft carpet."

Lloyd George would arrive late to meetings, and with little idea of the topic at hand, or even of the position Britain meant to take, he would begin to speak. One of the young English delegates recorded that he might start "most eloquently arguing the very case we were concerned to oppose. [A secretary] would scribble a note . . . which Lloyd George would glance at without interrupting the flow of his argument. Presently he would blandly explain that he thought he had done full justice to a view which, however, the British Government did not share, and would now expound our own real attitude."

Clemenceau, one of the young Americans noted, "had his desk in front of the fireplace with his back to the chimney. . . . Settled back, half-sunk in his armchair, with his eyes on the ceiling, he gave the impression of not listening more than half the time." Usually, when he wearied of a subject, he would frame a proposition or resolution and then inquire in rapid fire, "Y a-t-il des objections? Non? . . . Adopté"—and bang his gavel. He was, Nicolson wrote in his diary, "extremely rude to the small Powers: but then he is extremely rude to the Big Powers also." When he grew tired of the session altogether—especially as mealtime approached—he would pounce on any lull in a speech, declare c'est tout, drop his gavel on the table, "rise from his seat," one of the Englishmen said, and walk out of the room. Clemenceau presided, Lord Robert Cecil said, "with drastic firmness."

The decision of the major powers to listen to the small powers at the beginning of the conference was, in Nicolson's view, a horrendous "wastage of time and a falsification of proportion." The presentations of the small powers (which, for the most part, duplicated the written briefs they had submitted) did little more than give "the impression" to the members of the Council of Ten that "they were doing valuable and constructive work. Yet in fact they were doing nothing more than suffer, with varying degrees of courtesy, an exhausting and unnecessary imposition."

Of course, the big powers understood that their task was to prepare a treaty of peace with Germany—and so eventually left to their foreign ministers to work out additional settlements with Austria, Turkey, and Bulgaria, among others. But by proceeding as they did, in an effort to allow the Fourteen Points to set the agenda for the conference, they entangled themselves all at once in all the world's problems, from which they then labored to extricate themselves and establish some coherence. It was a goal that proved elusive.

Eventually the ten would create fifty-eight special subcommittees—some, as one of the young English aides said, "mainly as sops to starved vanities." But the multiplication of committees served not so much to organize work as to disorganize it, to generate such a massive amount of paperwork, of maps and charts, drafts and proposals and counterproposals filled with statistics and articles and amendments, with knowledge and ignorance of frontiers and corridors and watersheds that the young American aide Charles Seymour wrote home in dismay that "things are getting more rather than less complicated."

Now, when it came to trying to sort out the confusion and reach some decisions, Wilson entered the discussions already compromised. His Fourteen Points, despite their widespread popular success (or because of it), had aroused considerable anxiety in the ministries of Europe even before the conference began. To allay these worries, the president had sent an advisor to Europe in advance of the peace conference, to explain the Fourteen Points to

Clemenceau and Lloyd George. The advisor, Colonel Edward House, was a wealthy, amiable Texan who had been among those who had persuaded Wilson to run for president. House, according to the journalist William Allen White, had an "almost Oriental modesty . . . in constant and delightful agreement with his auditor. . . . He is never servile, but always serving; gentle without being soft. . . . He is forever punctuating one's sentences with 'That's true, that's true.' " But the southern colonel had a debilitating instinct for compromise, so that, when he met with Clemenceau and Lloyd George to explain the Fourteen Points, he explained them partly away.

Thus the idea of "open covenants openly arrived at" was not meant to exclude confidential negotiations in order to arrive at the open covenants. The principle of absolute freedom of navigation was not intended to preclude Britain's use of naval blockade, which the British considered one of their principal defenses. The idea of removing all economic barriers did not mean that a country could not protect its home industries by imposing tariffs. The reduction of national armaments was understood to apply most especially to Germany.

When Wilson entered the room with Clemenceau and Lloyd George, the president was already perceived as less than the toughest of negotiators or the most purely principled of politicians. And furthermore his compromises were understood by the others not as the end of what he must do but as the beginning.

Nor was Wilson's only antagonist to be Clemenceau. When the issue arose as to what would be done with the colonies taken from Germany, most of the delegates assumed they would be divided up among the victors. Wilson had another idea. Since "peoples and provinces" were not to be traded about like "chattels and pawns in a game," he thought all these colonies ought to be made independent—and then taken under the protection of the League of Nations. The League would see to it that the colonies were governed democratically and not abused by the larger powers. To oversee the colonies, the League would appoint protector nations. Thus, for example, Australia might become the protector for New Guinea, and New Guinea would become a "mandatory" under the League.

Billy Hughes, the prime minister of Australia, did not, for one, understand this idea. If the American president really meant to abolish colonies, that was a threat to the British Empire. But if Wilson meant only to disguise the real nature of colonial control, Hughes thought it contemptible.

Hughes, a small, pugnacious old man with an electric earphone (who seemed to enjoy pretending to be more deaf than he was so that he could shout), declared bluntly that he wanted New Guinea for Australia, whatever the arrangement was called.

This question, said Wilson, would have to be settled by the League.

In that case, Hughes said, he would want the League to settle in his favor.

Surely, Wilson replied, Hughes did not mean he wished to have New Guinea if it was opposed by the wishes of the whole world.

"Yes," Hughes shouted, "that's about it!"

Wilson said that a vote of the inhabitants would have to be taken to determine their wishes.

"Do you know, Mr. President," said Hughes, "that these natives eat one another?"

Wilson did not reply.

Lloyd George, thinking to come to Hughes's rescue, and aware of Wilson's interest in Christianity, asked the Australian prime minister whether he would not be willing to reassure the council that he would "allow the natives to have access to the missionaries."

"Indeed I would, sir," said Hughes, "for there are many days when these poor devils do not get half enough missionaries to eat."

As the negotiations went on, with Clemenceau trying to strike bargains, and Wilson spending his time with a committee drafting a covenant for the League of Nations—with most of the delegates trying to make deals and Wilson replying with statements of principle—the widespread admiration for the president waned.

At one point, Wilson was explaining to Clemenceau and Lloyd George how the League would establish a brotherhood of man where Christianity had not been able to do so. "Why," Lloyd

George recalled Wilson as saying, "has Jesus Christ so far not succeeded in inducing the world to follow His teachings in these matters? It is because He taught the ideal without devising any practical means of attaining it. That is the reason why I am proposing a practical scheme to carry out His aims."

Clemenceau, said the British prime minister, "slowly opened his dark eyes to their widest dimensions and swept them round the assembly to see how the Christians gathered around the table enjoyed this exposure of the futility of their Master."

But Wilson's high moral tone was not the most difficult aspect of his presence for the other delegates. His insistence that no great power should exercise a sphere of influence over former colonies, or over the new nations of Eastern Europe that were emerging from the disintegration of the Austro-Hungarian Empire, soon began to seem hypocritical and self-contradictory. After all, the United States was not offering to abandon the Monroe Doctrine, which declared a sphere of influence for the United States over the entire Western Hemisphere. The president's policies, advanced as disinterested, universal principles, were found to include exceptions when they impinged on American interests.

Wilson's insistence that the League of Nations be a peaceful gathering of nations, with no standing army, seemed to the French either useless or pernicious. The French, seeking guarantees against German aggression, wanted a military alliance, a standing army, and a French general at its head. No expression of ethical sentiment would suffice to secure their border against Germany.

The president was opposed to extracting large reparations payments from the Germans—though Lloyd George had promised his electorate to squeeze Germany "until the pips squeak," and the French were demanding full payment for the ravages of war. Ultimately, the financial pressure came from the United States. Italy and France owed vast sums to Britain and Britain owed vast sums to the United States. Wilson did not offer to forgive these debts.

Then, too, the generality of the president's principles seemed removed from the business at hand, and the amount of detail that needed sorting out was staggering, the conflicts of just claims alarming. While the area experts for France and England haggled over how Bosnia, Herzegovina, Croatia, and Slovenia were to be united with Serbia and Montenegro to create Yugoslavia, while a piece of Hungary was given to Romania, and the Czechs and Slovaks were joined into a new state of Czechoslovakia; while Austria was reduced to a small German-speaking area of six million people, lying principally to the east of Vienna, and Istria, the South Tyrol, and Trentino were given to Italy; as complaints were heard that only two-thirds of the new population of Poland would be Polish, and millions of Magyars were to be placed in Romania, and while fewer than ten million of the fourteen million inhabitants of Czechoslovakia would be Czechs or Slovaks, President Wilson was devoting his time and attention to drafting a covenant for the League of Nations.

"Mon cher," said the seventy-four-year-old French elder statesman Jules Cambon to a young British diplomat, *"Savez-vous ce qui va resulter de cette conférence? Une improvisation."*

Nicolson thought it resembled "a riot in a parrot house."

In spite of all the complexities of looking at the world in detail, Wilson did make steady progress in drafting a covenant for the League of Nations. The League was meant, most fundamentally, to provide a permanent organization for the peaceful resolution of disputes, and to be a place to which any imperfections that might inhere in the treaty could be taken for adjustment. He was tireless in this work, and clearly loved it. "The rest of us," said Lloyd George, "found time for golf and we took Sundays off, but Wilson, in his zeal, worked incessantly."

The president did have some sympathetic help in outlining the League. Both Jan Smuts of South Africa and Lord Robert Cecil had arrived at the conference with plans for a league of some sort. The French, too, had their champion of international government, in the elderly Léon Bourgeois. But Bourgeois had only one idea he wanted to put forward—that the League should have a permanent, standing international army, led by French generals.

Wilson took endless pleasure in explaining the virtues of his plan, and the others were captivated by his inspiring rhetoric, though jokes about the president were beginning to circulate in Paris with somewhat corrosive effect. "God," it was said that Clemenceau remarked, "had only Ten Points, but Wilson has Fourteen."

Above all, Wilson was eager to persuade Clemenceau and Lloyd George to incorporate the League into the peace treaty itself so that, no matter what the treaty might say, the League would exist to correct its faults and to usher in an epoch of democratic world government. It turned out to be astonishingly, suspiciously, easy to get Clemenceau and Lloyd George to consent to put the League into the treaty. As Clemenceau explained to his aide Jean Jules Henri Mordacq, "When the moment comes to claim French rights, I will have leverage that I might not have at this moment." Clemenceau would give Wilson his League right away, let Wilson celebrate his victory, and then present him with the bill.

Wilson was given his executive council, his secretariat and his secretary general. The new League was charged to undertake, as an early order of business, the reduction of the world's armaments, and the adjudication of disputes, in particular any that arose out of the treaty itself. Where Wilson met stiff opposition, however, was from Léon Bourgeois, and his insistence on a standing army. Such an army, said Wilson, would defeat the whole basis of the League, to say nothing of being impossible for Wilson himself under the American Constitution.

Wilson had made a tactical error. He had announced that he had to return to the United States in the middle of the conference in order to attend to business there. And all the delegates understood that the president would wish to return to Washington for this intermission with his League triumphantly in hand.

So the French now proceeded to conduct a filibuster. It took the British to intercede to save Wilson. Cecil took the floor to say he wished to speak "very frankly." The League, he said, was a gift from America and Britain to Europe—offering support to keep the peace in Europe, when it would be far easier for America and Britain to remain uninvolved. The alternative to Wilson's League was not a military alliance against Germany, but rather an alliance between America and Britain that would leave France out entirely. Cecil's speech had an instantaneous effect. Bourgeois dropped all talk of a standing army, and the League was approved as Wilson wanted it.

"This covenant," Wilson said, as he presented the finished covenant of the League to a full plenary session of the conference on February 14, "is definite in the one thing that we are called upon to make definite. It is a definite guarantee of peace."

"Many terrible things have come out of this war, gentlemen," the president went on, "but some very beautiful things have come out of it. Wrong has been defeated, but the rest of the world has been more conscious than it ever was before of the majesty of right. People that were suspicious of one another can now live as friends and comrades in a single family."

Several hours later, Wilson boarded a train at Gare du Nord for the coast and his trip back to Washington. It was perhaps the last moment in Wilson's life that he would feel triumphant.

Five days after Wilson left for Washington, on the morning of February 19, Clemenceau was being driven from his home to a meeting with Balfour and Colonel House, to continue negotiations in Wilson's absence. A twenty-three-year-old woodworker named Emile-Jules-Henri Cottin stepped out of the shadow of a kiosk at an intersection and fired a pistol twice into Clemenceau's limousine, crying, "I am a Frenchman and an anarchist!"

The car pulled away, and Cottin ran after it, firing another half dozen times. One of those shots hit Clemenceau, who slumped forward, saying, "The animal shoots well."

His driver circled back to Clemenceau's house, where the premier emerged from his car saying, "It's nothing." Three physicians arrived at once to tend the premier, who was put to bed coughing. A bullet had penetrated close to his heart, between his lungs. Clemenceau was not unaccustomed to bullet wounds; he had fought a dozen duels. But as he said to his secretary Jean Martet, "It is the one sensation that I hadn't yet had. I had never yet been assassinated."

Sarah Bernhardt wrote to Clemenceau on one of her small monogrammed cards: "I beg you, let me have some news of you. It is for me! For me alone! Thanks with all my heart!"

Within eight days, Clemenceau was back on his feet and attending meetings. The doctors had decided to leave the bullet in his chest. And every now and then Clemenceau would bring a meeting to a temporary halt with a fit of prolonged, deep, rumbling coughing. He never mentioned his wound, except in jest. Cartoons appeared in the newspapers of the indestructible Tiger. Clemenceau had replaced Wilson as the hero of the conference. Tough, courageous realism seemed the most dazzling manner of the day.

With Wilson gone, and Lloyd George popping back and forth to London to attend to business, the direction of the conference slipped almost completely into Clemenceau's hands. Colonel House had obtained the president's approval to bring matters to a readiness for his return. Balfour spoke for the absent Lloyd George.

Balfour introduced a resolution "to bring about a preliminary treaty with Germany," to have all the experts submit their final reports by March 8, a week before Wilson was due back, and to send an invitation to the Germans to come to Paris to receive the treaty ten days after Wilson returned. With that, Clemenceau, Balfour, and House went to work.

In Washington, meanwhile, Wilson was having an extremely difficult time with domestic politics. When he had invited the members of the Senate Foreign Relations Committee to attend a dinner in the White House, two members simply declined the invitation. Senator Henry Cabot Lodge, the chairman of the committee, left early. And Senator Frank Brandegee was quoted afterwards as saying, "I feel as if I had been wandering with Alice in Wonderland and had had tea with the Mad Hatter." Some of the conflict with Wilson was nothing more than party politics, but some was rooted in a suspicion of American involvement in international affairs. And there was particular anxiety that, to be consistent with Wilson's League of Nations, the Monroe Doctrine would be compromised. Whereas the League meant to abolish spheres of interest, the Monroe Doctrine, which stated that no European power could extend its system to any part of the Western Hemisphere, did establish a United States sphere of interest in the Americas. Wilson saw no contradiction; others did.

When Wilson returned to Europe on March 13, he was met by Colonel House at the port of Brest. The two men adjourned to Wilson's stateroom. They were closeted until after midnight. It had grown very quiet aboard the ship when, at last, Edith Wilson heard her husband's door open and Colonel House take his leave.

"I opened the door connecting our rooms," Mrs. Wilson recalled. "Woodrow was standing. The change in his appearance shocked me. He seemed to have aged ten years. . . . Silently he held out his hand, which I grasped, crying: 'What is the matter? What has happened?'

"He smiled bitterly. 'House has given away everything I had won before we left Paris.' " House had agreed, in the interest of speeding up the work of the conference, to arrive at a "preliminary" treaty of peace with Germany. The preliminary treaty dealt with military terms for Germany, boundaries, reparations, and a number of other matters.

By the terms that had been negotiated for this preliminary peace, the French had gradually won their diplomatic war of attrition on minor points until the treaty had come increasingly to resemble an arrangement for the permanent military and economic control of Germany by a military alliance of Britain, France, and America.

"He has compromised on every side," Wilson told his wife. ". . . his own explanation of his compromises is that, with a hostile press in the United States expressing disapproval of the League of Nations as a part of the treaty, he thought it best to yield some other points lest the conference withdraw its approval altogether."

What was worst of all, to Wilson's mind, was that House had given away the League itself: the covenant of the League had been completely removed from the preliminary treaty. Some were saying that the present conference would establish a treaty—and then the League would be put off for a future congress to discuss.

In fact, House had kept the president fairly well informed of the Paris negotiations while Wilson was in the States, and Wilson seems not to have grasped that the American position had been persistently worn away, perhaps because he had been distracted by domestic politics.

But then the president threw back his head and said, "Well, thank God I can still fight, and I'll win them back."

In his first twenty-four hours back in Paris, Wilson met informally with a group of delegates, speaking to them as though there had been no changes as far as the League of Nations was concerned during his absence. Evidently he hoped Clemenceau and Lloyd George would hear of these informal conversations and take the tactful hint. But Lloyd George, for one, was irritated to hear what Wilson had to say, "talking of matters that have already been settled as though they were still open for discussion." Wilson let another twenty-four hours pass, and then, as he imagined it, struck back. He issued a press release saying that there was no truth to the rumors that the League of Nations would not be a part of the treaty of peace.

Unfortunately, the president's statement had no effect on Lloyd George or Clemenceau. Whereas Wilson had just returned from a very difficult ordeal with his domestic political opponents, Lloyd George had just won a landslide election victory after the war and Clemenceau was about to win a clear vote of confidence from the chamber of deputies. All three leaders had demanding domestic constituencies to satisfy, but the strategies of Lloyd George and Clemenceau had the strong backing of their constituents, and Wilson's strategy did not.

Just as Wilson was issuing his press release about the League, Lloyd George had left for the country for the weekend with some of his advisors. The British prime minister, like Wilson, had had an opportunity to review what had been done in Paris during the previous several weeks, and it struck him that the terms the negotiators had agreed to were rather harsh. As he considered the course of negotiations at leisure that weekend he was not persuaded that Wilson's views were entirely useful, but he did not think Clemenceau's ferocity correct either.

And so Lloyd George proceeded to follow the instincts he had developed in his years in the House of Commons. He looked for compromises and adjustments he might make to convert a "hard" peace into a softer one. "He is taking the long view," as his secretary Frances Stevenson wrote in her diary, "about the Peace & insists that it should be one that will not leave bitterness for years to come, & probably lead to another war."

In the years to come, many historians would argue that Clemenceau's plan of a tough settlement might have been successful if it had been enforced; or, on the other hand, that Wilson's plan for a temperate settlement that did not breed resentment among the

Germans might have been successful—but that Lloyd George's instinct for compromise produced a treaty that contained the worst of both positions, hard enough to produce bitterness, soft enough not to be able to contain the consequences of that bitterness.

Lloyd George returned from his weekend with a memorandum outlining a refurbished British policy. British policy henceforth would be that no large blocs of population should be shifted, no Germans placed under Polish control. No humiliating peace should be drawn up that would push the Germans toward bolshevism. No reparations payments should be demanded that could not be paid by the generation that made the war. No disarmament agreements ought to apply to Germany alone. The Rhineland should remain a part of Germany, though France could either be given the Saar Valley or compensated for the French coal mines ruined in the war. America and Britain should guarantee French security with a military agreement.

And finally, at Lloyd George's suggestion, he and Clemenceau and Wilson, along with Orlando of Italy, sent all their advisors away, including even their translators, and just the four of them gathered in a little semicircle of armchairs in front of the fireplace in the study of Wilson's house in the Place des Etats-Unis to get down to serious negotiating. Lloyd George sat closest to the fireplace, then Clemenceau, then Wilson—then a table, and on the other side of the fireplace, Orlando, and next to the fireplace, an empty chair in case the Big Four wanted to call in a visitor. It was, as Wilson's aide Ray Stannard Baker said, "a dark, richly furnished room"—its walls containing a Rembrandt, a Delacroix, a Hobbema, several Goyas—"looking out upon a little patch of walled garden with an American sentinel pacing up and down the passageway."

At first they had no recording secretary present, and no one took notes. Clemenceau and Lloyd George thrived in this atmosphere—the atmosphere of the journalist's office or the cabinet room, where the give-and-take is fast paced and direct, deals are made and remade, myriad possibilities are kept in the mind at once, combinations are shifted and shifted again. Orlando, the only one of the four who did not speak English, was lost at once and was allowed to bring a translator into the room; still, even with his translator, the Italian could not keep up with the rapid talk. Wilson, pretending he was up to it, was soon disoriented, and his assistants began to notice that he was misplacing correspondence and exhibiting other evidences of confusion. In dealing with the "swift arrows of Clemenceau's Latin intellect," Nicolson said of Wilson on another occasion, and "with the kingfisher darts of Mr. Lloyd George's intuition," Wilson seemed "a trifle slow-minded."

"The president's slowness amongst the Europeans was noteworthy," said Keynes. "He would not all in a minute take in what the rest were saying, size up the situation with a glance, frame a reply, and meet the case by a slight change of ground; and he was liable, therefore, to defeat by the mere swiftness, apprehension, and agility of a Lloyd George." And now, with Lloyd George's eagerness to compromise, the president found it harder and harder to resist Clemenceau's steady wearing away of the Fourteen Points and Four Principles.

Nor was Clemenceau averse to purchasing Lloyd George's support. On the issue of reparations to repair the ravages of war, there was a difficulty in knowing how to justify giving some share of reparations to Britain, since the war had not been fought on British soil, thus the British had no damages to repair. Therefore, Lloyd George argued that reparations should be paid also for "damage to persons"—including disability pay and the costs of pensions for veterans. The experts were alarmed at this idea: the cost of pensions could inflate reparations enormously, fixing a sum the Germans could never pay. Clemenceau let it be understood he was ready to support Lloyd George.

Concerned that high reparations would ruin the German economy, Wilson argued that some top figure must be fixed that Germany could reasonably pay, or that some time limit be set so that future generations would not be obliged to pay for their fathers' sins. Too high a bill would produce chaos, bitterness, and a rage for retaliation.

Lloyd George suggested a way to slip around these irreconcilable differences: let no specific number, and no time limit, be named in the treaty, he suggested. Rather, let a commission be appointed to assess what the Germans could pay. If it was found the Germans could not meet their assessment, then the assessment could be adjusted.

The idea had a certain appeal. It permitted the politicians to appear in their home countries as though they intended to have revenge against Germany—which Lloyd George would find useful —but keep their options open for a reasonable program to let Germany rebuild. Clemenceau was somewhat concerned that the Germans would be let off too easily, but Wilson feared that the Germans would be beggared.

Wilson, Lloyd George concluded, was afflicted with a "pervasive suspiciousness." And indeed his suspiciousness, the delicacy of his position on the Monroe Doctrine, his sense that he was being bamboozled by both Lloyd George and Clemenceau, began to take its toll on the president. Since his return to Paris, Wilson was "so busy," said Ike Hoover, the White House usher, "he never dresses for dinner anymore. He goes right to that meal in the clothes he has worn all day. This is so different from his usual custom that I mention it to illustrate what is happening to him." Some delegates noticed that a muscle near Wilson's left eye had begun to twitch.

As conversations went on during the next week, it became apparent that the makings of a deal had taken shape in Clemenceau's mind. The crucial need for the French was for maximum reparations and security against German aggression; the French thought they could achieve the latter by taking and holding the Rhineland. Wilson's most crucial need, for the sake of his constituents back home, was a recognition of the Monroe Doctrine.

The conversations revolved obsessively around the same topics: talk of reparations in the morning, the League in the afternoon; the next day, reparations all day; the next day, reparations in the morning and the Rhineland in the afternoon; the next day, the Monroe Doctrine; the next day, the Rhineland and the Saar in the morning, reparations in the afternoon.

Among the English experts, Keynes was saying that, despite the dreadful appearance of destruction in France, the actual cost of rebuilding France would probably not be more than 2.5 billion dollars—and that the maximum Germany could afford to pay was about 10 billion.

Such careful estimates were of little interest to Clemenceau, who had a less than complete concern for what the Germans could afford to pay and keep a viable economy going. And as he pressed Wilson harder and harder to make a deal—to violate the Fourteen Points with agreements over the Rhineland and reparations, in order to keep his League and his Monroe Doctrine—Wilson understood his choices were reduced to making a deal or leaving the conference, going home, and accepting the consequences of whatever disorder might come with no treaty at all. One of his aides happened upon the president as he considered his dilemma, pacing up and down, and saying, "My God, I can't go through with it."

On March 27, Wilson made an essential concession to Clemenceau. Although the League of Nations made it both irrelevant and wrong, Wilson agreed to enter a military alliance with France and Britain to secure France against an attack by Germany. Having made such a concession that so fundamentally contradicted his ideals and his desires, Wilson awaited Clemenceau's concession in return. Instead, what he got were more demands for concessions.

Clemenceau now said he must insist—since Wilson still refused to yield on the Rhineland—on ownership of the Saar basin with its rich coal mines. Wilson said that would be impossible; the French had no rights to the Saar. In all its history, the Saar had once, and for a mere twenty-three years, belonged to France; but it was indisputably German territory, inhabited by Germans who wished to remain a part of Germany. Giving it to France could only be regarded as planting the cause of a future war.

Clemenceau was concerned that France, whose coal mines had been destroyed during the war, would be entirely dependent on the Saar for coal. Thus, if Germany got the Saar, Germany could virtually fix French industrial prices by the price of coal and so dominate French economic policy.

Clemenceau accused Wilson of being pro-German. Perhaps he ought simply to resign from the negotiations, Clemenceau told Wilson, and let his place be taken by President Poincaré and Marshal Foch, and then Wilson would see what real French hard-liners were like.

Wilson was outraged. Did Clemenceau mean to say that if he didn't get what he wanted, he would quit? "In that event," Wilson, who in recent days had so often wanted to quit himself, said, "Do you wish me to return home?"

"I do not wish you to go home," Clemenceau replied, "but I intend to do so myself." And with that, Clemenceau got up and walked out.

The president was put into a panic, and looking to Lloyd George for support, he found none.

"The truth is," Lloyd George said to Lord Riddell as they drove out of Paris for a picnic lunch and a tour of Versailles, "that we have got our way. We have got most of the things we set out to get [most of them, if the truth were told, without even having to try]."

Clemenceau sent André Tardieu to consult with Colonel House to see whether a compromise could be worked out. Lloyd George sent J. W. Headlam-Morley to sit in for the British. And these three worked out an arrangement: a special administrative regime would be established; France would get the coal from the Saar for fifteen years; at the end of that time, a vote would be taken in the Saar to see whether the inhabitants wanted to be part of Germany or of France. Wilson insisted to Colonel House that this violated the Fourteen Points; but House, anxious for *some* agreement, replied that there were "many who thought otherwise."

Wilson gave in, and was met at once with more demands from Clemenceau. On reparations, the British and French agreed to drop some indirect costs of the war, such as interest charges on war loans. Wilson allowed reparations to cover pensions to soldiers. Reprimanded by some of his aides, who remained steadfast Wilsonians, that this agreement was illogical, the president burst out, "Logic! Logic! I don't give a damn for logic!"

Clemenceau was persuaded now to accept Lloyd George's proposition to name no specific amount of reparations, but rather refer the matter to a commission. And Wilson consented. Then Clemenceau pressed Wilson to agree to a forty-year, rather than a thirty-year time limit on the payment of reparations.

The president, said Ray Stannard Baker, was "at the end of his tether." If the relentless demands went on many days longer, Wilson thought "he might have to make a positive break." And, indeed, on April 3, at six o'clock in the evening, a break of sorts did occur. The president was suddenly seized, as his personal physician Cary Grayson said, "with violent paroxysms of coughing which were so severe and frequent that it interfered with his breathing." He was put to bed at once.

Grayson thought Wilson might have been poisoned. The president's fever rose to 103, and he sank quickly into exhausted coughing and vomiting that went on through the night and continued over the next two days. Grayson revised his diagnosis to influenza.

In the years since, a number of physicians have had an opportunity to review Wilson's symptoms in Paris and his earlier medical history. The president had evidently suffered a succession of minor strokes, beginning at least as early as 1896, when he noticed a sensation of numbness in the fingers of his right hand and of weakness and slight pain in his right arm—and was not able to write well with his right hand for almost a year, so that he learned to write, and to play golf, left-handed. In 1906, he had awakened one morning to discover that he was blind in one eye—and his vision was slightly impaired for the rest of his life. In 1908, he had noticed another minor attack against his right hand. In subsequent years, he was afflicted from time to time with the sort of irritability, impulsiveness, and blinding headaches that are often associated with cerebral vascular difficulties. His medical history, and his symptoms in Paris, are consistent with the possibility of his having suffered another stroke.

The negotiations now continued in front of the fireplace in Wilson's study, with Colonel House sitting in for Wilson. From time to time the colonel would rise, move to the back of the room, open what appeared to be a solid, well-filled bookcase, and step through a secret passageway into Wilson's bedroom, where the president lay ill. As well as he could, Wilson guided House in closing the deals.

Clemenceau, as Frances Stevenson wrote in her diary, "was very pleased at Wilson's absence, could not conceal his joy. 'He is *worse* today,' he said to D. [David Lloyd George], and doubled up with laughter. 'Do you know his doctor? Couldn't you get round him & bribe him?!' The old man did not attempt to conceal his feelings on the subject."

With Wilson out of the way, a secretary was called into the room to make notes on the agreements made in front of the fireplace, and Clemenceau and Lloyd George wrote the treaty, paragraph by paragraph, clause by clause, working over every detail. One of the first things they did was to settle on reparations: that there should be no limit either to the amount the Germans would pay, nor the time in which they were liable to pay it. This was set down as a final conclusion. With the acceptance of the reparations clause, Wilson's defeat was complete.

As Nicolson recalled the moment, "the vessel upon which we had all embarked so confidently was foundering." The young liberals in the British delegation were dismayed. In the end, said Nicolson, "the collapse of Wilson meant the collapse of the Conference."

On Sunday morning, April 6, Wilson rose in his sickbed and called for Colonel House. The colonel was off on a luncheon outing at Versailles, but by four 'o clock in the afternoon, Wilson was conducting a meeting. He sat up in bed with his old sweater around his shoulders, attended by House, Secretary of State Lansing, and a couple of others. With their counsel, Wilson determined to send a message to Clemenceau and Lloyd George saying that, unless a treaty were written to conform to the Fourteen Points, the president would be obliged to return home, or else to insist upon conducting the conference in public.

Cheered up, Wilson commenced to summon other advisors to his bedside for consultations. He had his ship ordered ready to return to the United States, and he told his aides to circulate the news that the ship was being readied.

On the afternoon of April 8, the president returned to the discussions in front of the fireplace. The subject of the Saar was under discussion. Lloyd George had suggested that morning that the Saar be split off from Germany and made a separate state, like Luxembourg, and placed in a customs union with France.

It was at this point that Wilson—while still insisting that France could not take over the Saar—lit on the interesting notion that Germany should own the soil of the Saar, and France the subsoil, and its coal. After fifteen years, which would give the French time to restore their own coal mines, the people of the Saar could vote to determine their own future. Clemenceau and Lloyd George embraced this solution at once.

Had Wilson had such ingenious compromises to suggest in other areas, the treaty might have been very clever indeed. But the next compromise that was worked out—on the Rhineland—was cobbled together without inspiration, as Colonel House hustled back and forth between Wilson and Clemenceau during the next three days.

"Today," as one of Wilson's aides wrote in his diary, "when I went into his study, he looked old and worn. . . . I saw him standing with Grayson close to the window. The sash had been thrown up and Grayson was exercising the President by standing with him foot to foot, and with clasped hands pulling him vigorously back and forth. The President turned to me with the remark, 'Indoor golf.' "

By the fifteenth of April, Wilson and Clemenceau had reached a compromise on the Rhineland: the German side was to be demilitarized; the French would occupy their side of the Rhine in three strata—and the French would withdraw from these territories piecemeal, at three five-year intervals, finally giving the Rhineland back to Germany. If the Germans did not make a reparations payment, the French would stay until reparations were paid. The agreement seemed inadequate to the French, and a violation of principle to Wilson, and it would be a source of resentment for the Germans: but the exhausted negotiators agreed to it.

Reparations had been settled, and the Rhineland, and the Saar; Wilson was given the League and the Monroe Doctrine; Lloyd George had a share in reparations and, with the dispersal of the German navy and merchant marine, an assurance of the continuance of British mastery of the seas; competition with a German colonial system was ended. A good many minor issues remained, but the outlines of the treaty had been settled, and a wonderful feeling of ease and accomplishment descended on the negotiators in front of Wilson's fireplace. As Clemenceau remarked to his aide Mordacq, "At last, I've got almost everything I wanted."

To be sure, the crisis had not passed for Orlando, and for some of the representatives of other, smaller powers. In fact, Italy's interests were being given such short shrift by the Big Three that Orlando was finally the one who left the conference in a huff and went back home.

The issue was whether Italy or Yugoslavia was to get Fiume. According to a secret treaty of 1915, on the terms of which Italy had agreed to enter the war against Germany, Italy was to receive as spoils at the end of the war a slice of the Dalmatian coast, the islands of the Dodecanese, Trieste, and some other territories, and to give the port city of Fiume to what was to become Yugoslavia. The course of the war, Wilson's Fourteen Points, and the way of negotiations at the conference had rendered the treaty of 1915 obsolete. Now Orlando demanded Fiume—which was of no use to the Italians except that it would help them ruin Yugoslavian trade. Clemenceau and Lloyd George were open to haggling, but Wilson adamantly refused. As one Italian contemptuously remarked to Nicolson, Wilson, having compromised his Fourteen Points repeatedly with France and Britain, was now trying "to regain his virginity."

Orlando stormed back to Rome. He was greeted with pride by the Italians, his claim to Fiume fiercely supported by a popular young Fascist newspaper editor, Benito Mussolini. Eventually, Orlando would be lured back to the conference, but he was never given what he told the others he would need in order to remain in office in Italy. After the conference was over, Orlando was summarily voted out of office amidst a clamor finally led by Mussolini and his Fascist supporters.

In other areas of negotiation, there was the sense that subjects of immense importance were now settled half-attentively in an atmosphere of incessant distraction. While a revolution continued to rage in Russia—and the British and French and Americans backed the White Russian Army in its efforts to fend off the Bolsheviks— while Churchill proposed drawing up a definite plan of war against the Bolsheviks, and Wilson insisted the United States was not at war with Russia and would not become involved in a war, an American delegation that had actually been to Moscow discovered, on its return to Paris, that no one wished to receive its report on the state of Russia.

While the German military commenced to grumble about how

they had been "stabbed in the back" by their civilian government and ought, perhaps, not to accept any peace treaty at all; while the Poles edged toward a small war in Vilna, and toward a war with Russia elsewhere; while a revolution seized Budapest; while the Estonians threatened to make a separate peace with Russia and the Finns marched on Petrograd; the Yugoslavians attacked the Austrians and the Bulgarians were imprisoning Greeks, the negotiators in Paris gave Shantung to Japan, in violation of the Fourteen Points, and in such a way as to make the Japanese resentful in any case.

Balfour presented the case for a Zionist state in the Middle East, both because it was a "belated act of justice to the Jews" and also because it would "prove a protection to the wasp waist of our empire, Suez." Feisal, descendant of the prophet Mohammed and Emir of Arabia, accompanied by Lawrence of Arabia, labored to make a case, as Secretary of State Lansing thought, for creating an Arab kingdom out of the wreckage of the old Ottoman Empire, an Islamic kingdom that Feisal might lead, if it could successfully play off against each other the two major powers of France (who reckoned Syria as within its sphere) and Britain (who reckoned their sphere as taking in Palestine, including Balfour's new state, Transjordan, Iraq, and Kuwait).

The vexations were overwhelming. Clemenceau, asked by a persistent representative of Belgium whether there was any further service he might render his native land, said, "Yes . . . Go and drown yourself."

The treaty was finished in a maelstrom of confusion and turmoil and irritability, with Lloyd George saying he thought the covenant for the League of Nations was a "ridiculous and preposterous document," even as he consented to include it in the treaty, and the Italians saying they reserved their right to freedom of action on Fiume, the Chinese saying they would not sign the treaty because of the gift of Shantung to Japan, the Portuguese saying they had never in the past signed a treaty that did not ask for the blessing of God on its provisions, and Marshal Foch demanding an opportunity to appear before the diplomats to say he objected to a time limit of fifteen years for French occupation of the Rhineland.

Because the treaty was still not in a completed form that all the diplomats could review, even though it was about to be presented to the Germans, André Tardieu read a forty-four-page summary of its contents aloud. Since most of the diplomats in the room did not understand French, and the length of Tardieu's summary precluded the possibility of translation, few of the delegates understood at all what was being said, or what was to be given, finally, as their treaty of peace, to the Germans. "I don't think in all history," said Field Marshal Sir Henry Wilson, "this can be matched."

When at last German Foreign Minister Brockdorff-Rantzau presented a detailed, formal reply to the treaty he had been given, he replied with anguish: that the Germans had laid down their arms on the promise that a peace would be made according to President Wilson's Fourteen Points, and they must now insist that the Allies stick by their original, and binding, agreement; that they repudiated the allegation that they alone were responsible for starting the war; that they believed they had been attacked by czarist Russia and that Germany had invaded France only to forestall an invasion that the French (still bitter from 1871) planned to launch against Germany; that, in any case, to strip Germany of its armed forces, many of its mines, six and a half million of its population, one-tenth of its factories, one-sixth of its farmland, its merchant marine, and its colonies, to oblige it to build ships for the Allies, provide coal to the French, and then, after all this, to pay an unknown amount of reparations for an unknown period of years, would condemn the German people to starvation.

"Those who will sign this treaty," said Brockdorff-Rantzau, "will sign the death sentence of many millions of German men, women, and children."

The Germans had a counterproposal, which they now presented. It consisted of sixty-five thousand words, amounting, in effect, to an alternate treaty. The Germans sought to enter the League of Nations at once. They agreed to disarm, providing their disarmament was a prelude to general disarmament. They could not agree to cede the Saar, but they would agree to supply France with coal. They would not surrender any territory, except after a vote of its inhabitants had been taken so that, in accord with Wilson's Fourteen Points, the people were given the opportunity to exercise their right of self-determination. They could not agree to give the "Polish Corridor" to Poland, though they would agree to make several cities "free ports" so that Poland would have access to the sea. They would give up Shantung, but otherwise suggested a committee be set up to hear the German case for having mandates, under the League of Nations, over some of its former colonies. They agreed to pay $25 billion, but under conditions that made it clear (deducting the value of ceded properties, disallowing interest, and using several other devices) the real cost to Germany would be $7 billion.

Remarkably, many of those who had helped write the Allied treaty thought the German proposal was not bad. Andrew Bonar Law, former Chancellor of the Exchequer, wrote a note to Lloyd George stating, "The document is a very able one, and in many particulars is very difficult to answer." Jackie Fisher, First Lord of the Admiralty, declared the German document "the most brilliant treaty that victors had ever imposed upon conquered."

It may be that, if the Allies had allowed the Germans to participate in the process of writing the treaty from the beginning—or allowed them to participate now—all of them together would have written an acceptable and enduring treaty. But if the diplomats had learned anything from history, they had learned the lesson of Vienna: that allowing the French to send Talleyrand into the negotiations in 1815 had completely upset the plans of the victors. And so the Germans were firmly excluded.

Lloyd George was thrown into a frenzy, and immediately summoned from London every member of the cabinet who could be spared. On the evening of May 31, the cabinet ministers who had rushed to Paris dined with the prime minister. Winston Churchill, secretary for war and air, led the attack on the treaty, but the drift of the dinner table conversation was all against the treaty in any case. "It was amazing," said Sir Henry Wilson, "what unanimity there was in criticizing *all* the terms." The talk went on until midnight, and resumed the next morning at breakfast, and then, later that morning, the full empire delegation gathered in Lloyd George's apartments, where again, as E. S. Montagu, the secretary for India, said, "The strangest thing about the proceeding . . . was the unanimity." The treaty, said Smuts, was "an impossible document. . . . To sign it would be a real disaster . . . comparable in magnitude to the war itself."

Emboldened, Lloyd George told his delegation that he would go to Clemenceau and Wilson and insist that concessions be made on Poland and the Rhineland, on Germany's admission to the League, and on reparations. If there were no concessions, Lloyd George requested the cabinet's authority to say that the British army and navy would not be available to enforce the treaty. And to that the cabinet gave its unanimous agreement.

When Lloyd George took his proposals into a meeting with Clemenceau and Wilson, Clemenceau could not contain his scorn. The British were not suggesting any concessions, Clemenceau observed, at the expense of Britain. Lloyd George did not suggest that Britain return any of its captured ships or surrender colonies to Germany or assist in any way in helping Germany restore its overseas trade.

As for the suggestion that the period of the occupation of the Saar be reduced from 15 years, Clemenceau would not consider reducing it even to 14 years, 364 days. He had made as many concessions as he could; Foch and Poincaré and others were prepared to throw him out of office if he compromised more than he had already. "We know the Germans better than you," Clemenceau said to Lloyd George and Wilson. "We do not have to beg pardon for our victory."

On the morning of June 3, the Americans had a grand gathering of their delegation in Secretary of State Lansing's study at the Hotel Crillon. Thirty-eight delegates were present. Wilson, Lansing, House, and several other advisors sat in large armchairs facing a semicircle of experts. Wilson was his old genial self, going the rounds shaking hands, and giving a word of praise to each individual for some piece of work he had done.

Evidently, the president expected to hear from his delegation how well he had handled the negotiations, and how absurdly the British were behaving. Instead, two of his young economics experts questioned the reparations agreements. Lansing broke in to suggest that each group of experts might prepare a memorandum of what might be changed in each of their areas of expertise—but at that, Wilson became alarmed. He did not want his delegation to misunderstand him; there might be some minor revisions to be made in the treaty, but on the whole he would not favor revision just because some terms seemed hard. "The terms *are* hard," said Wilson. "Nations should learn once and for all what an unjust war means."

"The time to consider all these questions," said the president, "was when we were writing the treaty, and it makes me a little tired for people to come and say now that they are afraid the Germans won't sign it, and their fear is based upon things that they insisted upon at the time of the writing of the treaty; that makes me very sick."

The meeting was adjourned. The treaty was not altered. And the Allies, including Lloyd George, communicated their decision to stand firm in a formal note to the Germans. All that remained was for the Germans to designate someone to sign the treaty.

The German government collapsed; its ministers resigned. A debate ensued in Germany whether to refuse to sign the treaty, to hold out for better terms, or to resume the war. A group of senior German officers worked out a strategy to sacrifice western Germany, withdraw to the east, and make a last stand in the old bastion of Prussia. Along the frontiers of the Rhine, Marshal Foch inspected the Allied troops, to make certain they were ready to march once more. But in the end, a newly formed German government consented to send delegates to Versailles to sign the treaty.

"I see," Nicolson wrote in his diary, "nothing but blackness in the future."

When Wilson returned to the United States to seek Senate ratification of the treaty, only fourteen Republicans and four Democrats were unalterably opposed to it. Colonel House advised the president to be conciliatory to his opponents, but Wilson said, "House, I have found one can never get anything in this life that is worthwhile without fighting for it." He fought the Senate, refusing even minor revisions, insisting that the treaty be approved exactly as it was. Senator Lodge requested some documents from the president, including records of the Paris negotiations. Wilson declined. Plagued by headaches, his hands shaking, the president set out on a twenty-seven-day trip across the country to win support for the treaty. He traveled eight thousand miles and delivered forty speeches before he was stopped by a stroke that paralyzed an arm and a leg, and then by another stroke that deprived him of his speech.

He was brought back to the White House, where he recovered and relapsed. The treaty was defeated in the Senate, but its defeat caused such a clamor that it was brought up again for a vote. Modifications were made. The changes apparently gave it some chance of adoption in the Senate. Wilson rose up from his sickbed to send a message to his Democratic supporters to vote *against* the revised treaty. The treaty, with its League of Nations, was defeated by a margin of only seven votes.

Six

THE RULE
OF UNINTENDED
CONSEQUENCES

In our robust moments we welcome the fact that our actions have consequences. We prefer to forget that actions may have unintended consequences that are often vastly more durable and far-reaching than those we intended.

When Columbus set sail in 1492, he was looking for the spices and the gold of the Orient. He was not intending to lead the way for Cortés's conquest of Mexico. Nor, on a less momentous note, did he pay much attention to the abundance of novel foodstuffs to be seen when he finally reached the New World after two months at sea. On October 15, 1492, he wrote in his ship's log that he had spotted some green, fertile islands that "may contain many things of which I do not know because I do not care to land and explore them, being anxious to find gold." Five hundred years later, nutritionists could not help but notice that the diet of the Mayans (zucchini, tomatoes, carrots, beans, potatoes, fish and other seafood, composed of 65 percent carbohydrates, 15–20 percent proteins, and 20 percent lipids) corresponded closely to the current recommendations of the American Heart Association for a heart-healthy

177

diet. The foods of the New World, carried back to the Old, and incorporated into the core diet there, created the modern Mediterranean diet, which is now the world standard for a healthy diet to lower the risk of disease and increase the probability of long life.

When the diplomats at the Paris conference of 1919 drew up their final treaty to present to the Germans, it was certainly not their intention to assist the rise of a Hitler.

Nor was it the intention of the British Foreign Office to help bring on World War II by dismissing the clandestine efforts of a group of German military officers to enlist foreign assistance in a plot to assassinate Hitler on the eve of his invasion of Czechoslovakia.

It was not the intention of the United States government, in opposing the Communist party in Italy after World War II, to allow the Christian Democratic party and its leader Prime Minister Giulio Andreotti of Sicily to become so embroiled with the Mafia as to make it nearly impossible afterwards for the Italian government to work itself free of criminal influence.

It cannot have been the conscious intention of Prime Minister Margaret Thatcher and, later, of Prime Minister John Major, by approving the sales of military components by the Matrix Churchill Corporation to Iraq, to assist Saddam Hussein on his way to making Iraq a nuclear power, threatening the whole of the Middle East.

It was hardly the intention of Mikhail Gorbachev, when he embarked on his reforms in the Soviet Union, to split up Czechoslovakia and Yugoslavia, producing a war in Bosnia-Herzegovina, fueling not only a resurgence of nationalism but also of tribalism. Nor was it his aim to bring about the reunification of Germany, causing a rise in German debt as West Germany absorbed East Germany, leading the Germans to raise their interest rates, thus causing strains within the European community that might destroy it and provoking political analysts to worry again about "the German problem." It is hardly likely that all unintended consequences can be anticipated, nor that all would be avoided even if they were anticipated. Had Gorbachev thought these were potential consequences, he might have felt he had little choice but to accept them. But it is certain that history has no end of such consequences, and they can be a plague on the goals of even the wariest of practitioners.

In diplomatic history, perhaps no more awesome example of the rule of unintended consequences might be found than the meeting in 1945 of President Franklin Roosevelt, Prime Minister Winston Churchill, and Generalissimo Joseph Stalin at Yalta, where they gathered to ensure for each one of their countries the rewards of their victory over Germany and the other Axis powers, and the peace in which to enjoy them.

ROOSEVELT, CHURCHILL, AND STALIN AT YALTA, 1945

"The military situation was considerably improved," said Roosevelt, since they "had last met."

"This was certainly true, and . . . the Soviet armies were moving very successfully onto the line of the Oder" River in Germany, Stalin replied.

On his way to Yalta, said Roosevelt, he had "made a number of bets on board the cruiser . . . whether the Russians would get to Berlin before the Americans would get to Manila."

Roosevelt, age sixty-three, looked tired, worse than tired; thin and drawn and ill. Stalin, three years older than Roosevelt, had held up better under the relentless strain of war, though he too looked gray.

It was four in the afternoon, February 4, 1945. The first formal plenary session of the conference of the Big Three was scheduled to begin in an hour, and Stalin, as host, had come to pay an informal call on the president in his quarters. Roosevelt's translator, Charles Bohlen, was making notes as he translated. They had greeted each other, according to Bohlen, "as old friends, as in a sense they were," having gone through the war together as allies, meeting from time to time to consult on common strategy, and meeting now to make plans for the end of the war, and the aftermath. Roosevelt, however tired, had taken Stalin's hand and greeted him warmly. "Stalin," noted Bohlen, "his face cracked into one of his rare, if slight, smiles, expressed pleasure at seeing the President again."

Roosevelt and his entourage had been put up in the Livadiya Palace, an imposing white limestone pile, formerly a summer palace of the czars, set high on a mountain slope overlooking the resort area of Yalta on the Black Sea. Roosevelt had been given a suite, looking out over the sea—a living room, dining room (formerly the czars' billiard room), bedroom, and a private bath—and the rest of his party were spread out among the other forty-five or so rooms, more or less disconsolate at having to share the few other baths.

Yalta is set on the southern edge of the Crimean peninsula. Tolstoy summered there, and Chekhov and Gorky, along with actors and opera singers, the czars and many of the Russian nobility. It has a dry, sunny climate, breezy in the summer, crisp but not cold in the winter. It was in the forties just then, with blue skies and a warm sun. Long-needle pine forests covered the mountains above the coast. Where the forests give way to parks and gardens there are cedars, tall plane trees, cypresses, magnolias, olive trees, wistaria. Many of the houses had tiled roofs, which gave the town a Mediterranean cast.

Stalin and his aides and ministers were settled six miles away in a palace that had once belonged to Prince Yusupov, one of Rasputin's assassins, it was said. The British were several miles further, in a large villa that had been designed in the mid-1800s by an English architect. The villa looked a mixture of Scottish and Moorish, with gardens and terraces overlooking the Black Sea, and just two bathrooms. And as Churchill was the first to discover, bedbugs.

"It's a big house," Britain's Undersecretary of State Alexander Cadogan wrote his wife, "of indescribable ugliness . . . with all the furnishings of an almost terrifying hideosity." But the British thought the Russians were doing their best to make everyone comfortable, despite wartime shortages and the fact that the German army had recently gone through the Crimea, stripping summer palaces of plumbing fixtures, locks, doorknobs, and whatever else they could remove. Nearly everything had been brought down from several of Moscow's best hotels and hurriedly installed. The Russians were unfailingly attentive to their guests. When one of the Englishmen made an offhand remark about the lack of lemon twists for martinis, a potted lemon tree appeared the next day at the British villa.

The conversation shifted from the weather to the natural beauty of the area and the evidence of the Germans' recent presence.

The president remarked that "he had been very much struck by the extent of German destruction in the Crimea," since he had arrived at Yalta, "and therefore he was more bloodthirsty in regard to the Germans than he had been a year ago, and he hoped that Marshal Stalin would again propose a toast [as he had at the Teheran conference] to the execution of 50,000 officers of the German Army."

Stalin agreed. The Germans "were savages and seemed to hate with a sadistic hatred the creative work of human beings."

Stalin turned to business, asking about the military situation on the western front. Roosevelt said that General George Marshall would be giving a detailed outline at the plenary meeting, but that "the main blow of the Anglo-Allied armies on the Western Front would take place in March."

Stalin spoke briefly about the position of the Soviet troops on the eastern front.

Roosevelt asked Stalin how he had gotten along with General Charles de Gaulle at their recent meeting.

De Gaulle, said Stalin, was "a very complicated person." And then, less tactfully, de Gaulle was "unrealistic, in the sense that France had not done very much fighting in this war, and de Gaulle demanded full rights with the Americans, British, and Russians who had done the burden of the fighting."

Stalin did not need to point out that the Russians had suffered 20 million dead and the destruction of thousands of Soviet towns and villages that had left another 28 million homeless. The Germans had suffered 4.5 million dead, Great Britain 450,000, France about 500,000, Italy about 410,000. The United States lost about 290,000 soldiers. In central and eastern Europe, civilian casualties included about 6 million Jews and 4 million non-Jewish civilians. Yugoslavia and Hungary had both suffered about 400,000 casualties, Poland and Romania about 300,000 each, Austria about 300,000. In all, 50 million died in World War II.

Some areas of the Soviet Union were almost entirely bare— without buildings, uninhabited, or inhabited by only a few remaining farmers sowing grain by hand. The productive capacities of the Soviet Union had been diverted almost entirely to war.

As the French and English diplomats had repeated so often during the Paris conference of 1919, a victorious nation expected to be compensated in proportion to the sacrifices it had made in blood and treasure. And naturally enough, the first topic on the agenda for this conference, the topic that would serve as the foundation for all others, was a review of the military situation.

If Stalin based his claim to a large say in the constitution of the postwar world on past sufferings, Roosevelt based his on the realities of the future. The American president presided over what was soon to be the richest and most powerful nation the world had seen. The United States had emerged from the war with its own lands and factories and financial structures untouched; indeed, far from being destroyed or weakened by the war, the United States had been immeasurably strengthened. America had not only equipped fifteen million of its own troops, but, by Lend-Lease, supplied planes and tanks and trucks and jeeps and guns and ammunition and shoes to its Allies. Its productive capacities and resources were enormous. In an age to be increasingly dominated by technology, the United States had the technology, including the atomic bomb. At the end of the war, the Russians might possess an immovable position in Europe; the United States would hold irresistible economic and military power.

The president mentioned that he had had a conversation with de Gaulle in Casablanca two years before, and de Gaulle had compared himself, as a political leader of France, to Clemenceau and, as a spiritual leader, to Joan of Arc!

De Gaulle, said Stalin, "does not seem to understand the situation in France," and that, in fact, the current French contribution to the Allied effort was "very small."

Still, said Roosevelt, he thought it would not be a "bad idea" to give the French a zone of occupation in Germany, along with Britain, the Soviet Union, and the United States.

Stalin wondered, since it was clear the French had not earned it, "for what reason" they should be given a zone.

Only, said Roosevelt, "out of kindness."

Indeed, said Stalin—doubtless puzzling over whether Roosevelt had some ulterior purpose—"that would be the only reason."

It was shortly before five o'clock then, and Stalin and Churchill had agreed, since Roosevelt was confined to a wheelchair, to make it easier for the president by conducting their meetings at the Livadiya Palace.

Roosevelt suggested that they go into the next room, and with Stalin at his side, the president was turned in his wheelchair and escorted out of the living room into the palace's grand ballroom, a room with a handsomely molded ceiling, marble columns along its length, windows looking into an interior courtyard on one side, and at the far end of the room, a vast fireplace.

A round table had been set up in the center of the room, with chairs enough for a few more than two dozen. To this first meeting, Stalin had brought with him his foreign minister Vyacheslav Molotov (a bit "mulish" in his negotiating techniques, in the estimation of Britain's Undersecretary Cadogan), his assistant commissar for foreign affairs Andrei Vyshinsky, who had served through Stalin's ferocious purges of the thirties as the state's leading prosecutor ("a great villain," said Cadogan, "but quite a pleasant companion" at the cocktail hour), the ambassador to Great Britain Fedor Gusev, and the ambassador to the United States, Andrei Gromyko ("frog-face," Cadogan called him), his translator Pavlov, and his top military men, General of the Army Antonov, Air Marshal Khudyakov, and Fleet Admiral Kuznetsov.

Roosevelt had brought along the American ambassador to the Soviet Union, Averell Harriman (who had once instructed Cadogan about how international conferences usually develop, provoking Cadogan to confide to his diary, "I've forgotten a great deal more about that than he ever knew"), Secretary of State Edward

Stettinius, the translator Charles Bohlen, and his top military men, Fleet Admiral William D. Leahy, Fleet Admiral Ernest J. King, Major General Laurence Kuter, Major General John Deane, Brigadier General Frank MacFarlane, and General of the Army George C. Marshall.

The British party, under Churchill, consisted of Foreign Secretary Anthony Eden ("flapping in and out," said Cadogan, "and dropping papers all over the place"), the top military men Field Marshal Sir Alan Brooke, Marshal of the Royal Air Force Sir Charles Portal, Admiral of the Fleet Sir Andrew Cunningham, General Sir Hastings Ismay, Field Marshal Sir Harold Alexander, the translator Major A. H. Birse. Churchill was fitted out for this occasion in a handsome uniform with ribbons on his chest. The strain of the war had told on Churchill, as it did on the others, but he remained ebullient and irrepressible.

If the USSR had made the greatest sacrifices, and the United States was emerging as the most powerful country in the world, what was Churchill's claim to be at the conference table? It was Stalin who would soon answer that question in a toast he would propose to Churchill at dinner: to the prime minister, "the bravest governmental figure in the world." It was due, said Stalin, "in large measure to Mr. Churchill's courage and staunchness, [that] England, when she stood alone, had divided the might of Hitlerite Germany at a time when the rest of Europe was falling flat on its face before Hitler," and Great Britain, "had carried on the fight alone." In all history, said Stalin, there were few examples "where the courage of one man had been so important to the future history of the world." It was a great claim—no less great for the fact that Stalin made it, on Churchill's behalf, in the past tense.

Most of the men who sat around the table at Yalta were old acquaintances, and old hands at these conferences—having been to Casablanca in 1943 and to Cairo and Teheran later that same year. Many of the waiters and other domestic help the Russians had brought along from Moscow were familiar to the diplomats from previous conferences. Bohlen was delighted to discover that one of the waiters was a man he had known in Moscow before the war (and was even more delighted when the Russian waiter made a point of stocking Bohlen's room with an extra ration of caviar and vodka).

Roosevelt presided over the plenary sessions, and "at Stalin's request," Stettinius noted in his diary, "the meeting opened with a review of the current military situation."

The floor was given first to General Antonov, who spoke for the Russians, identifying which forces under which commanders had taken part in the astonishing Soviet offensive of the previous few weeks, in which Soviet troops had swept up into East Prussia in the north, up through Hungary in the south, and directly across Poland and into the middle of Germany, to the Oder River and the heart of the German Reich.

The Reich was collapsing. Two million East Prussians had left their homes and were fleeing frantically toward central Germany or to the coast. "Columns of refugees," according to the historian John Erickson, "combined with groups of Allied prisoners uprooted from their camps, and slave labour no longer enslaved in farm or factory, trudged on foot or rode in farm carts, some to be charged down or crushed in a bloody smear of humans and horses by the juggernaut Soviet tank columns racing ahead with assault infantry astride the T-34s. Raped women were nailed by their hands to the farmcarts carrying their families."

As the Soviet troops advanced, the Germans had blown up the gas chambers and crematoria of the concentration camps, taken their prisoners from the camps, and commenced the great European "death marches." From the concentration camps of Auschwitz and Birkenau and elsewhere, prisoners were marched out ahead of the advancing Russians; and those who fell were clubbed and beaten, and if they could not rise again, shot. At Stutthof, of twenty-five thousand prisoners in the camp, twelve thousand were killed just as the evacuation began.

Meanwhile, the American bombers came over Germany raining bombs down on synthetic-oil factories and civilians. Among the few left behind by the Germans at Auschwitz was a young Italian chemist, Primo Levi, who would later write, "We lay in a world of death and phantoms. The last trace of civilization had vanished around and inside us. The work of bestial degradation, begun by the victorious Germans, had been carried to its conclusion by the Germans in defeat."

The Soviet army had advanced to within forty miles of Berlin. Stalin was in the position of Czar Alexander in 1815: his troops were in the heart of Europe. And like Alexander, Stalin could see no reason to pull back.

There were those in the West who thought that Stalin meant to keep right on moving into Western Europe. Whether that was his intention or not, he had already attained the ancient dream of the czars—to take a tier of Eastern Europe and to hold it as a buffer to protect Russia from the invasions it had repeatedly suffered from the West: Napoleon in the nineteenth century, the Germans, twice, in the twentieth century.

Roosevelt broke in with a technical question about Russian supply lines: as the Russians advanced, had they altered the gauge of the railroads from the customary European gauge to the wide Russian gauge?

Yes, said Antonov, they had.

There was a bracing sense of finality about that. The president suggested that "as our armies are now approaching each other in Germany it was important that the staffs should discuss this problem so that there would be a definite place in Germany where the different gauges would meet." It was a delicate way of putting the matter of where the line would be drawn on the Russian advance. There were those who said that Roosevelt was not, at this time in his life, up to tough, careful negotiating. But he still knew how to frame an issue with unavoidable precision.

Stalin replied that the gauge of the railroads had been changed as the merest matter of necessity, to bring up Soviet supplies, and that "the greater part of the German railroad lines would remain of their customary gauge." Roosevelt's point was taken.

General Marshall reported on the Anglo-American forces on the western front. The troops under Eisenhower were approaching the Rhine, still far from Berlin. To the south, the First French Army was moving, though slowly, on Mülhausen. Further north, Field Marshal Sir Bernard Montgomery's troops were moving toward Düsseldorf. Marshall hoped that the Anglo-American forces would cross the Rhine in March, depending on ice and the current.

As far as a drive on Berlin was concerned, the Anglo-American troops were running late.

Operations on the western front had been limited, said Marshall apologetically, by a shortage of supplies due to the inadequacy of shipping, but supplies were now coming in sufficient quantities through Antwerp. The Russians, though they had not mentioned it, had been suffering from a similar problem. Though they were within striking distance of Berlin, they held back—and the western generals would wonder why. It seemed the Russians were giving the Anglo-American forces an opportunity to catch up with them. But the explanation may have been that the Russian supply lines were stretched dangerously thin. In the matter of supply lines, Stalin was an extremely cautious man.

Stalin remarked that the Anglo-Americans must know what the Russians hoped—that they would move as hard and as fast as they could on the western front, so that German forces would not be shifted to the east to fight the Russians. Stalin was being indirect: he had long been complaining fiercely that the British and Americans had been too slow in opening up a western front, forcing Russia to carry the burden and absorb the worst losses so that, at the end of the war, the West could take advantage of a weakened Russia.

Stalin's generals would mention to the British and Americans in their military meetings that the Russians wished the British and Americans would bomb German railroads in order to hinder the movement of German troops to the East. This wish was answered within days, when western bombers were directed to strike at the city of Dresden. A wave of 245 British bombers, followed three and a half hours later by 529 more, and followed the next morning by 450 American bombers, and then again the next day by 200 American bombers created a fire storm that raged through the city, packed with refugees, for seven days and nights. No one knows the final death toll: 39,773 bodies were counted. At least another twenty thousand were buried under the ruins, "or incinerated," as Martin Gilbert has written, "beyond recognition, even as bodies."

At the same time, Stalin said, he would like to know what the Russians could do for the British and the Americans.

Churchill replied at once that he wished to express profound gratitude and admiration for what the Soviet Union had done. And now that victory was in sight, it seemed imperative to him that "the two offensives should be integrated so as to get the best results."

Indeed, added Roosevelt, at the Teheran conference in November 1943, it had been agreed that each partner "would move as quickly and as far as possible against the common enemy." Now, however, "with our armies approaching each other it should be possible to coordinate more closely our operational plans"—and, it went without saying, to make some bargains over the disposition of the postwar world.

With that, the first plenary session of the Yalta conference was brought to an end. What had been said had been of a general but exact nature. The realities of guns and tanks and soldiers and sacrifices and geographical positions had been established as the starting point for discussions. Talk about postwar settlements would follow. The opening remarks of the conference had been brief but comprehensive. And so the diplomats, having done their work, adjourned for dinner.

The Big Three, with their foreign ministers and translators and a few others, went into the next room, where Roosevelt played host, while the military men and the lesser dignitaries in each delegation dined apart. This conference was a spartan affair compared to the Paris conference of 1919, or to Vienna in 1815 or certainly to the meeting of Henry VIII and Francis I. It lasted a week, and there were no concerts, picnics, receptions, balls, love affairs, parades. For dinner that evening, Roosevelt served caviar (which had become as common as cheese dip at these gatherings), beef with macaroni, sturgeon, chicken salad, fried chicken, and dessert: "a terrible party I thought," said Eden.

The conversation was agreeable enough, however, until a casual reference was made to the rights that the small nations would have in the postwar world. Stalin spoke quietly but firmly. The big powers had borne the brunt of the war, and they should have "the unanimous right to preserve the peace of the world." It seemed to him "ridiculous," for instance, to imagine that Albania "would have an equal voice with the three Great Powers who had won the war and were present at this dinner." His remark cast a bit of a chill over the dinner table.

Roosevelt smoothed over the moment. He agreed, he said mildly, that the Great Powers "bore the greater responsibility and that the peace should be written by the Three Powers represented at this table." Dedicated as he may have been to the ideals of the equality of nations and the rights of self-determination, Roosevelt was not about to make the mistake of following too closely in Woodrow Wilson's footsteps.

No question, said Churchill, picking up the topic a little less delicately, of the small powers "dictating to the big powers." Still, the prime minister said, "The great nations of the world should discharge their moral responsibility and leadership and should exercise their power with moderation and great respect for the rights of the smaller nations."

Andrei Vyshinsky turned to Charles Bohlen and said the Russians would never agree to the right of the small powers to judge the acts of the Great Powers.

Bohlen made a reference to the opinion of the American people.

The American people, replied Vyshinsky, "should learn to obey their leaders."

If Vyshinsky would like to visit the United States, said Bohlen, he would like to see Vyshinsky "undertake to tell that to the American people."

He would be glad to do it, Vyshinsky replied with a smile.

Churchill, endeavoring to restore the mood of the dinner table, raised his glass to toast the proletariat masses of the world. And so everyone drank to the proletariat masses.

But talk resumed at once about people's rights to self-government. No one, it appeared, could drop the subject, even though no one was eager to become entirely tied to it as Wilson had been in 1919.

Although, said Churchill, easing the conversation toward a digression, he was constantly being "beaten up" as a reactionary, he noted that he was the only one present "who could be thrown out at any time by the universal suffrage of his own people and that personally he gloried in that danger."

Churchill was off on a soliloquy about democracy. Stalin tried to divert him with a lighthearted reference to Churchill's unfounded fear of the electorate which, he suggested, so clearly loved the prime minister. But Churchill was not to be stopped now that he was rolling. Not only did he not fear the electorate, but he was "proud of the right of the British people to change their government at any time they saw fit." He thought, Churchill said, as his rhetoric began to rise to the moment, that "the three nations represented here were moving toward the same goal by different methods." The eagle, Churchill concluded grandly, "should permit the small birds to sing and care not wherefor they sang."

It was a splendid speech, and Churchill was evidently immensely pleased with it (as he would tell Lord Moran the next morning), but before too much more time passed, the president and Marshal Stalin both found a suitable moment to excuse themselves from the party and go to bed, leaving Churchill orating to Stettinius and Eden and Bohlen.

Meanwhile, at a separate British dinner for the lesser lights including Cadogan, Marshal Portal, and Churchill's physician Lord Moran, the conversation turned to how President Roosevelt looked. His health, like that of Woodrow Wilson in 1919, was a subject of constant concern and gossip. "Everyone seemed to agree," as Moran later said, "that the President had gone to bits physically; they kept asking me what might be the cause. . . . It was not only his physical deterioration that had caught their attention. He intervened very little in the discussions, sitting with his mouth open." He looked shrunken, and as though he were not taking everything in.

"He has all the symptoms," said Moran prophetically, "of hardening of the arteries of the brain in an advanced stage, so that I give him only a few months to live."

One of the lingering questions about the Yalta conference would be whether Roosevelt's physical condition had made him less effective at the negotiating table, whether he "gave away" more than he might have if he had been in stronger health. Eden thought not. The president's "handling" of the conference, he later said, "was less sure than it might have been," but not his judgment.

The prime minister got fairly good marks from his own aides. He "seems well," as Cadogan wrote to his wife, "though drinking buckets of Caucasian champagne which would undermine the health of any ordinary man."

The highest marks from ministers and aides and gossips, however, went to Stalin. "He never wasted a word," said Eden. "He never stormed, he was seldom even irritated. Hooded, calm, never raising his voice." He was, said Cadogan, "much the most impressive of the three men. He is very quiet and restrained."

The next afternoon, at the second plenary session of the conference, the Big Three turned to political matters. Roosevelt suggested that they concentrate on questions about Germany, and he opened with what he supposed was one of the easy issues. He thought they ought to discuss the temporary zones of occupation that each of them were to have in Germany once the war came to an end.

These zones had been sketched out and revised and agreed to months before. The American War Department had assumed that the zones would be "determined by the location of troops at the time of Germany's surrender or collapse," but the British, fearful that the Soviet Union would occupy all of Germany by the end of the war, had pressed for an agreement beforehand. In January 1944, the British had roughed out a three-part division of Germany into approximately equal zones. The Russians had accepted the British proposal in February of 1944, suggesting that Berlin, in the Soviet zone, be occupied jointly by the three powers. In time, the Americans accepted this Anglo-Soviet proposal. But now Roosevelt, as he had suggested to Stalin before the meeting began, wanted to discuss whether the French were to be given a zone that would be carved out of the existing British and American zones.

"I should like also," said Stalin, "to discuss . . . the dismemberment of Germany."

That could be added to the agenda, but the permanent treatment of Germany, said Roosevelt, as he understood it, "might grow out of the question of the zones of occupation, although the two were not directly connected."

Stalin wanted to be more specific. He wanted to understand exactly "whether or not it was the joint intention to dismember

Germany [permanently]. If Germany is to be partitioned, then in what parts [was it indeed the intention to divide it along the lines of the occupation zones]? It is well known that we twice exchanged views. First at Teheran when the President then suggested partition into five parts. The Prime Minister hesitated but said he also favored partition. I associated myself with the President, but that was only an exchange of views. The second time I exchanged views with the Prime Minister in Moscow. He talked of partition into two parts. . . . Hasn't the time come for decision?"

"In principle," said Churchill, "I think we are all agreed on dismemberment, but the actual method, the tracing of lines, is much too complicated a matter to settle here in five or six days."

In effect, Stalin had come to occupy Clemenceau's position in 1919: Germany ought to be deprived of its ability ever to wage war again; to be divided, stripped of its assets (and a large share would go to Russia to help repair the damage of the war); it was to be held down forever.

Stalin had come to believe that the essential thing was not so much the division of Germany—though he was not opposed to it —but the establishment of a permanent organization, perhaps based on the zones of occupation, to keep Germany down. The British and American planners came to have doubts about dismemberment—fearing that the destruction of Germany at the center of the European economy might destroy the economy of Europe and America. That belief would come to dominate the thinking of both the British and the Americans. But at Yalta there was hardly unanimity among all the advisors and experts.

Only Stalin remained faithful to Clemenceau's solution, and believed the British and Americans agreed with him still.

Stalin pressed for a definite agreement on the matter. Churchill demurred. They need not mention dismemberment in the terms of surrender, he said; the Germans were to surrender unconditionally; then it would be up to the Allies to do whatever they wanted.

Roosevelt seemed a trifle impatient with Churchill. Stalin had not asked for a detailed plan, only a decision on the principle: "Are we going to dismember or not? [Marshal Stalin] wants the matter settled in principle but not as to details. The Prime Minister . . .

is not yet ready to lay down the limit; that requires study. . . . That is the only difference. Shall we all agree that Germany should be dismembered? As at Teheran, I am very much personally in favor of decentralization."

The president suggested that they agree to the principle of dismemberment, and that they ask their foreign secretaries to come to the meeting the next day with a plan for dismemberment.

"You mean," said Churchill, "a plan for the *study* of the question of dismemberment, not a plan for dismemberment itself?"

"Yes, for the study of dismemberment."

"His Majesty's Government would be prepared now to assent [to the] principle of dismemberment and to set on foot the best body to study the method."

And so, in the end, Churchill grudgingly assented to assign to the foreign ministers the task of *studying* the *method* of dismemberment. It may be that he was holding back out of a worry that an agreement to dismember Germany would, as a matter of course (and, as it turned out, they did), designate the occupation zones as the lines of division of the new Germany, that the Soviets would dominate their own dismembered zone, strip it for reparations, and absorb eastern Germany into their sphere of influence.

On the other hand, Britain's chiefs of staff, along with a War–Foreign Office group known as the Post Hostilities Planners, uncertain whether a postwar Germany might favor the West or the East, was advocating a near mirror image of that presumption of Soviet policy. They suggested that the West might absorb a part of Germany into a North Western European Group, as a bulwark against the Soviet Union.

Would Germany be left united and unmolested so that it might revive and be a strong part of the European economy? Or would it be united only so that it could be bled for reparations? Would it be divided and left on its own, or divided and absorbed by East and West? While these issues remained uncertain, Churchill may have thought his best strategy was to bring the matter to some sort of impasse and mire it, for the time being, among the foreign ministers.

Roosevelt wished to return to the matter of a French zone of occupation.

If the French were given a zone, said Stalin, that was one thing; but they must not be given a place with Britain and America and Russia on the Allied Control Commission that administered the zones. That would "bring up many complications." In short, Stalin did not want another Western power to maneuver around.

But the French, said Churchill, "have had long experience in occupying Germany. They do it very well and they would not be lenient. We want to see their might grow to help keep Germany down."

In fact, said Stalin, he "could not destroy the truth, which was that France had contributed little to this war and had opened the gate to the enemy" at the beginning of the war. The control commission ought to be "run by those who have stood firmly against Germany and have made the greatest sacrifices in bringing victory." As far as he was concerned, the French could have a zone so long as they had no position on the Big Three's control commission, which Stalin hoped would be the principal instrument for postwar political control in Europe. He was not merely negotiating an occupation zone; he meant to have the postwar world controlled by the Big Three, not the Big Four.

If the French have a zone, said Eden acerbically, "how can they be excluded from the control machinery?"

"They could be controlled," said Stalin, "by the power from which they obtained the zone." He would concede the point on giving the French a zone. But let the foreign ministers discuss the relationship of that zone to the control commission. (If Churchill could mire the issue of German dismemberment among the ministers, Stalin could send this issue there too, while they all saw what other bargaining chips were available for trading.)

The Russians wanted to discuss the question of reparations. They had a proposal to make. Stalin turned to Ivan Maisky, an assistant commissar for foreign affairs, to present it.

The Russians proposed two forms of reparations: those to be taken immediately after the war (factories, plants, machinery) and yearly payments of goods (not cash) over a period of ten years. To restore Russia, "and for the security of Europe, it is necessary to cut down German heavy industry by 80 percent." To make Germany pay required very strict three-power control. Then each country would make reparations claims according to the physical damages and casualties they had suffered. The losses of the war were so immense in Russia that the Russians could never be entirely compensated, but when reparations were parceled out on a proportional basis, the Russians felt they were entitled to the largest share.

Churchill had reservations. "I remember well," he said, "the last war and the sad experience in reparations that followed. It was with great difficulty that one billion pounds was finally extracted from Germany and that was due to the fact that Germany received much larger amounts in loans from the United States. . . . I do not want to repeat that experience."

He recognized that the Russians had suffered great losses, and agreed that reparations were due Russia, but "we must also consider the phantom of a starving Germany and who is going to pay for that. If eighty millions are starving are we to say, 'It serves you right,' and if not, who is going to pay for feeding them?" If you wish a horse to pull a wagon, said Churchill, "you would at least have to give it fodder."

Yes, said Stalin, "but care should be taken to see that the horse did not turn around and kick you." In any case, said Stalin, "there will be food for them."

Roosevelt agreed with Churchill's reservations. "I envision a Germany that is self-sustaining but not starving. . . . Our objective is seeing that Germany will not starve in helping the Soviet get all it can." Nonetheless, he said, he would willingly support Soviet claims to reparations since he felt "that the German standard of living should not be higher than that of the Soviet Union."

The experience of 1919, said Maisky, would not be repeated, because the Russians did not propose taking cash—only goods. The time period would be limited to ten years. And the Germans would not starve.

As with the matters of dismemberment and zones of occupation, the Big Three were not eager to reach a conclusion at this first review of the issue; they had only to agree to agree, and it was Churchill who ended the conversation. "I agree," said the prime minister, on the setting up of a reparations commission to consider "the priorities to be assigned . . . [and] the guiding principles."

On that note, the Big Three adjourned their second plenary session, and went in to dinner. They had now put on the table their principal points for negotiation about Germany. Soon enough the hardest questions—whether Germany should be strong enough to help the European and American economies, or reduced to a tenth-rate pastoral country; whether its wealth would be used to help Russia rebuild, or the Russians were to be told to find the wealth elsewhere—would all recur, become tangled with questions about zones of occupation and dismemberment; and the fundamentally differing interests of the Big Three would begin to pry them apart.

But with the main issues now referred to the foreign ministers to hash out and bring back to the plenary sessions, the conference began to take on a comfortingly familiar shape. "We have reduced the Conference to such an orderly procedure," Cadogan wrote home happily, "that one day is very like another. We work in the morning till 11:30, when we have a meeting of Foreign Secretaries, followed by lunch. . . . Then follows a meeting of the Big Three, which goes on usually till about dinner time." The foreign ministers would try to hash out an agreement, and take their work to the Big Three for approval.

And as for daily life, the delegates had all found some way to settle into the routine and make themselves at home. "Give the Englishman real discomfort," said Lord Moran, "and he becomes cheerful." Cadogan was feeling positively buoyant: "bowls of fruit and bottles of mineral water in every bedroom," he wrote to his wife. "Also a decanter of vodka! The food is quite good, though, as usual in Russia, rather monotonous. And of course they have to be trained in the matter of breakfast. Caviar and mince pies for breakfast are all very well once in a way, but they pall after a bit. However we have now drilled them into giving us omelettes."

At the next plenary session, the Big Three took up a discussion, as Cadogan wrote, about the United Nations. "I was terrified of what the P.M. might say, as he doesn't know a *thing* about it—he has always refused to look at it—and here he was plunging into debate!"

The United States had proposed that the United Nations

would keep the peace. Germany would be disarmed, police power would be concentrated in the United Nations; disputes among small nations would be controlled. Britain, Russia, the United States (and perhaps China) would have special positions in the United Nations as permanent members of the Security Council, where final decisions as to whether the UN would go to war against any nation would be made. Acting together, the permanent members of the council would police the world and suppress trouble. It was to be Woodrow Wilson's League of Nations with something like Clemenceau's military alliance to keep the peace. To protect the permanent members of the council from having the United Nations turn on them, the American proposal stated that, before the UN could go to war, a unanimous vote of the Security Council was required. Thus, each member had a veto to protect itself against the UN going to war against it.

In order that this arrangement would not seem entirely undemocratic, the Americans proposed that any country would have the right to bring charges against any other nation in the Security Council, including the permanent members of the council. If a member of the council thus became party to a dispute, that member would abstain from voting on the issue. And on these issues, a simple majority vote in the council would be decisive.

Stalin was puzzled. On the one hand, members of the Security Council had veto power; on the other hand, they would abstain from voting. They would not vote on a matter that concerned them unless it meant war, in which case they would vote. So really, no member of the Security Council could be forced to do anything if they chose to make it an issue of war; and thus, in the final analysis, the provision for a majority vote was just window dressing, a grant of permission to the small powers to talk, but not to decide on any issue on which the major powers wished to reserve their powers.

Stettinius explained that on matters in which a peaceful settlement was possible, a member would abstain; on major questions—admission of new members, expulsion of members, questions of military enforcement—members of the council would have a veto.

Suppose, Stalin said, that Egypt demanded Britain return the Suez Canal. Would that matter be resolved peacefully, and Britain abstain from voting?

Churchill rejoined with Hong Kong. If China were to demand that Britain quit Hong Kong, China and Britain would abstain from voting on "the methods of settlement of this controversy." But Britain would not be required to return Hong Kong to China unless the British "felt that this should be done," since the British could veto such a decision.

Stalin remarked that he would like some time to study the proposal. It still seemed unclear to him (as well it might). The veto power would render the provision for majority voting a sham on the great issues of politics. He could not believe the small powers would not see through this. He could not bring himself to believe that mere ineptitude accounted for the design of this voting formula. He suspected that some plan lay behind it.

Stalin was not alone in being skeptical of the American design for the United Nations. Churchill thought that Roosevelt only wanted to give China a vote on the Security Council so that China would side with the United States in efforts to liquidate the overseas British Empire. Roosevelt, said Eden, "hoped that former colonial territories, once free of their masters, would become politically and economically dependent upon the United States."

To balance the Chinese vote, the British had proposed that permanent membership on the Security Council also be given to the French, whom they hoped to transform into their European partners.

Then Roosevelt thought it would be a fine idea to add Brazil, one of its Latin American friends, to the Security Council (and to add five other Latin American countries as founding members of the General Assembly, which would give the West a decisive majority in the assembly).

Stalin began to argue that the sixteen Soviet republics, like the members of the British Commonwealth, were constitutionally independent political entities. Perhaps the Soviet Union should have sixteen votes in the assembly. When the Americans expressed their "shock" at that idea, the Russians proposed that at least two or three republics, say the Ukraine, Lithuania, and Byelorussia, having made such a great contribution to the war, should be taken into the UN as independent members. (They had been, as it happens, expressing some restless desires for a more independent status within the Soviet Union, and Stalin no doubt felt this would help to mollify them.)

But these petty squabbles, Stalin now resumed at Yalta, should not be allowed to go on. The "main thing," he said, was to prevent quarrels in the future between the three Great Powers. Whether they were joined together in the United Nations, or on the control commission in Germany, if the three Great Powers were unified, there would be peace in the world; if they fought with one another, no one could guarantee the peace. The most important task for the Big Three "was to secure their unity for the future," whatever the organization they designed for the purpose.

Everyone around the table could agree on that. "If we three come together," Churchill had said to Lord Moran several months earlier, "everything is possible—absolutely anything." And Roosevelt had reassured Stalin just a few months before Yalta, "All three of us are of one mind."

The question of voting in the United Nations was set aside for further study, and the Big Three turned to the subject that would consume most of their time, and their passions, at Yalta: the question of Poland.

The Russians, having come at the end of the war to occupy Poland, meant to move the border between Poland and Russia back west into Poland, up to the so-called Curzon Line. The Curzon Line had been established as the Soviet-Polish border in 1919; but after the Bolshevik Revolution, the Poles had taken advantage of the continuing turmoil to invade the Soviet Union and move the border 150 miles to the east into Russia. Now, Stalin wanted to restore the Curzon Line. But, in order to compensate Poland for this loss of territory, the Soviets would move the western border of Poland further west, into Germany, up to a line marked by the Oder and the western Neisse rivers.

Having driven the Germans out of Poland, the Russians had recognized a new Polish government that they had established in the hands of the Communists in the Polish city of Lublin. The Lublin government was pliant to the Soviet Union, and Stalin meant to have the Lublin Poles recognized by Britain and America as the legitimate government of Poland.

First of all, said Roosevelt, to reassure Stalin at once, "I am in
favor of the Curzon Line." Still, he said, "it would make it easier
for me at home," among Polish voters, "if the Soviet Government
would give something to Poland." At the Teheran conference, Roosevelt had suggested that Russia concede a little piece of territory
over the Curzon Line that would include the oil fields around the
city of Lvov. "I am not making a definite statement, but I hope
Marshal Stalin can make a gesture in this direction.

"But the most important matter is that of a permanent government for Poland. The Lublin government," the president said,
"represents a small portion of the Polish people." The United
States favored reconstituting the government to include some of
the Poles who had gone into exile in London during the war.

Churchill joined in: "I have made repeated declarations in Parliament in support of the Soviet claims to the Curzon Line. . . .
However, I am more interested in the question of Poland's sovereign independence and freedom than in particular frontier lines.
. . . This is what we went to war against Germany for—that
Poland should be free and sovereign. . . . Great Britain has no
material interest in Poland. Her interest is only one of honor,
because we drew the sword for Poland against Hitler's brutal
attack."

"The Prime Minister," Stalin replied, "has said that for Great
Britain the question of Poland is a question of honor. For Russia it
is not only a question of honor but also of security."

Throughout history, he said, "Poland has always been a corridor for attack on Russia"—twice in the past thirty years alone.
"This is because Poland was weak. It is in the Russian interest as
well as that of Poland that Poland be strong and powerful and in a
position, in her own and in our interests, to shut the corridor by
her own forces. The corridor cannot be mechanically shut from
outside by Russia. . . . It is necessary that Poland be independent,
strong and democratic. It is not only a question of honor but of life
and death for the Soviet State. That is why Russia today is against
the Czarist policy of the abolition of Poland."

Nonetheless, it was clear from what Stalin said that if it was
not possible to create a strong and independent Poland, friendly to

the Soviet Union, then Stalin would feel constrained to take over Poland and "shut the door from the outside."

As for the Curzon Line, "I must remind you that the Curzon Line was invented not by Russians but by foreigners. The Curzon Line was made by [the British Lord] Curzon, Clemenceau and the Americans in 1918–1919. Russia was not invited and did not participate. This line was accepted against the will of the Russians on the basis of ethnological data." And he could not "be less defenders of Russia than Curzon and Clemenceau.

"Now about the government. . . . We had the opportunity in Moscow to create a Polish government with Poles. Both London and Lublin groups met in Moscow. . . . [But the London Poles] were against the agreement and hostile to the idea. They called the Lublin government 'bandits' and 'traitors.' Naturally the Lublin government paid the same coin to the London government. It is difficult to bring them together."

Once the Polish question had been opened up it could not easily be put away. In fact, neither Roosevelt nor Churchill cared much for the Poles or for Poland, except as a vivid symbol of the triumph of democracy that their people believed must result from the war against Hitler. Before the Americans had set out for Yalta, Secretary of State Stettinius had chatted with Henry Stimson, the American secretary of war. Stimson said he thought it was not "worth a quarrel with Russia" to dispute the Curzon Line. As for having a government of Lublin Poles or London Poles, it did seem "as if the Russians, with their possession, have 99 and 44/100 percent of the law" on their side. When the delegates had all first arrived at Yalta, and before the sessions had begun, Churchill was saying to Lord Moran, "I don't think much of the Lublin Government, but I suppose they are the best you can get."

Nonetheless, Roosevelt and Churchill had supported the London Poles throughout the war and did not want to desert them if there was any chance of saving them, or at least without the show of a struggle.

At their next plenary session, the Big Three returned at once to the question of the Polish government. The previous evening,

Roosevelt had given a letter to Stalin, saying that he agreed that the Poles should be consulted about putting their government together. So Roosevelt suggested that the Big Three invite the various Polish factions to Yalta to hammer something out.

Whether Roosevelt meant his proposal seriously, or only as a way to call Stalin's bluff, it was an easy maneuver for Stalin to outflank. After he had received Roosevelt's note, said Stalin, he had had his men make some phone calls. Unfortunately, the Lublin Poles could not be tracked down at the moment, and he was afraid there would not be sufficient time to find everyone and get them to Yalta. In the meantime, the Soviet foreign minister had a proposal to put on the table.

Molotov proposed that the Allies formally agree to accept the Curzon Line in the east, and the line of the Oder and western Neisse rivers in the west, as the borders of Poland; and in order to compromise on the matter of the Polish government, that "some democratic leaders from Polish *émigré* circles" be added to the Lublin government. Evidently, the Russians hoped this would be enough to soothe Roosevelt and Churchill—and to get them to agree on the Polish borders.

Roosevelt replied at once that he thought "some progress had been made," although he didn't care for the word *émigré*. In fact, said the president, they could find enough Poles within Poland to satisfy their purposes; there might be no need at all to bring in members of the Polish government in London. Evidently, Roosevelt calculated that if he dropped the London Poles, maybe Stalin would drop the Lublin Poles, and a completely fresh start could be made.

Churchill said that he, too, didn't like the word *émigré*. The word had originated, said the prime minister, "during the French Revolution and meant in England a person who had been driven out of a country by his own people." But the Poles had been driven out "as a result of the brutal German attack." He therefore preferred to refer to them as "Poles temporarily abroad." Like Roosevelt, however, he made no brief for the London Poles to be among those added to a reconstituted government.

Churchill was not quite so ready, however, to accept the western Neisse River as the western border of Poland. He preferred the eastern Neisse. It would be a pity, said Churchill, "to stuff the Polish goose so full of German food that it got indigestion."

As a follow-up to this exchange, the next morning, Roosevelt sent a letter to the British and Soviet delegations, suggesting that they agree to form a brand-new "Presidential Committee," composed of leaders of several Polish factions, who would meet to form a temporary government that would be representative of the Lublin government, the London government, and other democratic groups inside Poland. That temporary government would arrange for elections at an early date, and meanwhile, all the Big Three would recognize the temporary government as the Provisional Government of Poland. That would give them all an entirely fresh start.

At the plenary session that afternoon, Molotov withheld Soviet approval of Roosevelt's proposal. It was impossible, he said, "to ignore the existence of the present Polish government" in Poland. It could be enlarged, but it did exist, and it did enjoy "great prestige and popularity in the country." As for forming a presidential commission, "I am afraid instead of one we will then have two difficult problems—that of the government and that of the presidential commission. This will increase our difficulties, not decrease them." Altogether, said Molotov, "it would be better to talk on the basis of the existing situation and then how to improve it."

Roosevelt was chagrined. He understood that if the existing government was kept in place, and only a few new people were added to it, nothing much would change.

"Of course," said Churchill, "we are at the crucial point of this great conference. This is the question for which the world is waiting." If the Big Three could not all agree on which Polish government to recognize, "this will be interpreted all over the world as a sign of cleavage between the Soviet government on the one hand and the U.S. and British governments on the other. The consequences would be most lamentable in the world and would stamp the conference as a failure."

Churchill's remark was lost on no one: on the issue of Poland, Europe would either be divided, or not, into two hostile spheres of influence. This was the crucial point of the conference.

Stalin took a moment before replying. "I can assure you that these [Lublin Poles] are really very popular [in Poland]. . . . They are the people who did not leave Poland. They have come from the underground."

The Poles in London, said Stalin, "are not liked in Poland because during the time of stress they did not seek the underground. Perhaps this attitude is a little primitive but it must be taken into consideration."

At the moment, the Poles were celebrating their liberation from Hitler; they were celebrating that liberation with the leaders of the Lublin government, and so, although the Lublin leaders "may not be great men, [they] enjoy great popularity."

Of course, free democratic elections must be held; but in the meanwhile, he saw little difference between the position of de Gaulle and that of the Polish provisional government. "Neither had been elected, and he could not say which one enjoyed the greatest degree of popularity—yet we had all dealt with de Gaulle and the Soviet government concluded a treaty with him. Why should we be so different with regard to the Polish government?"

Roosevelt and Churchill seemed deflated by this comparison to de Gaulle, as it was within their sphere of influence.

"How long," asked Roosevelt, signaling that he was recognizing finally that he could not budge Stalin, "before elections could be held?"

"In about one month," said Stalin, "unless there is a catastrophe on the front and the Germans defeat us . . . I don't think this will happen."

"Free elections," said Churchill, "would of course settle the worries of the British government at least."

Once again, the Big Three seemed headed toward another compromise. Roosevelt suggested that they refer the question, as the others had been, to the foreign ministers for a final formula.

Before they adjourned, Stalin said, he would like to bring up one other matter. He would like to know what was going on in Greece. He did not—he added quickly and pointedly—wish to make any criticism of British conduct in Greece. He sought information.

"It would take too long to talk about Greece now," said Churchill. "I could talk about it for hours."

"I only wanted to know for information," Stalin responded. Greece, after all, fell within the British sphere of influence. He would not dream of interfering there—any more than he wanted Britain to interfere in Poland. "We have no intention of intervening there in any way," he repeated, in case Churchill had not got the point.

The next afternoon—one presumes he had a chance to discuss it with Stalin—Molotov opened the plenary session with what appeared a change in the Soviet position. The Soviets were eager, he said, to accommodate the wishes expressed by Stettinius earlier in the day, and so he had an amendment to offer to their Polish agreement that he felt would be acceptable to everyone: "The present Provisional Government of Poland should be reorganized on a wider democratic basis with the inclusion of democratic leaders from Poland itself and from those living abroad."

Also, at one point in much earlier discussions, a phrase had been added to say that the ambassadors of the three big powers would be responsible for overseeing Polish elections. It was a minor matter, but Molotov now felt that that should be eliminated, since he felt certain it would be "offensive to the Poles and would needlessly complicate the discussion." In any case, it was always the duty of ambassadors to observe and report, so that no such statement was necessary. However, the Russians would like another new phrase added specifying that the democratic factions participating in the elections would naturally be "anti-Fascist," that is, those who had fought against the Nazis.

Now, Churchill felt a significant advance had been made on the Polish question, although he did wish to make a few suggestions. Finding themselves close to agreement, "we should not put our feet in the stirrups and ride off." It would be "a great mistake to hurry this question—it is better to take a few days of latitude than to endanger bringing the ship into port."

Possibly Churchill thought he might hold the final terms of the Polish settlement back as a bargaining counter, to see what trades could be made on other points. In any case, he said, he would like to have some time to study this proposal. And in the meanwhile, he thought they might do well to turn to some of the other topics that the foreign ministers had been discussing earlier in the day to see what progress they were making on those matters.

Unfortunately for Churchill, this was not the perfect moment for this suggestion. It happened that, aside from Poland, the ministers had been busily discussing certain questions about the United Nations, including the matter of placing former colonial territories —in particular those of the soon-to-be-defeated Germans and Japanese—under United Nations trusteeship where they would be administered by UN members appointed as trustees, rather like Woodrow Wilson's plans for the League of Nations.

The ministers had agreed, reported Stettinius, that the permanent members of the UN Security Council would consult each other on machinery for territorial trusteeships.

Churchill exploded. The Americans, it seemed to him, had been discussing putting some pieces *even* of the British Empire into United Nations trusteeships. He did not "agree with one single word of this report on trusteeships." He had not "been consulted, nor had he heard of this subject up to now." But, he wanted it clearly understood, "under no circumstances would he ever consent to forty or fifty nations thrusting interfering fingers into the life's existence of the British Empire. As long as he was [Prime] Minister, he would never yield one scrap of their heritage."

Stettinius, "it appears," according to Moran, "was a good deal rattled by the violence of this outburst, and hastened to explain what he was saying did not apply to the British Empire. The P.M. appeared a little mollified. . . . [But after] the P.M. sat down he kept mumbling: 'Never, never, never.' "

This extraordinary outburst, said Eden, gave immense pleasure to Stalin, who was delighted to have some respite from the attack on *his* sphere of influence, and to watch Churchill squirm when the British sphere came under pressure. Stalin rose from his chair, "walked up and down, beamed, and at intervals broke into applause."

The Americans, Moran thought (as Eden and Churchill had come to realize, too), were the Britons' biggest problem on the matter of the empire. Stettinius, much subdued, read the rest of his report on the topics the foreign ministers had discussed earlier in the day.

But in fact, the Big Three were eager to get back to talking about Poland, and after they all took a brief intermission to study one another's proposals, they resumed their places around the table to listen to Roosevelt's remarks.

"I find," said the president, "that it is now largely a question of etymology—of finding the right words." (Roosevelt, said Eden, was "deluding himself.") Where Molotov referred to the Polish provisional government, Roosevelt suggested they refer to the "Polish provisional government now functioning in Poland"—which transformed it, presumably, into only one of the provisional governments of Poland, the one that was functioning in Poland as distinguished from the one that was functioning in London.

Stalin thought about this for a few moments and then he countered with the suggestion that they call the Lublin government "the Polish government which acts in Poland."

By this time, certainly, it was all but impossible to know whether these changes in words made the position of the Lublin government more or less entrenched: that it merely happened to act in Poland might make it seem as though it had less of a claim to be the legitimate government of Poland but, at the same time, referring to it simply as "the Polish government" made it seem quite firmly established. As heads swam around these wordings— with Molotov saying the Poles would need to be consulted, and Roosevelt suggesting it be referred again to the foreign ministers— Churchill had another point to make.

Stalin had said just the day before that Poland had been liberated by the Red Army, and that a new situation had been created in Poland that called for a new arrangement. Churchill thought that was an important "new fact," and one they ought to emphasize. (It would make it easier, though Churchill did not say so, for the British to partly scuttle the London Poles and arrive at a new compromise if Churchill could tell the British people that there was this important "new fact" to be taken into account.) "It is ornamental but it is important to us."

Churchill was working his way toward compromise with the Russians. And yet he was not yet entirely comfortable. He still had some remaining public relations problems. He would have some hard explaining to do back home. He must say, Churchill went on, the British suffered for lack of information from Poland; perhaps the Poles were indeed capable of having a fair election, but he thought the Russians, Americans, and British ought to be allowed to have observers present for their elections. "These are no idle requests. In Egypt whatever government conducts the elections wins."

"I," said Stalin, "do not believe much in Egyptian elections. It is all rotten corruption there. They buy each other."

"Anyway," said Churchill, "we seek this formula."

"What percentage of the people read and write in Egypt?" Stalin asked. "In Poland 70 percent can read and write."

"I do not know the Egyptian percentage," Churchill replied, "but I meant no comparison with Poland. I only wanted fair elections. . . . I must be able to tell Parliament that elections will be free and fair."

"This can be done in the presence of the Poles," said Stalin, "with various people present."

"In Parliament," said Churchill, "I must be able to say that the elections will be held in a fair way."

And then the prime minister dismissed the people he was defending with a casual phrase: "I do not care much about Poles myself."

"There are some very good people among the Poles," said Stalin, now the sympathetic defender of the virtues of the Polish people. "They are good fighters. Of course they fight among themselves, too. I think on both sides there are non-Fascist and anti-Fascist elements."

"I do not like this division" among Fascists and anti-Fascists, said Churchill, perhaps thinking of the British-backed government in Greece. "Anybody can call anybody anything. We prefer the terminology democratic parties."

"I want this election in Poland," said Roosevelt, jumping into the conversation, "to be the first one beyond question. It should be like Caesar's wife. I did not know her but they said she was pure."

"They said that about her," Stalin replied quickly, "but in fact she had her sins." And so, he implied, would the Polish elections.

Once again, however, even as the Big Three came within a hairsbreadth of agreement on the Polish government, they backed away from making any final commitments—leaving it to the foreign ministers to discuss it again and bring it back once more to a plenary session.

What was clear by this point in the negotiations was that Stalin was absolutely determined to hold his own on Poland. In the face of that determination, there was little that Churchill and Roosevelt could do. They might have threatened—as Wilson did in 1919—to walk away from the conference and go home. But at the time of Yalta, the war was not yet won. Cooperation among the Allies was still essential for victory over Germany and Japan. They might have withheld agreement on some other agenda item, to trade it for a concession on Poland. But Poland was not at the top of either Roosevelt's or Churchill's list of priorities. They had nothing they were willing to trade. As Secretary of War Stimson had perceived at once, Stalin's possession of Poland made conversation supererogatory.

"In politics," Stalin once said, "I believe one should be guided by an estimation of forces." And at Yalta, on the issue of Poland, Roosevelt and Churchill bowed to that calculus.

On other issues, the negotiating was easier. Stalin, having held onto Poland, gave way on other issues, no doubt in the expectation of being accommodated in return. When the Big Three returned to the question of giving France a zone of occupation in Germany and a seat on the Allied Control Commission, Stalin gave Churchill and Roosevelt their way.

On the several questions about the United Nations, Stalin again accepted the wishes of Churchill and Roosevelt—going along, finally, with the American voting procedure in the Security Council (anything could be raised for discussion, but the permanent members were entitled to veto any taking of action), even though he continued to think that a fraudulent distinction was being made for the sake of having it appear that the smaller nations had more power than they did.

The Russians also backed off their request to have all sixteen of their republics admitted as members of the UN Assembly, though they did ask to have two or three republics given independent seats. Churchill, who didn't want to lose any of the members of the Commonwealth as voting members of the UN, spoke in defense of the Russian request. His "heart went out," said Churchill, "to mighty Russia which, though bleeding, was beating down the tyrants in her path." Roosevelt managed to resist Churchill's rhetoric, although in the end, he did agree to admit two Soviet republics as initial members of the UN.

Stalin also consented to Roosevelt's suggestion that they issue a joint Declaration on Liberated Europe, in which the Big Three pledged themselves to enable those people who were liberated from fascism "to create democratic institutions of their own choice." This, noted the declaration, "is a promise of the Atlantic Charter [that Roosevelt and Churchill had signed in 1941]—the right of all peoples to choose the form of government under which they will live—the restoration of sovereign rights and self-government to those people who have been forcibly deprived of them."

Stalin, evidently understanding this as an expression of an obligatory lofty rhetoric, found the declaration perfectly accept-able. It contained no enforcement provisions.

The British had a little more difficulty with it. Churchill al-lowed that he "did not dissent" from the declaration "as long as it was clearly understood that the reference to the Atlantic Charter did not apply to the British Empire." The Atlantic Charter had pledged America and Britain to seek no territory and to respect the rights of people everywhere to choose the form of government under which they lived. Churchill, sensible of the wish of India to be independent of the British Empire—indeed aware of the restiveness of a good many colonial peoples—wanted it understood that, "as far as the British Empire was concerned the principles already applied": there was no more Britain needed to do to give self-government to people.

Stalin, listening to this exchange, could be pardoned if he were to have supposed the declaration might not be held any more strictly against Russia than against Britain.

Roosevelt had already violated the principles of the declaration even before he brought it up. A couple of days earlier, Roosevelt and Stalin had chatted alone about the war against Japan in the Far East.

The president hoped, he told Stalin, that it would not be

necessary for American troops to invade the Japanese islands—but rather, that bombing alone could win the war. Waves of American bombers were just beginning to fly out of the Marianas to drop incendiary bombs on the cities of Japan, and the wood and paper houses of the Japanese went up even more dramatically than the stone and brick of Dresden. In just a few weeks, Tokyo would be hit by 325 bombers carrying incendiaries: in one night sixteen square miles, 267,000 buildings, 89,000 lives would be consumed in a fire storm so hot that it caused the water in the canals of Tokyo to boil.

Stalin agreed with Roosevelt's desire not to have to engage in a costly invasion of the Japanese islands. He said he would be happy to provide air bases in the Far East for the Americans.

Of course, Roosevelt wanted more than air bases to carry the burden of the war against Japan. He presented Stalin with a paper outlining American wishes to have the Soviet military enter joint planning with the Americans. Stalin said he would like to discuss "the political conditions under which the USSR would enter the war against Japan."

The Japanese would be required, at the end of the war, to give up all their external territories. Stalin wanted to have returned to the Soviet Union everything Japan had obtained from the czars in a treaty of 1875 and in the Russo-Japanese war of 1904–05.

Roosevelt said at once that he had no difficulty with Russia's desire to have the southern half of Sakhalin and the chain of the Kurile islands that stretched from the tip of Japan northward to Russia's Kamchatka peninsula. The two men agreed that Russia would also have guaranteed use of the Chinese-owned railways that ran through Manchuria down to the Chinese warm-water port at Port Arthur and Dairen.

To be sure, said Roosevelt, he had not yet had a chance to discuss this with the Chinese, but he thought Dairen could be internationalized (never mind the rights of self-determination for the Chinese). In truth, said Roosevelt, who seemed consistently to gnaw away at the British Empire, he thought Hong Kong should be internationalized, too.

Later on, when the British heard of the deal Roosevelt had made with Stalin, they were in a snit. It was, said Eden, a "discreditable byproduct of the Conference," and he thought the British should not put their names to the agreement. But then, what upset Eden more than anything else was the growing conviction that Roosevelt, who so disliked "imperialist" countries, was well on his way to substituting American economic hegemony for the old imperialism.

As for Korea, Roosevelt said to Stalin, he had a rather "delicate" matter to discuss. "Personally," the president did not feel it was necessary to invite the British to participate in a United Nations' trusteeship of Korea. Rather, he thought that the Americans, Russians, and Chinese might manage Korea. Nonetheless, said Roosevelt, he felt that the British might resent this.

Indeed, said Stalin, the British "would most certainly be offended. In fact . . . the Prime Minister might 'kill us.' " In Stalin's opinion, the British should be invited to share the trusteeship.

Roosevelt did not insist on squeezing out the British. He moved down his agenda to talk about a trusteeship for Indochina —which would squeeze out the French.

Stalin did not disagree.

And then the president turned the conversation to China. The United States, said Roosevelt, "had been trying to keep China alive" for some time.

China, Stalin assured him, "would remain alive." Furthermore, Stalin said, he thought that Chiang Kai-shek, America's choice of leader for China, should "assume leadership" in bringing the Communists into his government—just as (though Stalin refrained from saying it) the Polish Communists in Europe would assume leadership in bringing democratic elements into their government. Thus Stalin did not hesitate a moment to undercut his fellow Communist Mao Zedong and defer to Chiang Kai-shek in China.

In sum, Stalin recognized America's interests in China, Japan, and elsewhere in the Far East.

When it came to discussing the Middle East, however, all three powers drew back. Russia and Britain had invaded Iran in 1941 to overthrow the pro-Nazi Shah Mohammed Reza Pahlavi; and they had agreed at that time to withdraw their troops at the end of the war and, meanwhile, not to compete with one another over Iran's oil. In 1942, when the United States had arrived in the area, American oil companies had soon followed. And so the British, in competition with the Americans, had begun to seek oil concessions. And then the Soviets had tried to get the Iranians to sign a five-year oil concession. With that, the United States at once had begun advocating that the Iranians grant concessions to no one, and when the Soviets had continued to press for oil rights, America had undertaken to "protect" Iran from Soviet pressure.

This led to an impolite squabble among the foreign ministers at Yalta which got Eden so out of joint that he mentioned it informally to Stalin. Eden had barely begun to speak when Stalin laughed and said, "You should never talk to Molotov about Iran. . . . If you want to talk about it, talk to me." And when Eden did, Stalin said, "Yes, I understand. I'll think about it." The subject was left unresolved at the Yalta conference.

On questions about Bulgaria and Romania, the West deferred to Russia. On Greece, Stalin deferred to Britain. ("Poor Neville Chamberlain," Churchill would say to some of the members of his cabinet after he got back to London, "believed he could trust Hitler. He was wrong. But I don't think I'm wrong about Stalin.")

On Yugoslavia, Russian and Western interests were harder to sort out. Once again, as in Poland, there was a government in place, that of Josip Tito, who had led the partisan forces during the war. And once again, there was a government—or at least a monarch, King Peter II—in exile in London. By the time of the Yalta conference, however, Tito's government was firmly in place in Yugoslavia. The British and Americans had no hope of removing Tito, and the Russians, in fact, were having a good deal of difficulty controlling him. At Yalta, the British proposed several modifications to arrangements in Yugoslavia, and Stalin declined to accept them. Even if the Russians had accepted the British proposals, it is doubtful that anyone could have forced the Yugoslavians to abide by them.

By the time the Big Three returned to the difficult issues of Poland and Germany in the closing days of the conference, a manner of give-and-take had overcome them. The questions about the

Polish government had been dissolved in a nice paragraph of diplomatic language.

The foreign ministers had come up with wording on the Polish government to which they all agreed: "A new situation has been created in Poland as a result of her complete liberation by the Red Army. This calls for the establishment of a Polish Provisional Government which can be more broadly based than was possible before the recent liberation. . . . The Provisional Government which is now functioning in Poland should therefore be reorganized on a broader democratic basis with the inclusion of democratic leaders from Poland itself and from Poles abroad."

Stalin, Churchill, and Roosevelt all liked this formulation, and so they gave it their approval and returned once more to the question of borders. The border with Russia, the Curzon Line, was accepted by all—but then hesitation remained over the western border, whether it would be set at the eastern Neisse or the western Neisse River. This the Big Three left unresolved, bowing to Roosevelt's argument that they should consult with the Poles before setting a western border.

On the matter of reparations, Stalin pressed for specific wording. He suggested that they agree that, in principle, Germany should pay reparations. That when a Reparations Commission would meet to discuss details, they take as the starting point the earlier American-Soviet proposal that there should be twenty billion dollars of reparations, with 50 percent going to the Soviet Union.

Churchill demurred. He had received instructions from his cabinet, he said, that no figures be mentioned.

Roosevelt said he was afraid that if figures were mentioned the American people would believe that it involved money, not reparations in kind, and that would arouse controversy.

According to H. Freeman Matthews, one of the American State Department men who was present taking notes, this was the only moment in the conference that Stalin became upset. He did not understand, he said, "why there should be any confusion . . . since the Soviet Union had concluded three treaties with Finland, Rumania, and Hungary in which the value of reparations in kind were definitely stated and that there had been no confusion as far as he knew."

If the British, Stalin told Churchill, "felt that the Russians should receive no reparations at all, it would be better to say so frankly." Reparations had been at the top of Stalin's agenda from the first day of the conference. He had talked on and on about the damage the war had done the Soviet Union, and of Russia's need, and its demand, for help in rebuilding.

Roosevelt mentioned something about confusion in America over the word "reparations."

But Churchill replied directly, at last, to Stalin's question by reading a telegram he had received from his cabinet. It would be "inadmissible," said the telegram "to state any figure until an investigation had been completed on the spot and that at any rate the figure of twenty billion was too great . . . it was beyond the capacity of Germany to pay." Such payments would make it difficult for Germany to pay its bills for imports—imports from Britain and America, for example. And if payments for reparations were put ahead of payment for imports it would mean that the countries from whom Germany imported goods would, in effect, "be paying for German reparations to those countries receiving them."

Stalin replied carefully. The Big Three had already agreed that there should be some reparations. He did not want to provoke Churchill into retracting that promise. He was only suggesting that the twenty billion figure be used as a starting point for later conversations.

The whole matter, said Roosevelt, ought better to be left to the Reparations Commission to sort out.

But, said Stalin, the Big Three should declare in principle that they agreed Germany should pay some reparations. He would be content, he said, retreating from naming his figure, to let the commission consider the amount without any recommendation of a figure. Everyone agreed.

The dinner that evening was to be their last dinner together, and the conversation rambled.

Churchill was anxious about the upcoming election in Britain. He thought he might face a tough challenge from the Left.

Left and Right, said Stalin, were terms without much meaning anymore. For instance, Edouard Daladier, a radical socialist, had dissolved the trade unions in France whereas Churchill had never molested them in England.

Nonetheless, said Churchill, he thought Stalin had an easier political time of it in Russia with only one party to deal with.

Yes, said Stalin, "experience had shown one party was of great convenience to a leader of a state."

As the diplomats broke up to return home, they all spent some time congratulating themselves on how well they had done. "Each of the three leaders," said Bohlen, "had achieved his major goals" —a remark both true and false at the same time. The issues discussed would come up again, and unpleasantly, at the Potsdam conference five months later, after Roosevelt had died and his place had been taken by President Harry Truman. The positions staked out at Yalta on Eastern Europe, Poland, reparations, the division of Germany, and other points of contention would eventually tear apart the erstwhile wartime allies—even as they told one another repeatedly, as Churchill said on one occasion, "everything depended on the unity of the three Great Powers and without that the world would be subjected to inestimable catastrophe."

In hindsight, it is hard to know what else each of the participants might have done differently. Given the position of Stalin's armies in Europe at the end of the war, the economic needs of the Soviet Union, and the Russians' historic fear of invasion from the west, Stalin could well feel that his actions in stripping eastern Germany of assets and seizing and clamping down on Eastern Europe were only necessary to the survival of the Soviet Union. But in his hope to achieve the ancient dream of czarist foreign policy— to take over a buffer of Eastern Europe to make Russia absolutely secure—Stalin took over more than he could maintain.

It was one thing for Stalin to take Eastern Europe, one thing to crush it and devastate it, and quite another to hold it. Perhaps the Soviet Union could not have held Eastern Europe in any event, given the brutality and ineptitude of Soviet policy; but when the Soviet Union was opposed by the United States and Western Europe, the two sides embarked on a competition that Stalin's successors could not sustain. And so, in an effort to secure and preserve the Soviet Union, Stalin, by overreaching, set his nation directly on the path to its ruin, and his policy must stand as a prime example of the perils of succumbing to the temptation of ruling what one can.

As for Churchill, presiding as he was over an empire that was irretrievably on its way down, he had little alternative but to attach Britain to the fortunes of the United States, to consent to the establishment of an American global hegemony, and to preside, as he said he never would do, over the liquidation of the British Empire.

The American policy makers, for their part, could only feel they were being pragmatic in understanding that, despite the wealth and power of the United States, they could not pry the Soviet Union out of Eastern Europe, short of a war that not even the Eastern Europeans wanted. At the same time, even as the American negotiators, and Roosevelt most of all, resisted drifting toward an adversarial relationship, the lines were drawn at Yalta over which much of the Cold War would be fought. And when Truman succeeded Roosevelt, whether he responded to the logic of the situation or intended to adopt a more adversarial stance, the effect was the same: the United States embarked upon the Cold War and the nuclear arms race, assuming an imperial role in the world that would erode the constitutional liberties and usages that these very men had hazarded their lives to protect.

Could all of these unfortunate consequences have been averted if any one of the Big Three had resolutely insisted on helping one another rebuild the physical and spiritual devastation the war had left behind, and refused to be pitted against one another as adversaries? Many historians have been quick to leap forward with their confident answers, whether yes or no, to the question. But on the evidence of history, no answer is entirely clear, save that, for all of the participants, among the most momentous consequences of the Yalta conference were those that none of them intended.

Seven

THE
FANTASY
OF REALISM

As we approach the twenty-first century, the nature of summits as they have recently been known is changing. No longer are there two superpowers to hold the balance between them, as the United States and the Soviet Union did for forty years through the era of the Cold War. Now there is only one great military power and a multiplicity of other considerable, increasingly assertive powers and would-be powers. The nationalities rearranged after World War I and repressed during the Cold War are no longer so easily managed by the Great Powers. The rivalry between East and West that made an enforced order in the Middle East and Africa and elsewhere no longer restrains the passions and aspirations and hatreds it once did. And the shape of summit meetings begins to look not so much like that of Yalta and the Cold War summits that followed as, once again, like a variation on the Congress of Vienna.

And yet, although the size and shape of the conference table changes, the same familiar puzzles of knowability, surprise, contingency, unintended consequences, and others remain with us—indeed, may well become more acute.

218

Because the twentieth century has developed such sophisticated techniques of handling and analyzing complex information,
it would seem reasonable to imagine that a large enough body of
well-processed data must inevitably yield a guide to policy. But, as
the chemist Peter Coveney has written, "to predict the future," and
so suit our actions to the given situation and to the situation as it
will develop over time, "you would have to measure the initial
conditions with literally infinite precision—a task impossible in
principle as well as in practice."

Then, too, as Coveney knows, history is not merely the working out of initial conditions. The system, as Paul Veyne has written, "is not isolated: there constantly come onto the stage new data
. . . that modify the original data. It follows that if each link is
explicable, the concatenation is not, for . . . the system is not entirely explicable from the initial data." It is this that makes the
notion of realism a delusion.

How should one behave under these circumstances? Professional diplomats have dealt all their lives in this familiar world of
no certain ends, and endless means, hoping that their actions may
have some effect on the course of history. And the great practitioners and historians of diplomacy are in rare agreement about
what is required of such a person. Generally, diplomats of any
time or place would agree with François de Callières, whose *De la
Manière de Négocier avec les Souverains* was published in 1716. A
good diplomat, said Callières, must have "a spirit of attention and
application" that is not easily distracted by the pleasures of society;
a "right judgment" that is able to understand things clearly and
follow the main lines of significance without getting lost in details
or subtleties; a "quick penetration" to understand the "secrets of
men's hearts, and to take advantage of the least motions of their
countenances;" a "spirit fertile in expedients;" a "readiness of mind"
in order to deal with the unforeseen and avoid pitfalls; an "evenness
of temper" in order to "hear patiently" what is being said; a "free
access" that encourages others to come to him with information;
and an "easy and engaging carriage which invites affection." Above
all, said Callières, "the good negotiator will never base the success
of his negotiations upon false promises or breaches of faith; it is an
error to suppose, as public opinion supposes, that it is necessary

for an efficient Ambassador to be a past master in the art of decep-
tion. . . . Doubtless the art of lying has on occasions been successfully practiced. . . . But even the most dazzling diplomatic
triumphs which have been gained by deception are based upon
insecure foundations. They leave the defeated party with a sense
of indignation, a desire to be revenged and a resentment which will
always be a danger."

The twentieth-century English diplomat Harold Nicolson
listed a different, but compatible, set of requirements, mentioning
in particular truthfulness, precision, calm, patience, modesty.
Vanity, said Nicolson, might lure "its addicts into displaying their
own verbal brilliance, and into such fatal diplomatic indulgences as
irony, epigrams, insinuations, and the barbed reply. It may prevent an ambassador from admitting even to himself that he does
not know Turkish." And a diplomat must avoid self-satisfaction.
"Diplomats, especially those who are appointed to, and liable to
remain in, smaller posts, are apt to pass by slow gradations from
ordinary human vanity to an inordinate sense of their own importance. The whole apparatus of diplomatic life—the ceremonial, the
court functions, the large houses, the lacqueys and the food—
induces an increasing sclerosis of personality. Such people, as they
become older, incline to a slowness of speech, movement and perception which is almost akin to pompousness."

"These, then," Nicolson concluded, "are the qualities of my
ideal diplomat. . . . 'But,' the reader may object, 'you have forgotten intelligence, knowledge, discernment, prudence, hospitality,
charm, industry, courage, and even tact.' I have not forgotten
them. I have taken them for granted."

Underlying this practical advice on the ideal diplomat lurks an
idea of how the world works—what might even be called a philosophy of history—that diplomats share without having bothered to
articulate. The assumption of the diplomats, acquired after their
years of work around the world, is that individuals cannot create
the conditions in which they work, or transform events by themselves, but if they have a clear vision, unclouded by bias or unex-
amined assumptions, they might be able to "read" the historical
field accurately. And if they have the requisite patience and mod-

esty in addition, they may enter the historical field as one of its actors and have a hand in shaping events.

In the history of diplomacy, the full combination of the familiar old conundra that erode confidence in realism has not been more distinctly seen than in a recent meeting of the so-called G7 nations in London. There the leaders of the United States and the other major industrial nations were joined by Premier Gorbachev, of what was then still the Soviet Union, for his last hurrah—frustrated by the enduring custom of summitry, that one cannot come to the table as an equal member of the Club without something substantial to bring. The meeting of the G7 provided a demonstration of summitry as we are likely to know it on into the next century, with all its old mysteries intact, its new preoccupation with economics, its need to resolve more of the new problems by negotiation than by force, and with its practitioners trying to measure up to the demanding standards set by Callières and Nicolson for operating in the world as it is.

Bush, Gorbachev, Major, Mitterrand, Kohl, and others in London

By the last decade of the twentieth century, the Cold War was well over—Eastern Europe had come unhinged from the Soviet Union, the Berlin Wall had come down, the USSR itself was in a state of political turmoil and economic chaos, civil war raged in Yugoslavia, and the war led by the United States against Iraq in the Persian Gulf had concluded with an astonishingly impressive display of American military technology. The world order that had organized relations among nations since Yalta had caved in with remarkable suddenness. The world was possessed by dislocations and disasters on a scale such as those in the aftermath of World

War I or World War II or the Napoleonic Wars of the nineteenth
century—and political leaders were in search of a new world order.

It was generally agreed among analysts that if there was to be
any new order at all it would be based not only on the immense
military power of the United States, as the world's only remaining
superpower, but also on the combined economic powers of the
industrialized nations as a whole. (The CIA would announce in the
spring of 1992 that 40 percent of its budget and attention would
henceforth be devoted to the gathering and analysis of economic
information.) The world order would be a consequence, in large
measure, of an ability to manage the world economy with skill and
foresight. And it was agreed, certainly among the leaders of the
industrialized nations, that the managers of the world economy
would be, essentially, the seven nations whose leaders met in London in mid-July 1991—the members of the so-called G7, Britain,
France, Germany, Italy, Japan, Canada, and the United States. As
Le Monde said: "One sign of the times: the meeting of the Seven
now clearly eclipses the periodic Soviet-American 'summits.' "

This meeting was, in fact, the seventeenth annual summer
session of the G7 that had begun at Rambouillet, just outside Paris,
"with a handful of national leaders," as R. W. Apple put it in the
New York Times, "gathered in relative obscurity to talk about
economic problems," something of an exclusive club of the world's
most privileged. "But they have turned into the annual meetings of
the Board of Directors of the Planet Earth."

That the world at large had not elected the G7 to be its board
of directors did not go unnoticed. The economics editor of *The
European* noted that "the rich should not decide for the poor. It is
true, alas, that Indian or African economic weight is close to zero,
but this is not a reason for leaving them out of the decision process.
That is like running a democracy with the richer class ruling the
poor classes. Would that still be a democracy? . . . Who will have
the courage to say this in London? Nobody, I am afraid. But as we
learned from history, refusing to look at the facts will not change
them." The board of directors was not likely to take its lessons
from a newspaperman.

As the London *Economist* contentedly said, "The G7 has become the forum of choice for decisions that can shape the world. It

is small. Its members share some basic values. They account for more than half of the world's economic weight. Together, if they so wish, they can act as the world's governing council. Being a polite bunch, they may not wish to call themselves that. But govern, in essence, they could."

As suddenly as the old order vanished, it seemed, a new one was found to be already in place and prepared to try to shape the world anew. With the end of the Cold War, and its political oversimplifications, the world had once again become a place where Metternich might feel at home among the shifting and uncertain contingencies.

"There is an analogy," Flora Lewis wrote in the *New York Times*, "to the emerging management system in the 19th century Concert of Europe, worked out at the Congress of Vienna in 1815 after the Napoleonic wars. There was no blueprint, no charter for running Europe then, as there won't be now for trying to keep the world on keel. But there were understandings capable of absorbing most frictions for a century.

"That world order broke down cataclysmically in 1914, leading to the bloody inhumanities of the 20th century. There must be no temptation to revert to the 19th century patterns as the new concert of powers evolves, a danger already visible in Balkan rivalries and in nationalisms in Eastern Europe. The new concert must not set out to repress change, as the old one did, but to provide openings for peaceful accommodation to inevitable challenges."

This was Premier Mikhail Gorbachev's hope as he traveled to London in the summer of 1991, desirous of being accepted into the club, and of having it help him ease the plight of the Soviet Empire in collapse.

It is the very essence of summitry that someone believes if he can just get his message delivered, there is the basis for a mutually satisfactory deal. Certainly, this was the case with Gorbachev as he arrived at the international conference. Gorbachev was unable to pay for his military, his economy was in rout, his empire slipping away. And yet he was not without a certain power: the power that came from the dangers a collapsing Soviet Union might pose for the rest of the world. If he could articulate those dangers well, he might convince the others that it was in their own interest to help the Soviet Union.

Gorbachev had not been invited, of course. The Seven were intending to concentrate on developing a "medium-term strategy" for the world economy, encouraging the United States to reduce its budget deficit, and to reach some understanding about the different rates of unemployment, inflation, and interest that were affected by their governments' policies and that gave one or another of them competitive advantages in the world economy. There was some "very frank" and "very forceful" talk about trade, as Britain's Prime Minister John Major said—meaning in particular some effort to break a deadlock in talks about the General Agreement on Tariffs and Trade. According to Major, the obstacles to agreement were differences over agricultural policy, access to one another's markets, services, and "intellectual property." A United States Treasury official warned that bargaining could not start while the European Community insisted on large farm subsidies. Jacques Delors, the president of the European Community, suggested that "those who want to give lessons can start in their own homes. . . . I would remind you," said Delors, "that you cannot cite just one country without agricultural subsidies except a country with virtually no agriculture."

Into an atmosphere of difficult problems—of contingencies added to contingencies—that did not directly concern him, Gorbachev arrived, with an invitation only to talk to the members after they had finished their official meetings. He arrived early, deliberately, and like Talleyrand at Vienna, his presence and his problems immediately took center stage.

Gorbachev sought direct foreign aid and foreign investment to shore up his rapidly failing economy and to ease the transition to a market economy. Grigory Yavlinsky, a former deputy prime minister of the Russian Federation, had drawn up an economic plan in consultation with a team of economic advisors from Harvard. Yavlinsky's plan called for a new, democratic political treaty among the Soviet republics, followed by an economic treaty which would establish a common currency and recognize a common obligation on the foreign debt. This would be followed by restructuring Soviet enterprises, privatization of the economy, and price liberalization. All of this would be underwritten by Western aid and investment. Yavlinsky's plan became known as the Grand Bargain —an internal reform of the Soviet Union and a new relationship toward the West, in return for help from the West.

However, Yavlinsky's plan was not the only one available to Gorbachev. Valentin Pavlov, the Soviet prime minister, had attempted to spell out some details of defense spending cuts, a value-added tax, and the creation of a stock and commodity exchange. It was, said some critics, altogether a plan that moved more rapidly toward a market economy—or, according to other critics, one that was less specific than Yavlinsky's about its plans for economic reforms. It was, in any case, what Gorbachev was leaning toward.

The president of the European Bank for Reconstruction and Development, Jacques Attali, had been working with the Soviet premier on a ten-point program that would bring the EBRD in to help privatize small business and housing, improve food distribution, create a private banking system, and build telecommunications. Abel Aganbegyan, a former aide of Gorbachev's, had drawn up a compromise between what some felt were too sudden reforms and what others felt would move too slowly.

Yavlinsky was asked if it made sense to give aid to a Soviet Union that seemed on the verge of splintering into an undetermined number of independent republics. "Not helping," said Yavlinsky, "would make it worse, much much worse. Then you will have eight Soviet Unions, or eighty, the same problem many times over. Frankly, one Soviet Union has been enough."

Vladimir Shcherbakov, the first deputy prime minister, rang an alarm: "If there is turmoil, it would not only occur in the Soviet Union, but also elsewhere." Vitaly Ignatenko, Gorbachev's personal spokesman, agreed: "There could be turmoil," he said, "in the whole world."

Like Talleyrand, Gorbachev was treated with a combination of extreme care and circumspection by the representatives of other countries.

Germany, Italy, and France were generally inclined to give Gorbachev help. Germany had already provided or pledged $31 billion in aid to the Soviet Union during the previous year—in return for the Soviet Union letting go of East Germany. And German Chancellor Helmut Kohl wanted other Western nations to pitch in. The Russians still had three hundred thousand soldiers on East German soil; if there was a collapse of the USSR, Chancellor Kohl might expect Russians to come flooding toward the West, to West Germany first. His motivation for doing something for the Russians was powerful though he protested "the Germans obviously can't do everything. Our resources are limited. We have no cash cow."

Kohl had met Gorbachev in Kiev the week before, presumably to give the Russian premier some advice. An "outbreak of instability in the Soviet Union cannot be in our interest," added Kohl's aide Dieter Vogel. "Up to now, Germany has been almost alone in aiding the Soviet Union. Now it is time for the other nations of the world to help, too."

President François Mitterrand of France was inclined to go along with the Germans, though not entirely enthusiastically. He thought it might be "a bit premature" to include the Soviet Union in international monetary institutions, or expand the G7 to the G8, although he hoped "it will happen someday."

The Italians were firmly on the Germans' side. "No one," said the Italian Prime Minister Giulio Andreotti, "wants to have it on his conscience that we didn't help."

The United States, Britain, and Japan were reluctant. Secretary of State James Baker announced, noncommittally, "Gorbachev will not leave here empty-handed."

"Nobody," said British Foreign Secretary Douglas Hurd, "wants to send President Gorbachev away discouraged; because we have all benefitted so much from the process of reform and want it to continue. . . . But equally I don't think anyone wants to start writing checks at this meeting."

Leaders of Eastern Europe, meanwhile—excluded, as had so often been the case in European diplomacy—clamored for attention, fretting over what might be done without their counsel and in violation of their interests. Several Eastern European leaders wrote letters to Prime Minister John Major, the summit's host, urging him to convey their wishes to the G7 that Eastern European countries be given access to Western markets and a greater inflow of Western capital.

Just how Gorbachev's request might fare in London was anyone's guess, but it was noted that, on Gorbachev's arrival, he received a note from Prime Minister Major, apologizing that "my economic summit duties prevent me from welcoming you and Mrs. Gorbachev this evening."

Gorbachev was met on his arrival at Northolt Airport by the queen's lord-in-waiting, Viscount Astor, and chauffeured into London by a British Foreign Office driver in a Daimler 4.2 litre, one of Britain's finest automobiles. In what some took to be a demonstration of British technology, on the way into the city, the car developed a rattle in its exhaust and had to pull into a Kwik-Fit at Golders Green. There, since no spare parts could be found, the car was fitted out with a temporary repair in its broken exhaust tubing by the installation of a Sunkist orange-drink can. The other heads of state had been provided with Jaguars or Rover Sterlings, though President Bush had his own two bullet-proof Cadillacs flown in from Washington and traveled about London with a fleet of sixteen limousines.

After Gorbachev was deposited at his quarters in London, he was chauffeured around town in an armor-plated Zil limousine that he had had flown in from Russia. In what was, perhaps, an unintended confirmation of the Sukhumlinov Effect—the principle, named in honor of a heavily decorated nineteenth-century Russian general, that the more medals a general wears on his uniform, the less chance his army has of victory in battle—Gorbachev was accompanied wherever he went by a twenty-three-car convoy.

Gorbachev stayed at Harrington House, the Soviet ambassador's residence on Kensington Palace Gardens; Bush stayed at the American ambassador's residence, Winfield House, in Regent's Park. The meetings of the G7 took place in Lancaster House, near St. James's Park, just next door to the Queen Mother's house, down the street from Buckingham Palace, across the park from the British prime minister's residence at Number 10 Downing Street.

Lancaster House, built in 1825, is a grand pile of Bath stone, with an astonishing interior double staircase suitable for sweeping entrances, splashes of gold gilt and riots of cherubs holding candelabra, paintings by Guercino and Veronese among others, and a capacious Long Gallery that had been graced by the manners and styles of many distinguished figures of history and was now furnished for these meetings with a new thirty-five-foot table equipped with microphones and headsets, and a glassed-in translators' booth stuck functionally at one end of the room.

Prime Minister Major—having only recently succeeded Margaret Thatcher—was making his debut on the international scene as Britain's leader, and he hoped, as his aides acknowledged, to make a good impression not just among his peers in the G7 but, perhaps even more importantly, among the voters at home—to be seen, finally, as a world figure considerable enough to succeed the formidable Mrs. Thatcher. He looked every bit the part in a sleekly tailored, single-breasted dark suit, and he had a decided bounce in his step.

Next to Britain's prime minister, Premier Gorbachev, in a double-breasted suit, looked just a little out of style, just a little like yesterday's news. But then, could it have been significant that Gorbachev's two staunchest supporters, Kohl of Germany and Andreotti of Italy, also wore double-breasted suits? Certainly not, although there were those who thought that the fact President Mitterrand was the only one at the G7 meetings to wear a light-colored suit might be meaningful—or, if not the shade of his suit, then the fact that he was the only one of the G7 to have left his wife at home when he came to the conference, or if not the fact that he left his wife at home then certainly the fact that he habitually arrived late for meetings.

Punctuality, it is said, is the courtesy of kings, the means by which they show a necessary respect for the sovereign equality of their peers. And yet Mitterrand was late for dinners or meetings three times in two days. Indeed, on at least one occasion when it was clear that his automobile was making its way in good time through the clogged traffic of diplomats and their followers, he stopped the car and got out and strolled through Green Park, setting off an alert among the security forces, and arrived ten minutes late at Lancaster House—displaying the eternal illusion of the independence of the French to the satisfaction of his conference peers —and the French back home.

In a photograph taken outside Lancaster House of the presidents and prime ministers and their principal ministers and aides, only one woman was present among the group of twenty-seven, Canada's Foreign Minister Barbara McDougall, a master diplomat, who said that the men were "very clubby," but that none of them had ever been "even remotely patronising"—having been moderately well trained, presumably, by the many years that Margaret Thatcher had been a prime minister among them. And yet, so it was gossiped, the men felt some sense of relief now that Mrs. Thatcher was gone, and the essential maleness of the club had been reestablished.

As a diplomatic occasion gathers momentum, with all its speeches and press conferences and gossip, its dinner toasts and postprandial conversation, moments that might or might not be snubs, remarks that might or might not be significant, apologies that might or might not be sincere, seating arrangements that are revised at the last moment, dress codes that are not quite violated, a certain loss of perspective is inevitable, and it is sometimes difficult even for a person of Metternichean sophistication to know what information is meaningful, or what is the sort of thing information theorists call noise.

President Bush looked a little as though he had just gotten out of bed, not a remarkable appearance ordinarily but one that might have raised a question among any pharmacologists who remembered that for the shipboard meetings the president had had with Gorbachev off the coast of Malta, Bush had been seen wearing a dime-sized transdermal scopolamine patch behind one ear. Transderm Scop, at that time a relatively new drug for seasickness, was an adhesive patch impregnated with a drug known as a belladonna alkaloid that seeps through the skin at a constant, low-dosage rate that lasts for three days.

Transderm Scop is an anticholinergic drug, which is to say it acts to inhibit the transmission of certain messages to the brain. Among its possible side effects are dryness of the mouth, drowsiness, a slight disorientation, blurred vision, slurred speech, dizziness, confusion, irritability, anxiety, loss of memory, nightmares, and hallucinations. A drug without side effects, physicians like to say, is a drug without effects. This is the medical equivalent of the political rule of unintended consequences. The question of whether the president was being too casually medicated for trivial concerns such as seasickness, jet lag, and sleeplessness would be raised openly six months later, after he vomited at a state dinner in Japan.

Inevitably, a certain spectacle of madness eventually takes over once a summit meeting is functioning at its optimum, and those in charge of security precautions in London—invigorated by recent activities of the Irish Republican Army—contributed to an overall sensation of smooth order. The French ambassador was waiting on the lawn of his residence in Regent's Park for guests to arrive for a Bastille Day garden party when the whole park was suddenly closed to traffic, keeping the ambassador's guests stranded in their cars because President Bush's motorcade was expected to pass by some time soon. Elsewhere, when the heads were ferried up to Kenwood Lakeside Concert Bowl for an open-air performance of *Tosca*, the voice of Placido Domingo was drowned out by the whup-whup-whup of security helicopters ferrying dignitaries back and forth overhead.

Of course, it may be, looking back some years from now, that the activities of the leaders of the G7 will not seem as significant as the activities of a small knot of people who gathered at the same time for what they called TOES, The Other Economic Summit, which was held near Lancaster House, at the Methodist Central Hall. The alternative summit featured workshops on the gaps in infant mortality and living standards between industrialized and developing countries, and noted, among other things, that the average caloric intake of the G7 countries was 34 percent above requirements, and in Bangladesh 22 percent below. The TOES delegates unfurled vast banners reading "Leaders fiddle while the world burns," and were entertained by a string quartet playing *The Ritual Firedance.* One of their members—Bruno Menser of Switzerland, who had spent seven years among the Penan tribe in Sarawak and, it was said, was wanted by the Malaysian police—chained himself to a lamp pole outside the Queen Elizabeth II Conference Centre, with a banner proclaiming: "Self-Determination for Tribal People in Sarawak."

When it came time for him to present his proposal to the G7 at a meeting in Lancaster House, Gorbachev set out before the delegates a twenty-three-page letter describing his ideas in general terms, along with thirty-one pages of proposals for economic cooperation with the West on such matters as converting military factories to civilian uses, stabilizing the ruble, and encouraging Western investments. Among other things, his letter spoke of a critical shortage of food, children's items and medicines in the Soviet Union. "The financial and credit system is in disarray, the state budget deficit is growing, export trade and currency earnings have gone down. . . . The ensuing hardships . . . may prove too heavy a burden, fraught with major social conflicts, and pose a threat to domestic transformations."

Gorbachev faced a situation at that moment not unlike that of Pope Leo I at Sirmione in A.D. 452. His job was to speak the truth as compellingly as he could, and hope that the truth would seize the imagination, and mobilize the fears, of those he addressed. And yet, while he might know a truth about the situation back home, it was impossible for him to know any better than Leo or Attila the whole historical field into which that truth would fall, what effect it would—or even could—have to alter the minds of those he faced across the table or to affect the immense upheavals that had yet to play themselves out in the Soviet Union.

"It is our strong feeling," said Gorbachev, "that the crisis can be overcome only if we make a radical shift toward a market economy. . . . We proceed from the assumption that it is primarily through our own efforts that we will have to address our currency and financial problems. . . . Measures are being taken to form a currency market, set a more realistic exchange rate for the ruble and make it convertible [what the Russians wanted, said one of Gorbachev's aides, was about 10 to 12 billion to help make the ruble convertible]. . . . By the end of 1992, it is intended to privatize, in some form or other, nearly 80 percent of the total number of retail outlets, public establishments, services and a number of enterprises in other sectors." Land reform was high on the agenda, said Gorbachev; people should be free to choose whether to continue working in a profitable collective or state farm, "or to go private and work their plot of land." He stood for a "mixed economy and equality of state, private, and all other forms of property ownership." Would such measures work? No one, certainly not Gorbachev, knew. The depth of unknowability of whether or how such practices would work in a country with no experience of capitalism, and with the prospect of unpredictable resistance of various surreptitious forms at every level of society, was stupefying.

Moreover, there was some vagueness in what Gorbachev had to say about these rights to choose between state and private enterprises, some question about just how "mixed" the premier meant the Soviet economy to be, some haziness about how "radical" his reforms would be in the end.

But if Gorbachev had had to wait anxiously in the wings before he had been able to present his case before the G7, he did not have to wait long for the response. The proposals were greeted instantaneously as neither specific nor sweeping enough.

United States officials dismissed Gorbachev's plan as a vague "circular."

"A mishmash of ill-fitting proposals," declared the *Economist.*

It was "clear on the aim," one American official said, "but not on the means of getting there."

"It is blatantly clear," another of the Western diplomats said, "that Gorbachev does not understand privatization or open markets"—or else that he was unable, because of political pressures back home, to say "the right things."

Certainly it was true that the Soviet premier operated under extraordinary political pressure from back home and, whatever understanding he might reach with Western leaders, he ran the risk of returning home with a plan that the politicians and people in his own country would not accept—like President Wilson after the Paris conference of 1919.

He was under fierce attack from the conservatives among the military and the Communist party bureaucracy in Moscow. The hard-line conservative Moscow party leader Yuri Prokofiev noted that the party had not been consulted about laws governing land ownership, about privatization or about entrepreneurial activity, and yet was expected to "bear responsibility for the actions of its leader and his numerous mistakes." Gorbachev, said Prokofiev, was in London begging to be admitted into a club bound by "archaic market conceptions."

While Gorbachev was in London, a meeting of the Communist party was called in Moscow on July 17, and the party members adopted a resolution declaring "resolute opposition to the reckless imposition on our society of institutions and mechanisms of the West." The members of the party also called for the convening of an emergency congress that would be empowered to change the entire party leadership—that is to say, to throw out Gorbachev.

At the same time, Gorbachev was under attack from the "radical" democrats in the Soviet Union, too, led by Moscow's mayor Boris Yeltsin, who felt that he was moving too slowly and conservatively to meet the needs of his disintegrating country. The economist Boris Pinsker, speaking for the more radical Russians, not only predicted that Gorbachev would be given "a polite but complete refusal" by Western leaders but went on to say that "this is correct policy on the part of the West, because the country's current leadership is not worth giving a kopeck."

No doubt Gorbachev hoped he might get a sympathetic reception from Western leaders, which he could then take home to buttress his position—a tactic he had used in the past to great advantage. But his political credit was running out in the West, too.

Questions could not be kept from rising in people's minds: what power did Gorbachev actually possess in the Soviet Union to carry out his promises? Could he deliver what he pledged, or was he hoping, as Henry VIII and Francis I had hoped at the Field of the Cloth of Gold, that an impressive show on the international stage would buttress his position at home? And would the appearance of power in London in fact be translated into the reality of power in Moscow?

For that matter, when it came to judging the reality or illusion of power at this G7 meeting, what powers did the West actually possess to rescue the Soviet Union? Given the West's own economic problems, were there resources available to prop up the disintegrating Soviet economy? Or were the deliberations of the Western leaders in part a charade to appear to the world that they possessed vast economic power that might on closer inspection be a chimera? On the other hand, would the mere appearance of help, the infusion of only a few billion dollars, give just that degree of apparently crucial help that would keep Gorbachev in office, and persuade the Soviet people to go along with reforming their economy?

After a dinner Gorbachev had with Prime Minister Major, one of the prime minister's aides remarked crisply that Gorbachev had "failed to provide convincing replies to a set of detailed questions" on how he intended to go about creating a free market economy. Major concluded that the G7 leaders found him too vague on his plans for property rights, liberalized prices, control over government finances, privatization of enterprises, the legal framework to underpin a market economy, and the relations between the central government and the constituent Soviet republics—as comprehensive a trashing of Gorbachev's proposals as might be imagined.

In case that was not enough, the prime minister added that, "We are very concerned to insure that not only the Soviets pass the legislation for economic reform, but they actually implement the legislation so that the economic reform itself can actually come about."

James Baker was even harsher: "I don't think," he said, "you get to a market economy by providing assistance to a disintegrating command economy."

The impression was inescapable that the leaders on both sides were still captives to some degree of the lessons of their recent past: that Western leaders, suspicious of anything the Russian leaders might say, were still in the habit of driving as hard a bargain with the Soviet Union as they could, and that Gorbachev had not quite yet given up communism. In fact, grumblings were to be heard that Gorbachev had not forthrightly espoused capitalism, that he had drawn up many plans, but their effects were still to be seen. The past holds us in its grip whether we know it or not.

There were, in addition to these broad criticisms of Gorbachev's proposals, some other, quite specific problems rooted in history. The Japanese would not favor helping the Soviet Union until the Soviets returned the Kurile islands, which they had seized from Japan at the end of World War II.

Nor was President Bush inclined to spare the Soviet Union now that it was on its knees. There was a "political problem," said Bush, "that we've got about helping the Soviet Union as long as they're propping up the one totalitarian dictator—Communist dictator—in our hemisphere," in Cuba. And there was the matter, too, of seeing to it that the Soviet Union continued to disarm. (Indeed, during these few days in London, Gorbachev would dutifully sign a treaty on nuclear missiles that was, at the least one could say of it, not considered an unfavorable treaty by most American military advisors.)

The Soviet Union remained one of the world's great reservoirs of natural resources, said Martin Feldstein, a former advisor to the Reagan administration and, at the time of the London summit, the head of the National Bureau of Economic Research; if the Soviet Union needed more hard currency, said Feldstein, let it pledge current stocks and future production of oil. "It is difficult," he said, in words that might have been spoken of the Germans by Clemenceau in 1919, "to see why they fall into the category of the deserving poor."

In the *New York Times,* William Safire, in a column titled "The Great Panhandler," suggested that the Soviet Union "stop wasting assets making tanks and planes and paying a huge standing army, and to stop subsidizing Cuba at the rate of $4.5 billion a year. . . . Now 30 percent of all Soviet production goes for arms; U.S. expenditure is 6 percent, everyone else less than 3 percent. . . . But if I demobilize the Red Army, Gorbachev says, not only do I lose my power base, but I will have an army of unemployed. If I bring troops home from Germany, where will they live? Answer: use the money saved on war production on home production. Give former soldiers a piece of land as their private property . . . homes will get built as never before."

British, Canadian, Japanese, and American officials all referred pointedly to the Soviet Union's gold reserves, its vast natural resources, and its continued high defense spending as indications that the Soviets had not exhausted their own resources before begging for help.

Still, some felt that the G7 was being unduly hard on the Soviet Union. Gorbachev hoped that the Soviet Union would be admitted to membership of the International Monetary Fund, for the potentially vast financial aid that could come from the IMF. But instead of offering the Soviets membership in the IMF, the G7

offered "associate" membership—a category invented on the spot
to seem to give the Soviets something without granting them full
membership. In this way the IMF could negotiate programs of
budget cuts and other economic adjustments, just as it does with
any member state that requests a loan. "But there would be a
crucial difference," as Anatole Kaletsky, the economics editor of
the *London Times*, pointed out: "the Soviet Union would not be
able to borrow a penny from the Washington-based fund to cushion
the pain of these adjustments as do the governments of Latin
America, Africa and Eastern Europe. To borrow from the IMF,
Moscow would have to become a full member. That is simply 'not
practicable' for at least two years," according to the United States
Treasury Under Secretary David Mulford. And according to the
British, it might not be practicable for five years.

Why was the Soviet Union to be denied membership? "Communist countries like China and Poland have been in the IMF for
more than a decade. Czechoslovakia was admitted last year within
eight months of its application being lodged in January. China was
admitted virtually overnight, despite an almost complete absence
of information about its economy." But, said David Mulford, the
IMF had just completed a two-year review of the relative voting
powers within the IMF, calculated according to a complex formula
taking into account the size of each member's economy, its reserves, and its international trade.

In this reassessment, Japan's share had risen from 4.52 to 5.59
percent, while Britain's had declined from 6.62 to 5.35. As a result,
Britain fell from second place within the pecking order to fourth,
equal to France. America's voting rights, at 19.1 percent, were
unchanged, although there was some anxiety in Washington that
the United States share might fall, at the next reassessment, to near
15 percent, the level required to exercise a veto over the most
significant IMF decisions. If the Soviet Union were admitted to the
IMF, the size of its economy would place it within striking distance
of the top five nations. And if its economic reforms were successful,
the Soviet Union might well, within a decade, replace Britain at
the head table.

Even so, denying full membership to the Soviet Union struck
some observers as illogical. "When even Albania is about to become

a member," said the *Times* of London, "such double standards are wrong."

But not even the intricacies of IMF politics exhausted the contingencies bearing on the question of aid to the Soviet Union. The Board of Directors of Planet Earth was not without its internal rivalries. As the *Wall Street Journal* commented on the eve of the London summit, "scratch the surface of almost any issue" that would be raised at the summit, and "you are likely to find a U.S.-European spat. . . . Across a wide range of issues, from trade to foreign aid to interest rates, the U.S. and Europe increasingly find themselves at odds."

What was at work was not just the resolution of the old conflict between the USSR and the West—a formal writing to the end of the Cold War after all the years of tense and sometimes bloody hostility, but a positioning for the new competition between the United States and Europe, and within Europe, in the 1990s and on into the twenty-first century, in the New World Order—the sort of competition for new advantage that had been seen among the victors in Vienna in 1815, in Paris in 1919, at Yalta in 1945.

The vast military power of the United States might just have been reasserted in the Persian Gulf War, and the president might be telling the United States Congress that his proposed North American Free Trade Agreement, which brought about 360 million people into a new, more open market for labor and manufacturing and trade in the Americas, "offers an historic opportunity to create the largest market in the world." But at the same time, Jacques Delors, the president of the European Community, liked to tell people that his twelve-nation group, with a population of 340 million, would soon be "the largest market in the world." The end of the Cold War had only allowed different competitions to flower.

"A newly self-assured Europe" was "on the rise," as the *Wall Street Journal* reported, and the Europeans, "confident in the strength of a unified European economy and freed from the Soviet threat," might be "less willing than ever to bend to U.S. pressure."

Nonetheless, on the question of the IMF, Britain, Japan, and the United States could agree: the "newly self-assured" Europeans bent to that combined pressure, and Gorbachev was offered only an associate membership. It would be up to him, in press conferences, to make that appear to be a triumph for the Soviet Union.

Gorbachev was "visibly concerned" by the negative response to his proposals to the G7. Evidently he had expected that he would be asked to make some adjustments or provide some more details on his intentions. But that was not requested; rather his ideas were simply rejected.

Some Soviet economists in London, fretting over this rejection, emphasized the difficulty of moving to a market economy while the existing Communist-run system was deteriorating and people were anxious about scarce supplies of food and consumer goods. To turn an army of unemployed soldiers loose under such circumstances hardly seemed a prudent thing to do.

The demands for a speedy transition to a market economy, said the Soviets, ignored both the problems of real political resistance and also the problems of the resistance of the physical world, of outmoded factories, broken-down trucks, and the confusion of how to make the chaotic economy work together.

Vladimir Shcherbakov complained that the G7 "Sherpas"—the senior officials involved in analyzing the proposals for the heads of state at the summit—had an "imperfect understanding" of the Soviet Union's situation.

According to Arkady Maslennikov, Britain had privatized 18 percent of its industry in Mrs. Thatcher's more than ten years in power. "We are talking about 80 percent and you want us to do it in two or three years. Be as serious about us as you are about your own country. Do not experiment on us."

Leslie Gelb, writing in the *New York Times*, had some sympathy for the Soviets, but not much hope that this summit meeting could succeed. "Here's why: Mr. Gorbachev's list of market reforms [is] significant, but not bold enough. That's because neither he nor Boris Yeltsin and the other democratic leaders have dared to tell the Soviet people how long and how hard the road to genuine reform will be. . . . The only mandate they have sought from the Soviet people is for reform without pain, a circumstance that does not inspire courageous decisons. Western leaders (with the exception of the Germans) do not add much realism. They speak as if the Soviets could establish democracy and free markets essentially with their own resources and without substantial Western aid. That is the diplomatic equivalent of baby talk."

The proposal of the Soviets, the Grand Bargain, said Gelb, "has been mangled and maligned by people who obviously never bothered to study it. . . . [It] does not seek to prop up the existing Communist regime, but to transform the U.S.S.R. into a federation of democratic republics with free markets. It does not call for Western aid in return for Soviet promises, but for aid only after Soviet performance of promises. And it makes absolutely clear that aid will be delivered only when and as the Soviets slash military spending and aid to Cuba and Afghanistan." The Grand Bargain, said Gelb, was a "common-sense framework" for Soviets and Westerners to work toward a common goal. "It is, thus and alas, a dream."

What could come of a Western refusal of aid? Awful, even cataclysmic surprises could not be ruled out. The warnings were of the fall of the Soviet government, a possible military coup, the disintegration of the Soviet Union into a number of small and warring republics, some of them armed with nuclear weapons that might become turned on others outside the Soviet Union itself, of the Red Army cut loose to wreak havoc on the Soviet Union, or to flood west in hope of food and shelter.

Set against these dreaded possibilities were cautions against pouring money down a sinkhole, of propping up a government that was to fall in any case, of trying to hold together a Soviet Union that was better off (and in the long term less threatening to the West) if it splintered apart, of using the pain the Soviets felt to force them to make even more concessions to Western desires, to disarm them, to make them pull back entirely from their allies and dependencies around the world. Reform, as Lenin said, would only postpone the cure. The gamble—whichever way the decision went—was enormous. The stakes—of possible destruction in the event Soviet disintegration led to armed conflict, of possible loss of lives, of loss of historic opportunity—could hardly have been greater.

In fact, the leaders of the G7 and their advisors at this summit were consciously grappling with the real and profound problems of history: with the sheer unknowability of the historical forces with which they dealt at the moment; with the question of the reality or illusion of their own power to affect the future of the Soviet Union and of Gorbachev's prospects of remaining in power and being able to do what was necessary; with the inevitability of surprises that confound even the best judgment; with the undeniable insistent presence of others in the USSR—conservative and radical—who could upset any decisions taken by the leaders at the London meetings, the infinitely complex web of contingencies that operated on all historical events; with the realization that there were no reliable lessons of history to depend on in this moment; with the near certainty that any decision would produce unintended and undesirable consequences.

All that the G7 leaders might know for sure was that they did not know whether they could, acting together, shape the course of events as they might wish, that none of them could act with any great confidence that they actually knew what to do.

In the end, it was the United States that had the power to make or break a deal with the Soviet Union. And in the end, President Bush's answer was no deal.

Mikhail Gorbachev was a living example of the fact that charm, warmth, wit, grace, tact, wiliness, finesse, resourcefulness, resilience, persuasiveness, wheedling, coaxing, threatening, maneuvering, manipulating, and all the other arts of a great politician could make a difference—though, finally, not enough of one.

He had arrived asking for billions, and received only some millions—35 to 80 million in technical assistance from Britain, 130 million in agricultural credits from Canada—nothing much, compared to his vast needs, and very little new: the promise of a "special association" with the IMF, the promise to "work together and intensify" efforts in the West to give the Soviets "practical advice," and even "technical assistance" in their efforts to change over to a market economy, a promise to keep in "close touch" with Gorbachev, and to encourage officials representing small business to go to Russia and meet with people there.

In short, as the hard-liners back in Moscow were saying, for Gorbachev the trip to London was "humiliating." Colonel Viktor

Alksnis, in Moscow, said the meeting "ended in a brilliant failure" for Gorbachev.

Gorbachev's proposal, declared Grigory Yavlinsky, had been too "foggy," and it had elicited a comparably "foggy" response from the West. Others said that Gorbachev's plan had offered too little, and the response from the West had been too limited. What would come of this mutual disappointment remained to be seen— whether the Soviet Union would gradually reconstitute itself as part of a new and peaceful order for the twenty-first century or help to fuel a new slide into chaos and bloodshed for the century to come, whether the West would eventually come to the assistance of the old Soviet Union, and whether that assistance would come in time, or be sufficient to do the job.

At their farewell dinner at Number 10 Downing Street, the G7 plus Gorbachev circled about the table exchanging menus for one another's autographs, dined on turbot in ginger butter and asparagus, lemon chicken and sliced nectarines, and joined together finally in a spontaneous outbreak of singing: "Money, Money, Money Makes the World Go Round."

As they faced newspaper and television reporters before they left London, they all tried to put a good face on things. "The ice," Gorbachev said, "has started moving. . . . And the icebreaker is on its way toward renewal." "I want to compliment President Gorbachev," said Bush. "He's shown enormous leadership in forging ahead with these plans. . . . " It was, Prime Minister Major stated, a "historic" occasion.

The cartoon on the front page of the British *Guardian* showed Gorbachev arriving at the Moscow airport customs counter, with arrows pointing in one direction for "something to declare" and in the opposite direction for "nothing to declare," as one customs agent asked another, "Which way will Gorbachev go?"

Less than six weeks later, hard-line Russians launched a coup in Moscow, although it was stopped, and civil war did not break out, and the hard-liners were defeated. Boris Yeltsin, President of the Russian Federation, assumed leadership in Moscow. The Soviet Union shattered into a collection of independent sovereign republics. All this happened without a bloodbath, without the army rioting against the people or against its own leaders, but rather with an uncommonly nonviolent transition to a new government—still beset by all the same old problems.

Within another eight months, in April of 1992, having watched all these near catastrophes in the former Soviet Union, the members of the G7 reversed themselves and said they were ready to accept Russia and the other former Soviet republics into full IMF membership, ready to help stabilize the ruble, ready to pave the way to increased trade, ready immediately to begin a flow of financial aid reckoned at about $150 billion in total value.

Whether this response of the G7 would prove too late or too little, whether the former Soviet republics could be salvaged without enormous suffering and bloodshed on into the 1990s and even into the next century, whether it would have made a difference if such aid had started nearly ten months or so earlier, or if the pieces had simply been put in place that much earlier so that aid had been ready to flow instantly when the moment was deemed right for other reasons: the answers to all these questions were as unknowable in the spring of 1992 as they had been in the summer of 1991 in London.

Those who had to make the decisions, like the rest of us in other circumstances, had little certainty on which to base their conclusions, and no choice but to act, to step out into the great unexplored territory of history.

A NOTE
ON SOURCES

For the most part, I have tried to mention my principal sources as they have come up in the text of each chapter—in part to remind myself and the reader that no material of history comes without a provenance, and also—because this is an extended essay and not a work of research—to avoid footnotes. However, for those readers who would like to know more of the sources on which I have relied, here is a selected bibliography.

For general considerations of historiography and diplomacy, I have found the following sources especially valuable for this book:

Ankersmit, F. R. *Narrative Logic.* The Hague, 1983.
Baron, Salo Wittmayer. *The Contemporary Relevance of History.* New York, 1986.
Barston, R. P. *Modern Diplomacy.* London, 1988.
Black, Max. "The Reality of the Past." In *Philosophical Analysis.* Englewood Cliffs, N.J., 1963.
Block, Marc. *The Historian's Craft.* Manchester, 1954.
Brady, Linda P. *The Politics of Negotiation.* Chapel Hill, 1991.
Breisach, Ernst. *Historiography.* Chicago, 1983.
Callières, François de. *The Art of Diplomacy.* Edited by H. M. A. Keens-Soper and Karl W. Schweizer. New York, 1983.
Cambon, Jules. *The Diplomatist.* London, 1931.
Clausewitz, Carl von. *On War.* Translated by Michael Howard and Peter Paret. Princeton, 1976.

Craig, Gordon Alexander. *Force and Statecraft.* New York, 1983.

Der Derian, James. *On Diplomacy.* Oxford, 1987.

Eban, Abba. *The New Diplomacy.* New York, 1983.

Eco, Umberto. *The Open Work.* Cambridge, Mass., 1989.

Eubank, Keith. *The Summit Conferences, 1919–1960.* Norman, Oklahoma, 1966.

Ganshof, François Louis. *The Middle Ages: A History of International Relations.* New York, 1971.

George, Alexander L. *Forceful Persuasion.* Washington, D.C., 1991.

Gould, Stephen Jay. *Wonderful Life.* New York, 1989.

Harmon, Robert Bartlett. *The Art and Practice of Diplomacy.* Metuchen, N.J., 1971.

Hexter, J. H. *On Historians.* Cambridge, Mass., 1979.

Iqbal, Afzal. *Diplomacy in Islam.* Lahore, 1962.

Kaufmann, Johan. *Conference Diplomacy.* Boston, 1988.

Kremenyuk, A., ed. *International Negotiation.* San Francisco, 1991.

Lauren, Paul Gordon. *The China Hands' Legacy: Ethics and Diplomacy.* Boulder, 1987.

———. *Diplomacy.* New York, 1979.

Lowenthal, David. *The Past Is a Foreign Country.* Cambridge, 1985.

Maqalhaes, Jose Calvet de. *The Pure Concept of Diplomacy.* Translated by Bernardo Futscher Pereira. New York, 1988.

Marwick, Arthur. *The Nature of History.* Basingstoke, 1989.

Mink, Louis O. *Historical Understanding.* Ithaca, 1987.

Munz, Peter. *The Shapes of Time, A New Look at the Philosophy of History.* Middletown, 1977.

Neustadt, Richard, and Ernest May. *Thinking in Time.* New York, 1986.

Nicolson, Harold. *Diplomacy.* London, 1963.

Panikkar, K. M. *The Principles and Practice of Diplomacy.* Delhi, 1952.

Plischke, Elmer. *Presidential Diplomacy.* Dobbs Ferry, N.Y., 1986.

Reychler, Luc. *Patterns of Diplomatic Thinking.* New York, 1979.

Ricoeur, Paul. *Time and Narrative.* Translated by Kathleen McLaughlin and David Pellauer. Chicago, 1984.

Rorty, Richard. *Contingency, Irony, and Solidarity.* Cambridge, 1989.

Satow, Sir Ernest Mason. *Guide to Diplomatic Practice.* London, 1979.

Scholes, Robert, and Robert Kellogg. *The Nature of Narrative.* Oxford, 1968.

Singh, Indu Prakash. *Diplommetry.* Bombay, 1970.

Stanford, Michael. *The Nature of Historical Knowledge.* Oxford, 1986.

Stock, Brian. *Listening for the Text.* Baltimore, 1990.

Strang (Lord Strang). *The Diplomatic Career.* London, 1962.

Unger, Roberto Mangabeira. *Social Theory: Its Situation and Its Task.* Cambridge, 1987.

Veyne, Paul. *Writing History.* Translated by Mina Moore-Rinvolucri. Middletown, Conn., 1984.

Watson, Adam. *Diplomacy.* London, 1982.

White, Hayden. *Metahistory.* Baltimore, 1973.

Wicquefort, Abraham de. *L'Ambassadeur et ses fonctions*. Translated into English by John Digby. London, 1716.

Winks, Robin. *The Historian as Detective*. New York, 1969.

Yale French Studies. *Rethinking History*. New Haven, 1980.

Zartman, I. William. *The Practical Negotiator*. New Haven, 1982.

ONE: THE PROBLEM OF KNOWING

I have relied especially greatly and gratefully on the Roman historians, on Gibbon, and on Maenchen-Helfen to provide very different views and kinds of material for this chapter. I have also benefited greatly not only from years of reading Lionel Casson but from having his personal guidance on this chapter as well as the guidance of Professor Arther Ferrill.

Ammianus Marcellinus. *Rerum gestarum libri*. Translated by Walter Hamilton. Middlesex, 1986.

Blockley, R. C. Ammianus Marcellinus: a Study of His Historiography and Political Thought. Bruxelles, 1975.

————. *The Fragmentary Classicising Historians of the Later Roman Empire, Eunapius, Olympiodorus, Priscus, and Malchus*. Liverpool, 1983.

Bouvier-Ajam, Maurice. *Attila, le fléau de Dieu*. Paris, 1982.

Brion, Marcel. *Attila, the Scourge of God*. Translated by Harold Ward. New York, 1929.

Brown, P. R. L. *The World of Late Antiquity*. London, 1971.

Cassiodorus. *A History of the Goths*. Inextant, but summarized in Jordanes.

Casson, Lionel. *Travel in the Ancient World*. London, 1974.

————. *Ancient Trade and Society*. Detroit, 1984.

Cunliffe, Barry. *Greeks, Romans and Barbarians*. London, 1988.

Feist, Aubrey. *The Italian Lakes*. London, 1975.

Gibbon, Edward. *A History of the Decline and Fall of the Roman Empire*. Edited by J. B. Bury. London, 1896–1900.

Goffart, Walter. *Barbarians and Romans*. Princeton, 1980.

Gordon, C. D. *The Age of Attila*. Ann Arbor, 1960.

Halliwell, William J. *The Style of Pope St. Leo the Great*. Washington, D.C., 1939.

Hambia, Louis. *Attila et les Huns*. Paris, 1972.

Huntington, Ellsworth. *The Pulse of Asia*. Boston, 1907.

Hutton, Edward. *Attila and the Huns*. London, 1915.

Jalland, Trevor. *The Life and Times of St. Leo the Great*. New York, 1941.

Jones, A. H. M. *The Decline of the Ancient World*. London, 1975.

Jordanes. *The Gothic History of Jordanes*. Translated by C. C. Mierow. Princeton, 1915.

Leo I. *Select Sermons*. Translated by William Bright. London, 1886.

L'Orange, Hans Peter. *The Roman Empire*. New York, 1985.

Ludlum, David McWilliams. *The Weather Factor*. Boston, 1984.

Maenchen-Helfen, Otto J. *The World of the Huns.* Berkeley, 1973.

Mueller, Sister Mary Magdeleine. *The Vocabulary of Pope St. Leo the Great.* Washington, D.C., 1943.

Pelikan, Jaroslav. *The Excellent Empire.* San Francisco, 1987.

Randers-Pehrson, Justine Davis. *Barbarians and Romans.* Norman, Oklahoma, 1983.

Thompson, E. A. *Romans and Barbarians.* Madison, 1982.

Wigley, T. M. L., M. J. Ingram, and G. Farmer, eds. *Climate and History.* Cambridge, 1981.

Zinsser, Hans. *Rats, Lice, and History.* Boston, 1935.

TWO: THE ILLUSION OF POWER

The foundation of contemporaneous information here comes from Edward Hall, but I am also deeply and repeatedly reliant on the immense detail in Joycelyne Russell, and on the view of the material that Sydney Anglo in particular, and the other analysts of theater more generally, have provided for this chapter. I have stolen Stephen Orgel's book title for the title of this chapter, and relied on his work for many of the dramaturgical insights as well. Professor Jay P. Anglin was my personal mentor for this chapter.

Anglo, Sydney. "The Evolution of the Early Tudor Disguising, Pageant, and Mask." In *Renaissance Drama*, New Series, 1, 1968.

———. "The Hampton Court Painting of the Field of the Cloth of Gold Considered as an Historical Document." *The Antiquaries Journal* 46, pt. 2 (1966).

———. *Spectacle, Pageantry, and Early Tudor Policy.* Oxford, 1969.

Axton, Marie. "The Tudor Mask and Elizabethan Court Drama." In *English Drama: Forms and Development.* Edited by Axton and Raymond Williams. Cambridge, 1977.

Berry, Edward I. "Henry VIII and the Dynamics of Spectacle." *Shakespeare Studies* 12, 1979.

Bristol, Michael D. *Carnival and Theater.* New York, 1985.

Caley, John. "Two Papers Relating to the Interview between Henry the Eighth of England, and Francis the First of France." *Archaeologia* 21, 1827.

Cohen, Raymond. *Theatre of Power.* London, 1987.

Ferguson, Arthur B. *Naked to Mine Enemies: The Rise and Fall of Cardinal Wolsey.* London, 1958.

Goodman, Anthony. *The Wars of the Roses.* Boston, 1981.

Hall, Edward. "The Triumphant Reigne of Kyng Henry the VIII." In *Lives of the Kings.* Edited by Charles Whilbley. London, 1904.

Holinshed, Raphael. The last volume of the chronicles of England, Scotland, and Ireland. London, 1577.

Jones, Dorothy V. *Splendid Encounters; The Thought and Conduct of Diplomacy.* Chicago, 1984.

Jonson, Ben. *Ben Jonson's Plays and Masques.* Edited by Robert Adams. New York, 1979.

Kenyon, J. P. *The Stuarts: A Study in English Kingship.* London, 1958.

Knecht, R. J. *Francis I.* Cambridge, 1982.

"Letters and Papers." *Letters and Papers Foreign and Domestic of the Reign of Henry VIII.* Edited by J. S. Brewer III. London, 1867.

Lindley, David, ed. *The Court Masque.* Manchester, 1984.

Mattingly, Garrett. "An Early Nonaggression Pact." *The Journal of Modern History* 10, no. 1 (March 1938).

Milton, Roger. *The English Ceremonial Book; A History of Robes, Insignia, and Ceremonies Still in Use in England.* New York, 1972.

Orgel, Stephen K., ed. *Ben Jonson: Selected Masques.* New Haven, 1970.

————. *The Illusion of Power.* Los Angeles, 1975.

————. *The Jonsonian Masque.* Cambridge, Mass., 1965.

Pollard, A. F. *Henry VIII.* London, 1951.

Rawdon Brown, Lubbock. *Four Years at the Court of Henry VIII.* London, 1854.

Ross, Charles. *The Wars of the Roses.* London, 1976.

Russell, Joycelyne G. *The Field of the Cloth of Gold.* London, 1969.

Scarisbrick, J. J. *Henry VIII.* London, 1968.

Seward, Desmond. *Prince of the Renaissance: The Life of Francis I.* London, 1973.

Starkey, David. *The Reign of Henry VIII.* London, 1985.

Stone, Lawrence. *The Crisis of the Aristocracy, 1558–1641.* Oxford, 1965.

Withington, R. *English Pageantry.* Cambridge, Mass., 1918–20.

THREE: *THE INEVITABILITY OF SURPRISE*

The main sources for the narrative from the Spanish point of view are Díaz and Gómara, with some references from Cortés's letters. The main source for the narrative from the Aztec point of view is Sahagún. Much of the military information, and the evaluation of it, comes from Norman Davies. For an overview of the conquest that more or less accords with the view of it in this essay as a revolution, see J. H. Elliott's chapter in the Cambridge History. Davies opposes this view. I am indebted to Professors Suzanne Alchon and George Scheber for their detailed guidance on this chapter.

Bancroft, Hubert Howe. *History of Central America.* San Francisco, 1882–1887.

Bandelier, A. F. "Art of War and Mode of Warfare of the Ancient Mexicans." In Reports of the Peabody Museum of American Archaeology and Ethnology, 95–161. Boston, 1877.

Bray, Warwick. *Everyday Life of the Aztecs.* Dorset Press, New York, 1968.

Burland, Cottie Arthur. *Montezuma.* New York, 1973.

Calnek, Edward. "The Internal Structure of Tenochtitlan." In *The Valley of Mexico, Studies in Pre-Hispanic Ecology and Society,* edited by E. Wolf, 287–302. A School of American Research Book. University of New Mexico Press, Albuquerque, 1970.

Carrasco, Pedro. "Social Organization of Ancient Mexico." In *Handbook of Middle American Indians; Archaeology of Northern Mesoamerica,* edited by Robert Wauchope, Gordon Ekholm, and Ignacio Bernal, pt. 1, vol. 10, 349–375. University of Texas Press, Austin, 1971.

Cartwright, Frederick F., and Michael D. Biddiss. *Disease and History.* Thomas Y. Crowell Company, New York, 1972.

Caso, Alfonso. *The Aztecs.* Translated by Lowell Dunham. Oklahoma, 1958

Cortés, Hernán. *Letters from Mexico.* Translated by Anthony Pagden. Yale University Press, New Haven, 1986.

Crosby, Alfred W. *"Conquistador y Pestilencia:* The First New World Pandemic and the Fall of the Great Indian Empires." *Hispanic American Historical Review* 47 (1967): 331.

Davies, Nigel. *The Aztec Empire: The Toltec Resurgence.* University of Oklahoma, 1987.

Díaz, Bernal. *The Conquest of New Spain.* Penguin Books, New York, 1963.

Dobyns, Henry F. "An Outline of Andean Epidemic History to 1720." *Bulletin of the History of Medicine* 38 (1963): 496.

Elliott, John H. *Imperial Spain.* London, 1963.

———. "The Mental World of Hernán Cortés." In *Transactions of the Royal Historical Society.* 5th ser., 17 (1967): 41–58.

———. "The Spanish Conquest and Settlement of America." In *The Cambridge History of Latin America,* edited by Leslie Bethell, 1: 149–206. Cambridge, 1984.

Gibson, Charles. *Tlaxcala in the Sixteenth Century.* New Haven, 1952.

———. *The Aztecs under Spanish Rule.* Stanford, 1964.

Johnson, William Weber. *Cortés.* New York, 1987.

López de Gómara, Francisco. *The Life of the Conqueror by his Secretary, Francisco López de Gómara.* Translated by Lesley Byrd Simpson. Berkeley, 1964.

Leon-Portilla, Miguel. *The Broken Spears.* Boston, 1962.

McNeill, William H. *Plagues and Peoples.* New York, 1976.

Nicholson, Irene. *Firefly in the Night.* London, 1959.

Prescott, William H. *History of the Conquest of Mexico.* Philadelphia, 1873.

Ramenofsky, Anne F. *Vectors of Death: The Archaeology of European Contact.* University of New Mexico Press, Albuquerque, 1987.

Sahagún, Fr. Bernardino de. *The War of Conquest.* Translated by Arthur Anderson and Charles Dibble. University of Utah Press, Salt Lake City, 1978.

Simpson, Howard N. *Invisible Armies.* Indianapolis, 1980.

Soustelle, Jacques. *Daily Life of the Aztecs on the Eve of the Spanish Conquest.* Penguin Books, New York, 1964.
Vaillant, George. *The Aztecs of Mexico.* New York, 1941.
Wolf, Eric. *The Sons of the Shaking Earth.* Chicago, 1959.

FOUR: THE PRINCIPLE OF CONTINGENCY

I have relied on Enno Kraehe, Henry Kissinger, Harold Nicolson, and Charles Webster as my essential guides—each coming at the material from a different time and point of view—in Vienna. And I have relied on La Garde-Chambonas and Hilde Spiel for providing much of the incidental color along the way. Of course, Talleyrand, too, was a great source of both ideas and atmosphere.

Alsop, Susan Mary. *The Congress Dances.* New York, 1984.
Arblay, Madame d'. *Diary and Letters.* London, 1846.
Bartlett, C. J. *Castlereagh.* New York, 1966.
Bernard, J. F. *Talleyrand.* New York, 1973.
Bryant, Arthur. *The Age of Elegance.* London, 1950.
Buckland, C. S. B. *Friedrich von Gentz's Relations with the British Government.* London, 1934.
———. *Metternich and the British Government.* London, 1932.
Burghersh, Lady. *The Letters of Lady Burghersh.* London, 1895.
Castlereagh, Viscount. *Correspondence.* Edited by his brother. London, 1852.
Cecil, Alger. *Metternich.* New York, 1933.
Cooper, Duff. *Talleyrand.* London, 1932.
Du Coudray, Helen. *Metternich.* New Haven, 1936.
Ferrero, Guglielmo. *The Reconstruction of Europe.* Translated by Theodore R. Jackel. New York, 1941.
Foreign Office, Great Britain. British and Foreign State Papers. London, 1838–1841.
Gooch, G. P., and A. W. Ward. *Cambridge History of British Foreign Policy, 1789–1919.* Cambridge, 1922.
Headlam-Morley, James. *Studies in Diplomatic History.* London, 1930.
Heeren, A. H. L. *History of the Political System of Europe.* Northampton, 1829.
Hinde, Wendy. *Castlereagh.* London, 1981.
Holborn, Hajo. *A History of Modern Germany.* London, 1969.
Hyde, H. M. *The Rise of Castlereagh.* London, 1933.
Kann, Robert A. "Metternich: A Reappraisal of His Impact on International Relations." *Journal of Modern History* 22 (1960).
Kissinger, Henry. *A World Restored.* Boston, 1973.
Kraehe, Enno E. *Metternich's German Policy.* Vol. 1–2. Princeton, 1983.
La Garde-Chambonas, Comte A. de. *Souvenirs du Congrès de Vienne.* Paris, 1901.
Lieven. *The Private Letters of Princess Lieven to Prince Metternich.* Edited by Peter Quennell. London, 1937.

Ligné, Prince de. *Fragments de l'histoire de ma vie*. Paris, 1928.

Longford, Elizabeth. *Wellington*. New York, 1969.

Marriott, Sir J. A. R. *Castlereagh*. London, 1936.

Metternich, Clemens. *Memoirs of Prince Metternich*. Edited by Richard Metternich. New York, 1881.

Milne, Andrew. *Metternich*. Totowa, N.J., 1975.

Nicolson, Harold. *The Congress of Vienna*. London, 1945.

Orieux, Jean. *Talleyrand: The Art of Survival*. New York, 1974.

Palmer, Alan Warwich. *Metternich*. London, 1972.

Phillips, W. A. *The Confederation of Europe*. London, 1913.

Seton-Watson, Hugh. *The Russian Empire, 1801–1917*. Oxford, 1988.

Simon, Walter. "Prince Hardenberg." *Review of Politics* 18 (1956).

Spiel, Hilde. *The Congress of Vienna: An Eyewitness Account*. Philadelphia, 1968.

Sweet, Paul R. *Friedrich von Gentz*. Westport, 1970.

Talleyrand-Périgord, Charles Maurice de. *Talleyrand Intime: Unedited Letters to the Duchess of Courland*. Paris, 1891.

———. *The Correspondence of Prince Talleyrand and King Louis XVIII during the Congress of Vienna*. Edited by M. G. Pallain. New York, 1881.

———. *Memoirs of the Prince de Talleyrand*. Translated by Raphael Ledos de Beaufort. New York, 1891–92.

Temperley, Harold William, and Lillian M. Penson. *Foundations of British Foreign Policy*. Cambridge, 1938.

Troyat, Henri. *Alexander of Russia*. New York, 1982.

Ward, Sir A. W. *The Period of the Congresses*. New York, 1919.

Webster, Charles. *British Diplomacy 1813–15*. London, 1921.

———. *The Congress of Vienna*. London, 1934.

———. *The Foreign Policy of Castlereagh*. London, 1931.

FIVE: THE FALSE LESSONS OF HISTORY

For more recent diplomatic events, the amount of documentary evidence available increases dramatically. Here the official American, British, and French collections of documents were the principal source for this chapter. I wrote a book on this subject in 1980. Then and now I was enormously indebted to Harold Nicolson for his detailed reporting of the event, his sense of atmosphere, and his intelligent insight into the conference. Keynes, Shotwell, and Seymour were also excellent guides through the conference. Richard Watt and Arno Mayer give good overviews. My book provides a more complete bibliography, but here are some of the principal sources.

Albrecht-Carrie, Rene. *Italy at the Paris Peace Conference*. New York, 1938.

Bailey, Thomas. *Woodrow Wilson and the Great Betrayal*. New York, 1945.

Baker, Ray Stannard. *What Wilson Did at Paris*. New York, 1919.

————. *Woodrow Wilson: Life and Letters.* New York, 1937–39.

Baruch, Bernard. *The Making of the Reparation and Economic Sections of the Treaty.* New York, 1920.

Black, C. E., and E. C. Helmreich. *Twentieth-Century Europe.* New York, 1969.

Blum, John Morton. *Woodrow Wilson and the Politics of Morality.* Boston, 1956.

Bonsal, Stephen. *Suitors and Suppliants.* New York, 1946.

Bruun, Geoffrey. *Clemenceau.* Cambridge, Mass., 1943.

Burnett, Philip Mason. *Reparation at the Paris Peace Conference from the Standpoint of the American Delegation.* New York, 1940.

Cambon, Paul. *Ambassadeur de France, 1843–1924, par un Diplomate.* Paris, 1937.

Clemenceau, Georges. *Clemenceau: The Events of His Life as Told by Himself to His Former Secretary, Jean Martet.* Translated by Milton Waldron. New York, 1930.

Constantine, Stephen. *Lloyd George.* London, 1992.

Cooper, John M., ed. *Causes and Consequences of World War I.* New York, 1972.

Cox, Frederick J. "The French Peace Plans, 1918–1919; The Germ of the Conflict between Ferdinand Foch and Georges Clemenceau." *Studies in Modern European History.* New York, 1971.

Elcock, H. J. *Portrait of a Decision.* London, 1972.

Erlanger, Philippe. *Clemenceau.* Paris, 1968.

Ferrell, Robert. *Woodrow Wilson and World War I.* New York, 1985.

Foch, Ferdinand. *Memoirs of Marshal Foch.* Translated by Colonel T. Bentley Mott. Garden City, N.Y., 1931.

Gilbert, Bentley. *David Lloyd George.* London, 1987.

Grayson, Cary T. *Woodrow Wilson: An Intimate Memoir.* New York, 1960.

Hankey, Maurice P. *The Supreme Control at the Paris Peace Conference, 1919.* London, 1963.

Hanotaux, Gabriel. *Le Traite de Versailles, du 28 juin 1919.* Paris, 1919.

Jones, Thomas. *Lloyd George.* London, 1951.

Keynes, John Maynard. *The Economic Consequences of the Peace.* New York, 1920.

————. *Two Memoirs, Dr. Melchior: A Defeated Enemy and My Early Beliefs.* London, 1949.

Lansing, Robert. *The Big Four.* Boston, 1921.

————. *The Peace Negotiations.* Boston, 1921.

Lentin, A. *Guilt at Versailles.* London, 1985.

Levin, Norman Gordon. *Woodrow Wilson and the Paris Peace Conference.* Lexington, Mass., 1972.

Link, Arthur S. *Wilson the Diplomatist.* Baltimore, 1957.

Lloyd George, David. *Memoirs of the Peace Conference.* New Haven, 1939.

————. *The Truth About the Peace Treaties.* London, 1938.

Lloyd George, Frances. *The Years That Are Past.* London, 1967.

Loades, Judith, ed. *The Life and Times of David Lloyd George.* Gwynedd, 1991.

Luckau, Alma. *The German Delegation at the Paris Peace Conference.* New York, 1941.

Maier, Charles S. *Recasting Bourgeois Europe.* Princeton, 1975.

Mantoux, P. J. *Les délibérations du conseil des quatre: notes de l'officier interprète.* Paris, 1955.

Mayer, Arno J. *Politics and Diplomacy of Peacemaking.* New York, 1969.

Mee, Charles L., Jr. *The End of Order.* New York, 1980.

Miller, David Hunter. *My Diary at the Conference of Paris.* New York, 1924.

Mordacq, Jean Jules Henri. *Le ministère Clemenceau: journal d'un témoin, novembre 1917–janvier 1920.* Paris, 1930–31.

Nicolson, Harold. *Peacemaking 1919.* Boston, 1933.

Noble, George Bernard. *Policies and Opinions at Paris, 1919.* New York, 1935.

Owen, Frank. *Tempestuous Journey.* London, 1954.

Payne, David Sylvester. *The Foreign Policy of Georges Clemenceau.* Durham, N.C., 1970.

Riddell (Lord Riddell). *Lord Riddell's Intimate Diary of the Peace Conference and After, 1918–1923.* London, 1933.

Roberts, J. M. *Europe 1880–1945.* London, 1989.

Schwabe, Klaus. *Woodrow Wilson, Revolutionary Germany, and Peacemaking, 1918-1919.* Translated by Rita and Robert Kimber. Chapel Hill, 1985.

Seymour, Charles, ed. *The Intimate Papers of Colonel House.* London, 1928.

———. *Letters from the Paris Peace Conference.* New Haven, 1965.

Shotwell, James T. *At the Paris Peace Conference.* New York, 1937.

Stevenson, David. "The Treaty of Versailles." *History Today* (October 1986).

Taylor, A. J. P., ed. *Lloyd George: A Diary by Frances Stevenson.* London, 1971.

———. *Lloyd George: Rise and Fall.* London, 1961.

Temperley, Harold W. *A History of the Peace Conference of Paris.* London, 1920–24.

Trachtenberg, Marc. "Reparation at the Paris Peace Conference." *The Journal of Modern History* (March 1979).

United States Department of State. Papers Relating to the Foreign Relations of the United States, The Paris Peace Conference, 1919. Washington, 1942–47.

———. Papers Relating to the Foreign Relations of the United States, 1918, suppl. 1, vol. 1. Washington, 1933.

Vansittart, R. G. V. (Lord Vansittart). *The Mist Procession.* London, 1953.

Walworth, Arthur. *America's Moment, 1918.* New York, 1977.

Watson, David. *Georges Clemenceau*. London, 1974.
Watt, Richard. *The Kings Depart*. New York, 1968.

SIX: THE RULE OF UNINTENDED CONSEQUENCES

I have relied here mainly on the documents in the *Foreign Relations of the United States*, but I am particularly indebted, too, to Russell Buhite and Diane Shaver Clemens for their works on Yalta. Yalta has, of course, been the subject of immense domestic political argument on the topic of whether Roosevelt was too complaisant with Stalin. There is an extensive bibliography on that subject alone, and I am indebted to the Center for European Studies at Harvard for holding, in 1991, a conference of historians who addressed this question among others in several days of discussion devoted to Yalta. I am grateful to Professor Ronald Steel for his personal help to me on this chapter.

Ambrose, Stephen E. *Rise to Globalism*. London, 1971.
Bohlen, Charles. *Witness to History, 1929–1969*. New York, 1973.
Brzezinski, Z. "The Future of Yalta." *Foreign Affairs* (Winter 1984–85).
Buhite, Russell D. *Decisions at Yalta*. Wilmington, 1986.
Churchill, W. S. *The Second World War*. London, 1952.
Clemens, Diane Shaver. *Yalta*. New York, 1970.
Dallek, Robert. *Franklin D. Roosevelt and American Foreign Policy, 1932–1945*. New York, 1979.
Davis, Lynn Etheridge. *The Cold War Begins*. Princeton, 1974.
Dennett, Raymond, and Joseph E. Johnson. *Negotiation with the Russians*. Boston, 1951.
Deutscher, Isaac. *Stalin*. London, 1966.
Dilks, D., ed. *The Diaries of Sir Alexander Cadogan, 1938–1945*. London, 1971.
Earl of Avon. *The Eden Memoirs*. London, 1965.
Edmonds, Robin. *The Big Three*. London, 1991.
Feis, Herbert. *Churchill-Roosevelt-Stalin: The War They Waged and the Peace They Sought*. Princeton, 1957.
Fenno, Richard F. *The Yalta Conference*. Lexington, Mass., 1972.
Gaddis, John Lewis. *Russia, the Soviet Union, and the United States*. New York, 1978.
———. *The United States and the Origins of the Cold War*. New York, 1972.
Gilbert, Martin. *Churchill*. Garden City, N.Y., 1980.
Hull, Cordell. *The Papers of Cordell Hull, 1908–1956*. Washington, D.C., 1974.
Laloy, Jean. *Yalta*. New York, 1988.
Leahy, W. D. *I Was There*. New York, 1950.
Loewenheim, F. L., H. D. Langley, and M. Jonas, eds. *Roosevelt and Churchill, Their Secret Correspondence*. London, 1975.
Maisky, Ivan. *Memoirs of a Soviet Ambassador*. New York, 1968.

Mastny, V. *Russia's Road to the Cold War.* New York, 1979.

Moran, Lord Charles. *Churchill: Taken from the Diaries of Lord Moran.* Boston, 1966.

Nadeau, Remi A. *Stalin, Churchill, and Roosevelt Divide Europe.* New York, 1990.

Ponomarenko, Konstantin Aleksandrovich. *Yalta: A Short Guide.* Simferopol, 1974.

Ponomaryov, B., A. Gromyko, and V. Khvostow, eds. *History of Soviet Foreign Policy, 1917–1945.* Moscow, 1965.

Rodine, Floyd H. *Yalta: Responsibility and Response, January–March 1945.* Lawrence, Kansas, 1974.

Ross, G., ed. *The Foreign Office and the Kremlin.* British Documents on Anglo-Soviet Relations, 1941–45. London, 1984.

Senarclens, Pierre de. *Yalta.* Translated by Jasmer Singh. New Brunswick, N.J., 1988.

Stettinius, Edward R., Jr. *The Diaries of Edward R. Stettinius, Jr., 1943–1946.* Edited by Thomas M. Campbell and George C. Herring. New York, 1975.

————. *Roosevelt and the Russians: The Yalta Conference.* Edited by Walter Johnson. Garden City, NY., 1949.

Sulzberger, Cyrus Leo. *Such a Peace.* New York, 1982.

Ulam, Adam B. *Stalin.* New York, 1973.

United States Department of State. *Foreign Relations of the United States.* Diplomatic Papers, The Conferences of Malta and Yalta, 1945. Washington D.C., 1955.

SEVEN: THE FANTASY OF REALISM

I am grateful to a number of people in the British and American diplomatic communities for sharing their knowledge of the G7 meeting with me. While they prefer not to be identified, the specifics in this chapter were all printed in the newspapers and journals, in any case, from July 14–21, 1991: The *New York Times*, the *Washington Post*, the *London Times*, *Private Eye*, the *Economist*, the *Guardian*, *The New Scientist*, *The European*, the *Wall Street Journal*, the *Financial Times*, *Figaro*, and *Le Monde*.

INDEX